DEAN TUCKER AND EIGHTEENTH-CENTURY ECONOMIC AND POLITICAL THOUGHT

DEAN TUCKER AND EIGHTEENTH-CENTURY ECONOMIC AND POLITICAL THOUGHT

George Shelton

ISBN 978-1-349-16505-6   ISBN 978-1-349-16503-2 (eBook)
DOI 10.1007/978-1-349-16503-2

© George Shelton 1981
Softcover reprint of the hardcover 1st edition 1981

All rights reserved. No part of this publication may be reproduced or transmitted, in any form or by any means, without permission

First published 1981 by
THE MACMILLAN PRESS LTD
London and Basingstoke
Companies and representatives
throughout the world

Photoset in Great Britain by
Rowland Phototypesetting Ltd
Bury St Edmunds, Suffolk

British Library Cataloguing in Publication Data

Shelton, W G
   Dean Tucker and eighteenth-century economic and political thought
   1. Tucker, Josiah
   2. Economists – England – Biography
   I. Title
   330'.092'4   HB103.T8

To my Mother and Father

Contents

	Preface	ix
	Note on Page References in the Text	x
1	Background	1
2	Bristol and the Methodist Controversy	17
3	Early Publications	37
4	The *Essay on Trade*	48
5	The Naturalisation Question	70
6	The 'Great Work'	88
7	Political Activities	133
8	Dean of Gloucester and 'Defender of the Faith'	162
9	American Affairs	182
10	The *Treatise Concerning Civil Government*	214
11	'A Well-Wisher to All Mankind'	240
	Notes	273
	Index	285

Preface

It is not difficult to understand why Dean Tucker has not been the subject of a biography. Not only was his life relatively uneventful, but, for those who were curious, R. L. Schuyler provided a convenient biographical sketch in the Introduction to his 1931 selection of Tucker's works. In recent years, however, a substantial number of his publications have been reprinted, and a full length study of his life and work may be useful.

I have chosen to discuss his writings more or less in order of appearance, relating them to his personal life when enough is known about it, and to his times where appropriate. Because he is best known as a controversialist, there has been a tendency to give his thought less weight than it might have received if he had been more dispassionate and more systematic. For this reason, I have examined his ideas at some length where they appear to warrant it. I have also quoted liberally from his incidental comments on a variety of subjects, because through them he offers us a kind of window on his age. Since his career as an author spanned almost half of the eighteenth century and since much of what occurred during that period is reflected in what he wrote, we get a generous sampling of the social as well as the intellectual history of his times.

I should like to extend my thanks to the University of Victoria for its generous study leave policy, and both the Canada Council and the University for financial assistance. Along the way I received assistance from librarians, archivists and private citizens too numerous to mention. It was much appreciated. Finally, I wish to express my gratitude to June Belton for secretarial help beyond the call of duty, and to my wife, Mary, for her patience and encouragement over the years.

GEORGE SHELTON

Note on Page References in the Text

Where a work by Tucker is referred to repeatedly, page references are given in the text. Where there are several successive quotes from the same page or pages, the reference is given following the last in the series and should not be taken as referring to that quote only or to those that follow it. Casual references to works by Tucker and all other references are covered by the Notes section, in which, also, the initial reference to any of the works cited will be found.

1 Background

The ancestry of Dean Tucker is not easy to establish. One of the reasons is that he himself had no interest in genealogy. 'For', as he once wrote, 'a blind, old, bedridden maiden aunt gave me such a surfeit for that kind of learning, that I have never liked it since . . . and as to family-antiquity, she assured me that we were descended from one Morgan who by having a round turret perched on the top of an hill, must have been a prince, – and indeed considering the situation of the place I think I might claim some relationship to the knights of the golden fleece. For I am sure my great ancestor Prince Morgan was a *sheep-stealer.*'[1]

There are certainly no clues in what survives of his correspondence. He never discusses his parents; the only family ever mentioned is a sister with eight children whom he had to support in later years.[2] The date of his birth has even been subject to confusion, with 1711, 1712 and 1713 given by different authorities. However, there seems little doubt now that he was born in December 1713 in Laugharne (sometimes called Langharne), Carmarthenshire, South Wales.[3] The parish register contains no record of his baptism,[4] but there is a notice on 30 October 1711 of the marriage of Josiah Tucker and Eliza Bradshaw. Presumably these were his parents, as we know his father's name was also Josiah.

This register does, however, introduce another complication, by describing this Josiah Tucker as a 'salt officer of Nevern, Co. Pembrokeshire', whereas the Dean's father is always referred to as a farmer. The records of the Revenue Service are of no help here, since they list the name of another man with the receipts for this period.[5] One can only assume that Tucker's father had some connection with the Salt Office but was not in charge of its operations at Laugharne.

The link with Nevern (or Neverne) can provide us with a hypothetical genealogy showing descent from Sir William Tucker, seneschal to Hugh de Lacy, constable of Chester in the reign of Henry II. This man was the forebear of Sir Owen Tucker, who fought at the battle of Poitiers under the Black Prince, and Thomas Tucker, who, in the reign of Edward III, received a grant of land at Sealyham in Pembrokeshire. One of his descendants was John Tucker, MA, who was named Vicar of Nevern in 1663 and died there in 1692.[6] The records of the parish church at Nevern show that the Rev. John Tucker was one of the most active incumbents it has had. He made an inventory of the church's possessions, which included an ancient cross of great historical interest, and took collections over the years for such worthwhile causes as the repairing of the church at St Alban's, the relief of the poor after the Fire of London and of Christians taken by the Turks, and one that would have earned the approval of the practical Dean: 'reducing bed of river Towy in Landovey to ancient bounds £0-5-0'.[7]

The parish register of Nevern shows that John Tucker had two sons, one of whom died young. There is no further record of the other, who was baptised Job in 1672, but it is possible that he was the father of the Josiah Tucker who settled in Laugharne.[8] However, that is as far as we are able to pursue the question of Tucker's ancestry. Probably this speculative family tree would have impressed the Dean even less than the researches of his aunt.

Laugharne, where he spent his childhood, was a fishing port and market town which, according to its historian, reached its population peak of about 1000 in the early nineteenth century, when it was described as the 'best-built town in Carmarthenshire' and could boast some elegant carriages. After that it went into decline. As late as the 1860s, when its history was written, the site of Bell House, where Tucker had lived, was still pointed out, but his connection with it now seems forgotten.[9] Today its only claim to fame is that it was the home for many years of Dylan Thomas, who wrote *Under Milk Wood* in a little garage overlooking the magnificent sweep of the bay. Located on the road which takes tourists to the beaches of the Pendine Sands, it slumbers on in picturesque decay, but in the early eighteenth century it must have been a lively little outport, judging by its customs and revenue returns.

If the elder Tucker was associated with the Salt Office, this would have brought his son into contact at an early age with the problems of economics and finance, for the salt tax was extremely unpopular. Years later, in his *Instructions for Travellers*, Tucker put the salt tax at the top of his list of taxes which should be eliminated.[10] It has even been accused of holding back the economic development of Wales, because it increased the cost of salting beef in a cattle-raising country.[11] But it was popular with the government because there was less fraud in its collection than in that of any other form of revenue, owing to the efficient organisation of the Salt Office.[12] This did not, however, prevent attempts to circumvent it, which added excitement to life along the Welsh coast. So as not to discourage exports, those who shipped salt or salt fish out of the country were entitled to receive back the tax which had already been paid. Thus, since salt entered for a foreign port was tax-free when it left the harbour, there was considerable temptation to make a false entry of destination and 'run' it back in. An account of such activities near Conway in 1712 throws light not only on the difficulties encountered by the salt officer in the course of his duties, but also on the social and political realities of the time.

> On the night in question the whole countryside had gathered with carts to smuggle several cargoes of salt entered for foreign parts. 'As he lay on his belly in the sands,' ran the officer's report '(for he durst not appear among them), he saw Sir Griffith Williams, Bart., one of the J.P.'s, riding upon a little mare' at the head of the company. On being detected, the officer was beaten, bound, blindfolded (with a leather smith's apron) and so violently used that he had to beg for his life. He was finally carried off and impounded in the magistrate's poultry house, where he was detained, still blindfolded for a day and a half and given nothing 'save a little buttermilk'. 'The officers cannot procure further information,' the report complained, 'for all concerned are tenants, servants or dependents on great men.' Before publishing a reward in the *Gazette* for information concerning the delinquents, the government thought 'fit to hint' its intentions to Sir Griffiths 'and respite till his answer'.[13]

Little more is definitely known about Tucker's youth than is known about his origins. His father is said to have inherited some land near Aberystwyth, to which place they moved when he was still a child. Again the documents fail us, for the elder Tucker's name does not appear in the list of wills probated in Wales at that time, and there is a vital thirty-year gap in the burial records of Llanbadarn Fawr parish church. The family name is also absent from the Cardiganshire freeholders list of 1760.[14]

Aberystwyth is mentioned briefly in Defoe's *Tour* of 1724 as being 'enrich'd by the coals and lead which is found in its neighbourhood, and we fancy'd the people look'd as if they liv'd continuously in the coal or lead mines. However, they are rich, and the place is very populous'.[15] This account must be treated with caution, however.[16]

Pococke, writing in 1756, long after Tucker left, does not mention mining at all: 'This place has a good harbour for small boats, of which they have several employed, chiefly in bringing limestone in from Milford Haven to make lime for manuring the land.' What struck him most was the character of the inhabitants:

> They are here a most profligate, lawless sort of people, and do justice themselves on all strangers, and even on gentlemen of the country who have differences with any persons in this place, and often send 'em off with severe chastisements. I saw an instance of it myself; they were assembled about the inn, and ready to redress a pretended grievance, until they saw it was without foundation, there being no justice of peace residing in their town.[17]

Perhaps we can find here one source of Tucker's later low opinion of the common people and his unwillingness to see their political power increased.

All that survives from this period in accounts of Tucker's life is a tale told by someone who probably knew him personally:

> The Dean was led to commercial speculation perhaps by a circumstance which took place in the little sea-port of Aberystwyth, where he lived in his early life. The town was divided into partizans of the House of Hanover and the House of Stuart. The latter, to gain over the inhabitants to their cause, used to tell them, that if their Prince (as the Pretender was then called) came in, they should be all smugglers. This assertion staggered a little our young politician, who, on turning it in his mind saw

plainly, that if they were *all* smugglers, it could not be worth any one's while to smuggle, as they would be all upon the same footing.[18]

Whatever the elder Tucker's financial circumstances, he was able to recognise his son's potential, and see that he received a good education. The boy was sent to Ruthin School at Ruthin, Denbighshire, in north-eastern Wales. At that time the headmaster was Mr Hughes, a noted grammarian and interpreter of the classics, as well as a strict disciplinarian.[19] It was an Elizabethan grammar school, endowed in 1595 by Gabriel Goodman DD, who was Dean of Westminster for many years. Tucker would have been taught and housed in the new building constructed in 1700 at a cost of £247 9s. 3d. It was 60 feet by 30 feet by 15 feet high, with five rooms above, where twenty boarders could be accommodated. The number of pupils in his time is not known, but in 1787 the school had the maximum allowed by the founder, 120, 'the greatest number that the two masters could teach in an efficient manner'![20]

When Carlisle wrote his description of the endowed grammar schools in 1818, he noted that the system of education at Ruthin was similar to that of the great public schools, with the Eton Latin and Greek grammars being used.

> The school hours are, in the summer from six, and in the winter from seven o'clock until nine, when half an hour is allowed for breakfast; – from half after nine to twelve business is renewed; but the boys who learn writing and arithmetic [which were optional subjects] stay in until one o'clock; – Dinner at half after one; – into school again at two, and remain there until five. The vacations are, one month at Christmas, – one month at midsummer, – and one week at Easter.[21]

Tucker must have done very well in his studies because he went up to St John's College, Oxford, as an exhibitioner. It is in connection with his arrival at Oxford that the first documentary evidence concerning the chronology of Tucker's life appears. In *Alumni Oxoniensis*, vol. IV, p.144, we find: 'Tucker, Josiah, s. Josiah of Llanbadarn Vawr, Co. Cardigan, pleb. St John's Coll., matric. 26 Jan. 1732–3, aged 19; B.A. 1736, M.A. 1739, B. and D.D. 1755.'

Unfortunately, the fact that he arrived there in 1733 and graduated in 1736 is all we know of his stay, except for an anecdote which is repeated in a number of biographical notices. Here is one version:

> The journey from his native place to the University was long, and at that period very tedious, on account of the roads. Our young student for some time travelled on foot. At last old Mr. Tucker, feeling for his son's reputation as well as for his ease gave him his own horse. . . . But upon his return, young Josiah, with true filial affection, considered that it was better for him to walk to and from Oxford, than for his father to repair on foot to the neighbouring markets and fairs. The horse was accordingly returned; and our student, for the remainder of the time he continued at the University, actually trudged backwards and forwards with his baggage at his back![22]

The distance involved was about 160 miles, which would have taken a good six days' walking. However, cold water is thrown on this story by another historian of Gloucestershire, who, after presenting his version of it, observes, 'Of the dutiful principles of Dean Tucker there can be no doubt, nor that there may be some temporary journey to Oxford on horseback; but the support of a horse at Oxford was utterly incompatible with the then circumstances of the student and the story must be in the main erroneous'.[23]

The eighteenth-century Oxford that Tucker reached after his long walk has been subjected to severe criticism not only by moderns looking back from an age with higher standards, but also by contemporaries who might have been expected to be more lenient. As one authority puts it, 'Butler and Adam Smith, Gibbon and Bentham constitute a formidable group of critics.'[24] There were complaints, of course, about a curriculum which seemed out of step with the times, but objection was taken also to lecturers who did not lecture and tutors who showed no interest in their pupils. Even more serious were accusations of corruption in the examination system.

Nicholas Amhurst, a former student who wrote virulently about Oxford in the 1720s, tells a story about three students who surprised a divinity professor one day by turning up for his lecture.

He informed them that three was not a quorum and left. To add insult to injury, it was claimed that the students had to pay fines for not attending lectures that were not given.[25] The crotchety antiquarian Hearne, writing in 1721, gives a clue as to the laxity and sloth typical of many Fellows: 'Whereas the university disputations on Ash Wednesday should begin at 1 o'clock, they did not begin this year till *two* or after, which is owing to several colleges having altered their hours of dining from 11 to 12, occasioned from people's lying in bed longer than they used to.'[26]

Modern scholars generally accept these criticisms as just. In the words of one, 'For a great part of the eighteenth century Oxford was a world of drab ideals, a small society where disillusioned Jacobites and half-hearted Hanoverians contended with each other, where scholars disinclined for study encountered teachers as indifferent as themselves, where dreamers found enthusiasm discouraged, education deadened, endowments ill-applied.'[27] Another refers to the reigns of the first two Georges as a 'dark age for most colleges'.[28]

However, it is not easy to be objective about education, a subject on which there will probably always be violently opposed views, and therefore the other side should also be heard. For every critic like Gibbon, there were probably many more like Berkeley, who considered the Oxford of his day an ideal retreat for learning and piety.[29] Much depended on the temperament of the student. If he were prepared to take advantage of the freedom provided by the system, his years at Oxford could be satisfying and productive. In the words of Dr Wallis, Savillian Professor and Keeper of the Archives at the end of the previous century, 'I do not know any part of useful knowledge proper for scholars to learn: but that if any number of persons (gentlemen or others) desire therein to be informed, they may find those in the university who will be ready to instruct them; so that if there be any defect therein it is from want of learners, not teachers.'[30] Thus, without denying that the Oxford of that era was seriously wanting in many respects, it can be said that, for someone from the wilds of Wales such as Tucker, who was interested in learning for its own sake as well as in preparing himself for a career in the Church, the opportunity to study there must have been gratefully welcomed.

Tucker's college, St John's, was also Amhurst's and as a result was not spared in his book. Not only had he unkind things to say about the President of the college, but, in addition, his description of the contents of the curio room of the college library is hardly meant to be complimentary. In addition to manuscripts and archives, the library possessed, among other oddities, St John the Baptist's thigh-bone, a dead bird-of-paradise, several large stones taken from a bullock's maw and a genealogy of the Stuarts from Adam to Charles I.[31]

The last item is indicative of the prevailing political atmosphere. Oxford was sometimes referred to as the 'Jacobite capital' of the kingdom.[32] An atmosphere of bitterness existed such as can only stem from devotion to a lost cause. There was sometimes even physical violence, and in the Blacow Affair of 1748 two undergraduates received two years imprisonment for riotous behaviour which included shouting support for King James and Prince Charles. St John's was one of the colleges which remained attached the longest to the old cause, being 'notoriously Jacobite' until at least 1730[33] and strongly Tory for twenty years more. If Tucker were already the staunch Hanoverian we know he was later, he must have found the spirit prevalent in Oxford on his arrival extremely unsympathetic. In any case, his attachment to his college was not affected. When, years later, his old tutor, who had become President, died, we find him actively lobbying for a successor.[34]

The period of Tucker's residence at Oxford is notable for very little except the birth of Methodism. John Wesley, who had gone up in 1720, was back teaching as a Fellow of Lincoln, and George Whitefield, who arrived in 1732, was Tucker's contemporary. Because of Tucker's role as an early critic of the sect, it would be interesting to know if he made their acquaintance at the time. He certainly must have been aware of their movement, for as early as 1732 the London press attacked them as 'sons of sorrow', suffering from a mental disease induced by superstition and enthusiasm.[35] However, they can have been little more than a curiosity, as in 1735, for example, the movement had only fourteen or fifteen members.

Whitefield apart, Tucker seems to have had no exact contemporaries who later became famous. William Pitt went up in 1727 and George Grenville in 1730; Samuel Johnson was briefly present in 1728-9; Blackstone did not appear on the scene until 1738 and Adam Smith only in 1740.

One event which occurred in his first year at the University is worth mentioning briefly. This was the Oxford Act, a formal graduation ceremony for Masters and Doctors, which attracted a substantial number of the public and, probably for that reason, had not been held since 1713. This one began on 5 July 1733, when Handel ('and his lousy crew – a great number of foreign fiddlers', as described by Hearne) performed his oratorio *Esther* before a large audience which had paid five shillings each for tickets. The following day a startling total of twenty-seven pieces of prose and verse were recited in the Sheldonian Theatre. The exercises for degrees in the various schools began on 7 July and the degrees were conferred over the following three days.[36]

An important part of the Act was the speech of the Terrae Filius. He was essentially a licensed jester who lightened the solemnity of the occasion with satire. Sir Christopher Wren, also a St John's man, had been one in the previous century. Over the years these speeches had become so scurrilous and indecent that the authorities had tried to have the institution suppressed. That is why the Act had ceased to be an annual affair. Amhurst had used the name as the title for his series of publications in the early 1720s. In 1733 no Terrae Filius was appointed, but a speech under his name appeared in print nevertheless, and ran to a fourth edition. The morals and habits of those in authority were, as usual, attacked: the Bishop of Oxford was referred to as a 'mitred hog' and the Fellows of Trinity were described as 'barrel-gutted'.[37]

Whether Tucker was present to hear the recitations and listen to Handel we cannot say – nor can we know whether he ever accompanied one of the local belles known as 'toasts' for a stroll in Merton Walks (later closed because of scandalous proceedings there) or if he witnessed a hanging at Gownsman's Gallows, where quite late in the century two undergraduates suffered death for highway robbery.[38] We can assume, however, that Tucker used his time sufficiently well to impress influential people with his potential, because he obtained an appointment to a rural parish in 1735 and was granted Holy Orders in 1736. This speedy commencement of a clerical career was not the general rule; many hopefuls cooled their heels in Oxford for years while waiting, often in vain, for the necessary patronage.

Much of Tucker's later career can only be comprehended through an understanding of the part played by the Church of

England in eighteenth-century England. Like the universities, it was an institution which, although in a somewhat decayed state, was yet in its own way serving the needs of the community. Just as the mediaeval church while fulfilling its religious obligations had to some extent been absorbed into the feudal system, so the Church of England, because it was the established church, had become an integral part of the system by which the country was governed. It functioned in the same loose and decentralised way as did the justices of the peace and the parish officials. However, this was really no problem, because, despite the fact that the power to appoint to the various offices and livings was widely dispersed, the composition of the clergy reflected reasonably well the actual structure of the society. The same kind of people as sat in Parliament and took part in local government dominated the Church. There was some division in the first half of the century, when Jacobitism still lingered on, but, whatever the differences amongst themselves, the same class remained firmly in command. There was little opposition from below, where curates struggled to make ends meet and the more ambitious clergy engaged in an unending quest for preferment. The *status quo* was not seriously challenged: it is significant that John Wesley, who did more than anyone to upset it, was himself a staunch Tory.

The eighteenth-century Church of England has been much decried by historians, who, while they might not themselves be active church-goers, have high ideals about what a church should be like. Judged by any such exalted standards, the Established Church did not measure up in terms of either the calibre of the individual clerics or the quality of their performance. But it should be remembered that this situation is far more characteristic of ecclesiastical institutions than the relatively short periods of revival and reform through which they pass – when a genuine spirituality may pervade them. Once the initial impetus provided by the founder or reformer has run its course, the organisation solidifies and form triumphs over content. The price paid for success and respectability is illustrated by what happened to the Wesleyan movement itself in later years.

Furthermore, the eighteenth-century Church was not just apathetic about what could be called 'active' religion: it was strenuously opposed to it – and for good reason. 'Enthusiasm', like alcohol, can produce exaltation, but often only at the cost of painful after-effects. Religious fanaticism, after all, had disturbed the peace of Europe for the previous two centuries. The Church of England from its inception had attempted to provide a spiritual home for Christians of various temperaments as long as they were prepared to eschew extremism. Like the political settlement, it was founded on compromise. The temporary but costly failure of this compromise in the seventeenth century only reinforced the feeling that the peace and good order of the kingdom were threatened if its subjects took their religious differences, and therefore, to some extent, their religion, too seriously. The fact that to the end of his life, John Wesley considered himself a member of the Church, and that the Church did not expel him, is a measure of the success of this policy.

The Church of England supplied buildings, a theology, a clergy, a ritual and all the expected trappings of a Christian communion. Although it could be too formalistic and remote from the daily lives of many Englishmen, it was broad enough to embrace not only those who wanted little more than the outward appearances of religion but also those who possessed a much more intense and personal faith. However, by its very nature it could not satisfy everyone. In the eighteenth century it was losing support at both ends: even its modest demands were excessive for many, who turned to deism or agnosticism, while to others, who demanded a more dramatic and emotionally satisfying form of worship, this was no religion at all. As the Dissenting churches were moribund, even to the extent of losing talented people to the Church of England in the early eighteenth century, there was nothing for the latter group until the Methodist movement appeared on the scene.

The Church of England was also open to the charge that as an established church it was forced to put political interests ahead of ecclesiastical ones. There is no doubt that this may have been a source of corruption from a purely religious viewpoint, but, of course, the doctrine of complete separation of Church and State is quite recent and only became possible when the religious passions loosed by the Reformation had moderated. The one thing most sects had in common was the desire to obtain control of the State so that they could impose their brand of truth on everyone else. It was only after a period of relative quiet, such as that enjoyed by England in the eighteenth century, that real toleration could gradually develop. Even then it was a tender plant, as the Gordon Riots of 1780 showed. It could be said, with some truth, that one of the main functions of the Church of England was to discourage religion – if one means by that term anything resembling the manifestations of hysteria which accompanied the sermons of Whitefield and the early Wesley – not to foster it. Nevertheless, elements within the Established Church were certainly aware of the need for improving the wretched lot of the deprived, and in their eyes usually depraved, portion of the populace, and were prepared to do something about it.

However, there is no doubt that the national church had political as well as religious functions. In addition to its general duty of attempting to maintain a proper degree of respect for authority, and resignation to their lot among the lower orders, the hierarchy was encouraged to engage in the political battles of the time in favour of the party in power. The bishops were especially important, since their twenty-six votes in the House of Lords were occasionally crucial. In the early part of the century, as a result of Queen Anne's appointments, they were split along political lines, but later the episcopal bench took on an overwhelming Whig cast – unlike, it may be said, the parish clergy. This was owing not only to the appointment of malleable men as sees fell vacant, but also to the fact that there was a method of keeping them in line afterwards. This was a consequence of the great differences in the incomes of the various bishoprics, ranging as they did from about £450 a year at Bristol to £7000 at Canterbury. A man was usually started off in one of the poorer incumbencies and only moved up after he had earned promotion by his services. If such co-operation were not forthcoming, he might spend years in the ecclesiastical wilderness. For example, Bishop Secker, who voted against the government twice, languished in the relative poverty of first Bristol and then Oxford for sixteen years, although this did not stop him from eventually becoming Archbishop of Canterbury.

Furthermore, the necessity of passing a substantial part of the year in the capital, in order to fulfil their Parliamentary obligations, as well as the hardships of travel, especially for the aged or infirm, made it difficult even for the most conscientious bishops to spend as much time in their dioceses as they should have done. There were a number of cases of bishops whose dioceses never saw them once. In addition to their presence at the House of Lords, the bishops, and indeed the lower clergy as well, had two other kinds of service to perform, if they were looking for preferment. One was electioneering and the other pamphleteering. With regard to the first Norman Sykes says,

> In an age when political education was imparted mainly through the pulpit, the ecclesiastical organisation of which the bishop was head together with his widespread influence with the clergy of his diocese furnished the most practicable means of party organisation then available throughout the country. Accordingly, few political ministers faced the fortunes of a general election without previous consultation and negotiation with their episcopal friends, nor were the majority of the episcopate unwilling to become parties in the enterprise.[39]

As we shall see, there is no evidence of this kind of organisation for the Bristol elections in which Tucker advised the Whigs, but it does indicate that the sort of contribution he made not only was not unusual in Georgian England but actually was expected.

Sykes also gives many examples of the link between clerical advancement and the authorship of pamphlets defending government policy. Since many of these were written over pseudonyms, their significance was owing not to the prestige of the author's office but to his skill as a polemicist. The career of Dean Swift, the finest of them all, and that of Tucker himself show, however, that ability in this area was no guarantee of a bishopric. Furthermore, bishoprics were awarded on grounds other than political expediency. Genuine merit was recognised at times; a chuch which could boast Berkeley and Butler as bishops had no need to apologise – at least, on intellectual grounds. As C. D. Broad says with such graceful irony,

> We all know how greatly Church and State have advanced in morality since the corrupt first half of the eighteenth century; and it is gratifying to think that a man like Butler would now be allowed to pursue his studies with singularly little risk of being

exposed to the dangers and temptations of high office or lucrative preferment.[40]

Bishop Butler is worth pausing over a moment, because of his connection with Tucker. Not only did the latter serve as his chaplain when Butler was Bishop of Bristol, and as one of his executors, but, further, the young Tucker obviously was strongly influenced by Butler's thought. He specifically recommended Butler's *Analogy* in his *Instructions for Travellers*.

Born in 1692, Joseph Butler was one of the outstanding Dissenters gained by the Church of England at this time. Although raised as a Presbyterian and educated at Tewkesbury Academy, he was ordained an Anglican priest after attending Oriel College, Oxford. His major appointments were: 1719, preacher at the Rolls Chapel, London; 1725, the lucrative living of Stanhope; 1736, Clerk of the Closet to Queen Caroline, who before her death the following year recommended him for a bishopric; 1738, Bishop of Bristol, to which office he added the Deanery of St Paul's in 1740; and finally in 1750, the bishopric of Durham. He died in 1752. His *Fifteen Sermons*, preached at the Rolls Chapel, were published in 1726, and his *Analogy of Religion* in 1736.

These two works had completely different fates. The *Analogy*, which arouses little interest today, went through twenty-eight editions and was not dropped as a classic at Oxford until 1860. The *Sermons*, although running only to six editions, are responsible for the high regard in which he is still held as an ethical philosopher. The reason for this difference is that in the *Analogy* Butler was defending the role of revealed as well as natural religion against the arguments of the deists. He did this by attempting to show that the assumptions made by the supporters of a special revelation, specifically biblical Christianity, were no more improbable than those on which the case for natural religion or deism rested. The popularity of the book for over 100 years indicates that Butler provided a satisfactory answer to the doubts of a large number of Englishmen who, while they accepted the existence of God without question, and were inclined by upbringing to accept also the particular teachings of the Church of England, felt the need for an additional intellectual prop. The fact that the *Analogy*, with its rather feeble resort to equal probability, served this purpose is a testament to the lukewarm nature of both their beliefs and their doubts. When those doubts became deeper and the existence of God was no longer taken for granted, as it had been by Butler's opponents, the deists, then his answers ceased to be relevant.

The *Sermons*, on the other hand, while resting on orthodox theology, can to some extent be detached and studied as one possible approach to the problems of ethics. Butler's fame seems to rest mainly on the supposition that he refuted once and for all the theory of psychological egoism, of which the most powerful proponent had been Hobbes. Put briefly, this is a denial that disinterested actions are possible. Much of the argument revolves around terminology and will not be discussed here. What is significant is that, in order to win his case, Butler is forced to give so much away. Although he places a great deal of emphasis on conscience – the voice of God within us – as the supreme authority in making ethical decisions, he ends up by practically equating it with self-love. He attempts to show that by obeying the dictates of conscience we are acting in our own best interests, if by that we mean avoiding the suffering occasioned by pangs of remorse in this world and divine punishment in the next. 'Cool self-love', as he calls it, or enlightened self-interest, taken over the long run, will always lead us to act in the same way as conscience: that is, to favour virtue over vice.

Butler can be variously interpreted, depending on which quotations are used for support, but most students of his ideas will probably admit that he skates very close to hedonism and utilitarianism in the process of avoiding them. Much depends on definitions of pleasure and pain or happiness and misery. What is interesting for us is that self-sacrifice is not held up as an ideal and that even benevolence can cease to be a virtue if indulged in to excess. Prudence seems to be the watchword. As we shall see, Tucker was not only firmly convinced that individuals will always look to their own interest but also thought that this was right and proper, and that the community would benefit if they were free to do so. For example, he saw an affinity rather than a conflict between commerce and religion.

It should be noted at this point also that, long before he published *The Wealth of Nations*, Adam Smith had written *The Theory of Moral Sentiments*, in which he attacked Mandeville's belief that 'private vice is public virtue'. This he did not by rejecting private vice out of hand, but by insisting that acting in one's own private interest, which was what Mandeville had in mind, was not necessarily vicious at all, but often desirable. Rephrased as, for example, 'the pursuit of private gain leads to public benefit', it becomes the basis of the famous 'invisible hand', whereby each, looking to his individual profit, increases the wealth of the whole, even if that is not his intention.

There is much to be said for Butler's contention that, over the long run, virtuous behaviour is in our interest, whether or not we accept with him the eternal sanctions of heaven and hell. But, even putting aside the important question of whether we can really know what will be the long-term effects of our actions, the ability to restrain ourselves from the immediate satisfaction of our desires while we engage in a reasoned calculation concerning implications for the future requires a coolness of temperament and lack of passion more likely to be found among retiring bachelor clergymen than among the rest of the populace. However, it was a common assumption during that age of rationalism, and, in a modified form, was precisely the sort of exercise a merchant had to practise in order to be successful. It was therefore an ethic which made sense in the thriving mercantile city of Bristol, which became Tucker's home in 1737.

2 Bristol and the Methodist Controversy

Bristol, to which Tucker came as Curate of St Stephen's in 1737, was at that time the second city in Great Britain. It replaced Norwich in that position at about the beginning of the eighteenth century, when its population was only 20,000. It prospered during the next 100 years, with its population increasing to 64,000 by 1801 (42,000 in the old city), but towards the end of the century other cities grew even faster, with the result that in 1801 Manchester–Salford had 84,000, Liverpool 78,000 and Birmingham 74,000. As always, London dwarfed the others, reaching 900,000 in 1801.

Nevertheless, throughout most of this period, Bristol, as the second port as well as the second city of the kingdom, remained a place to be reckoned with. Defoe noted in 1724, 'The merchants of this city not only have the greatest trade but they trade with more independency upon London than any other town in Britain. As 'tis evident in this particular, (viz.) that whatsoever exportations they make to any part of the world, they are able to bring the full returns back to their own port and can dispose of it there.'[1] This was because, as W. E. Minchinton points out, Bristol was a metropolitan centre in its own right; it could be called with justice the 'metropolis of the West'. The major reason for this was its geographical location.

> The upper reaches of the rivers, the Avon and Frome, at whose confluence it stands, were of little consequence as arteries of communication with its hinterland, although the Avon became navigable to Bath in 1726. But seaward the Avon placed Bristol at the focal point of two major systems of water communications, at the orifice of two funnels, which served through the centuries to direct the produce of the west to Bristol. The first was the Bristol Channel which linked Bristol with the ports of Somerset, Devon, Cornwall and South Wales and with more

distant ports: the second was the river and canal network of the Severn and Wye, still in course of improvement, which served the marches of Wales and the west Midlands.[2]

Bristol's hinterland actually extended as far as the north Midlands, until the building of the Bridgwater–Brindley canals later in the century allowed Liverpool to take its place in that area. Bristol was also a centre of the gradually improving network of roads serving this region. Its overall importance in domestic trade is indicated by the fact that in a number of commodities it made its own prices independently of those set by London. Each district sent its agricultural specialities to the Bristol market, which acted as an entrepot for transshipment, or as the consumer of large quantities itself: wheat from the Midlands, peas and beans from Gloucestershire, butter from south Wales, milk, eggs and poultry from Somerset, Gloucestershire and Wiltshire, cheese from Cheshire, and meat from South Wales. Industrial raw materials included timber from the Forest of Dean, tin from Cornwall and wool from Wales. For the importing and transshipment of iron, Bristol was the leading town in the country.

Given these advantages it was only natural that Bristol should be an important manufacturing centre also. This was owing not only to its favourable geographical location but also to the presence of large deposits of coal at nearby Kingswood. These were worked by large-scale operators such as Lord Beaufort, who in 1779 was mining at the 600-foot level, as well as individuals and small partnerships exploiting shallow pits in relative isolation from each other. It was the latter, cut off as they were from traditional social ties, who provided the first fertile ground for Wesley's evangelism.

The labour of these miners produced the cheap fuel on which Bristol's industries thrived. The best known of these was the manufacture of glass, particularly bottles and window glass. The multitude of 'glass-houses' was responsible for that smoky atmosphere about which travellers often complained, but they also made Bristol probably the leading glass-making town in the country. Zinc was smelted there by a process patented by the Quaker William Champion in 1738, and this, when combined with copper, made brass, which could be fabricated into a large number of useful articles. The manufacture of sugar flourished, with twenty refineries in operation by the end of the century. Soap-making, Bristol's oldest industry, maintained its importance as new ones appeared. The Churchman patent for chocolate-making was sold to the Quaker apothecary Joseph Fry in 1761, and Henry Overton Wills joined a local tobacco business in 1786. In addition to numerous distilleries and breweries, there were many importers of wine, who paved the way for Bristol's pre-eminence in the sherry trade. The usual variety of consumer goods required by any market, such as haberdashery, furniture and earthenware, were also, of course, produced there. With the profits from its manufacturing and trade, Bristol was able to supply capital for the development of its hinterland. Its first bank was founded in 1750, and even earlier, in 1718, it had acquired the first fire-insurance office outside London.

It also provided some of the amenities of a metropolis. There were newspapers, a social life of some pretension, a theatre which now ranks as the oldest in Britain, and in the Georgian terraces of Clifton it has left a legacy of eighteenth-century grace and style. For those in search of health and recreation, it possessed the Hotwells at St Vincent's Rock, which made it something of a spa until long after the greater attractions of nearby Bath were appreciated.

However, it was as a port in the seaborne trade that Bristol really made its mark. Although it fell from second place in 1700 to eighth in 1800, the decline was only relative. Whereas 240 ships arrived from outside Great Britain in 1700, by 1787 the total was 485, and the average tonnage of Bristol ships had increased from 105 to 144 tons. The total tonnage of shipping entering Bristol increased from 19,878 in 1700 to 76,000 in 1791.

There were a number of special factors about Bristol trade which must have influenced Tucker in some of his opinions. One was that it suffered badly during the wars of the eighteenth century. The volume of trade, which fell between 1744 and 1747, eventually revived only to fall again in 1756. American non-importation agreements delayed recovery after the Treaty of Paris, but a new peak was then reached in 1775, following which the American Revolution took its toll in falling trade and bankruptcies. Commerce increased again after 1783, reaching a new high in 1791 and 1792, after which the French Revolution led to a new decline. The loss of ships by enemy action was only partially made up by the acquisition of prizes, and many others were diverted from legitimate trade to privateering. On the other hand, of course, wars and even rumours of war could have a beneficial effect on some parts of the economy, as prices tended to rise – particularly those of sugar and slaves.

Bristol took no part in the East Indies trade, which was the monopoly of London merchants, but it dominated the Irish trade. However, although Cork, Limerick and other Irish ports accounted for the largest number of entries, this trade was mostly in Irish hands and therefore had little political influence. Furthermore, the West Indian trade was far more lucrative. Many ships dealt directly with the West Indian islands, especially Jamaica, trading in such staples as sugar, rum and molasses. Others touched there on the 'middle passage' of the triangular trade involving negro slaves from Africa. The slave trade itself, which was dominated by Bristol in the middle of the century, was largely usurped by Liverpool at the end. Other ships engaged in the Newfoundland fisheries, sometimes taking the fish and train oil directly to Spain and Portugal and returning with wine, olive oil and fruit. This trade grew in importance later in the century, especially as more and more Spanish wool was required by the clothing industry.[3] Although, because of economic forces beyond its control, Bristol would in any case have failed to maintain the special position it enjoyed until fairly late in the century, there is little doubt that its fall was hastened by its failure to compete aggressively enough with its rivals. The long delays in building a new exchange and expanding the port facilities were symptoms of a complacency noted by Professor Pares:

> It would not have been very genteel for fellow-members of a small dining club [there were only about 200 merchants of substance in the city], connected together by the marriage of their children to wage war to the knife by cutting freight rates or instructing their captains to snatch consignments from each other's ships or to utilize some of the other weapons in the armoury of competitive enterprise.[4]

However, the facts that industrial development in the hinterland of Liverpool had no counterpart in the Bristol region and that the port itself was unable to cope with bigger and bigger ships were probably more crucial factors.

Since Tucker was in Bristol for twelve years before his first economic writings appeared, he had plenty of time to absorb the views of the various parts of the community, including the relatively small group which dominated its economic, social and political life. As we shall see later, many of the aspects of the Bristol economy touched on above are reflected in his writings. First, however, it is necessary to look at some of the activities which engaged him during that intervening period.

After serving briefly as a curate in rural Gloucestershire, Tucker came to Bristol in 1737, as Curate of St Stephen's. Two years later he became Rector of All Saints, where he was to remain until his return to St Stephen's as Rector in 1750. The consecration of Butler to the see of Bristol in 1738 brought Tucker an influential friend and patron. He soon became Butler's domestic chaplain and in 1742 was installed as a minor canon at Bristol Cathedral. In his various capacities he saw Butler frequently and often used to accompany him as he walked about the Palace gardens after dark. It was on one of these occasions that Butler raised the question of whether certain occurrences in history can only be explained on the assumption that whole communities can be as subject to attacks of insanity as individuals. This notion appears to have deeply impressed Tucker, who mentioned it on several occasions, especially with reference to the madness of war.[5]

Little is known of Tucker's personal life at this period. At some point he married Elizabeth Woodward, the widow of Francis Woodward of Grimsbury, Gloucestershire. The plaque to her memory erected in Bristol Cathedral by her sons indicates that she was seventy-five when she died, on 17 November 1771. This would have made her seventeen years older than her new husband. The nature of their relationship is something of a mystery, since Tucker never mentioned her in his correspondence in the way he did his second wife. In fact, the few references in his letters to his personal circumstances imply that he lived alone. Whatever the truth was, it cannot have reflected much discredit on Tucker, because his enemies, who were prepared to use any ammunition that they could find, are silent on his private life. His wife had two sons from her previous marriage, one of whom, Richard, eventually became Bishop of Cloyne. That Tucker took a keen interest in his welfare is indicated by several references in his correspondence.[6]

Tucker's presence in Bristol at this time coincided with the beginnings of a movement within the Church of England which eventually became a great Protestant sect of its own – Methodism. As has already been mentioned, Tucker was at Oxford when Whitefield was a student and John Wesley a Fellow of Lincoln. Charles Wesley had, a few years earlier, when John was away at Epworth and Wroote, begun the methodical practice of religious devotion which gave the group its name. The Oxford Methodists, however, never numbered more than a handful and they have only a tenuous connection with the society as it was eventually shaped by the capable hands of John Wesley. The leader himself still had an important part of his spiritual pilgrimage to travel before he was clear as to the nature of his vocation. This involved his leaving Oxford in 1735 to spend two years as a missionary in General Oglethorpe's new colony of Georgia. The only significant result of this rather unsatisfactory episode was the acquaintance he established with the Moravian Brethren. This sect, which could trace its origins back a good half century before Luther's revolt, had experienced a revival under Count von Zinzendorf, who had established a model community at Herrnhut (or Herrenhuth), Saxony. Its members struck a sympathetic chord in the breasts of English churchmen, who had practically handed over the Anglican congregations in Georgia and South Carolina to them, and in 1749 obtained an Act of Parliament which encouraged them to settle in the British colonies.[7]

Wesley got to know the Moravian community in London before deciding to visit Herrnhut in 1738. He made the trip shortly after his famous 'conversion' experience of 24 May 1738, when, after hearing someone read from Paul's Epistle to the Romans at a society in Aldersgate Street, his heart was 'strangely warmed'. On his return from Saxony, Wesley worked with the society at Fetter Lane for a period before receiving a call from George Whitefield to come to Bristol.

Whitefield was for many years to be better known in the movement than Wesley. The reason lay in his oratorical powers. If this former pot boy from the Bell Inn at Gloucester had not committed himself to the ministry, he most certainly would have won fame on the stage, for it was his tremendous powers as an actor which swayed the thousands who swarmed to hear him preach. He had been in Georgia at the same time as Wesley but had set down firmer roots there and was to return many times to the New World and eventually to die there. However, in 1739 he was in Bristol electrifying congregations wherever he went. It was at this time that he began preaching in the open air, something he had already done in America. Several miles from Bristol lay Kingswood Chase, which had no parish church to serve the miners and therefore offered an ideal opportunity for his new approach. He preached his first sermon there on 17 February 1739 and a few days later laid the cornerstone of a school. But, as he wanted to get back to America and his beloved orphan school near Savannah, he needed someone to take over his work. That is how Wesley happened to appear in Bristol in the spring of 1739 and how he was persuaded to adopt the unorthodox method of outdoor or field preaching, which he practised so successfully the rest of his long life.

However, it was Whitefield who had upset the Bristol religious *status quo* and it was at him that the first protests of the Established clergy were directed. The latter were in somewhat the same position as was Luther when Tetzel attracted away his congregation with what seemed to him specious promises. Tucker's first known appearance in print occurred at this time. There is a broadsheet which was reprinted in the *Gentleman's Magazine*[8] and which contained several paragraphs dated Bristol, 30 March 1739, and signed George Whitefield. Underneath is a message dated 16 April of the same year and signed Josiah Tucker, reading as follows:

> This abstract of the life of Mr. Whitefield with his tenets of the new birth and principles of religion (being the substance of what he was endeavouring to propagate in private, and instill into some of my parishioners) was told me by a gentleman present at the conversation, who drew it up at my desire, as verbatim as he could recollect. The contents I afterwards carried to Mr. Whitefield to know from his own mouth, if he did maintain such positions; who acknowledg'd them to be his doctrine, and set his hand to the paper of which this is a true copy.

What Whitefield says in the document is that he thought he had led a religious life until he went to university, where a book called *The Life of God in the Soul of Man* opened his eyes. For two years he 'underwent a series of temptations, and continual buffetings of the Devil, which have in a high degree qualified me for the ministerial office'. Having experienced all the pitfalls personally, he felt 'better qualified than other people' to compose sermons, for he preached only what he felt; while others 'are forced to plod and rack their brains whole weeks in compiling a discourse, I am enabled to compile as fast as I can write'. He asserts that 'the Holy Ghost first appeals to the understanding, then over-rules the will; that its experiences are not to be described to an unregenerate person, any more than colours to a man born blind'.

Why Tucker felt compelled to publish this is not clear; possibly he believed that once Whitefield's pretensions were exposed, his influence would evaporate, or else he might have wanted to pin the evangelist down so that he could not squirm away from the questions which Tucker next planned to direct at him. Before moving on to them we might note, as a reflection of current opinion, that this item in the *Gentleman's Magazine* was followed by a long critical article reprinted from the *Weekly Miscellany*. In this a man who had seen Whitefield preach at Moorfields compared him to a mountebank pedlar of physics, who also drew large crowds by offering quack nostrums.[9]

Following that article we find 'Queries to Mr. Whitefield, by the Rev. Mr T-ck-r, Minister of All Saints, Bristol; *not answered*'. Tucker justifies his questions on the ground that he is replying to a person 'so readily disposed to bring mankind out of darkness and error'. He admits that he is personally 'unacquainted with this extraordinary and supernatural light', but that if it exists it 'must certainly tend very much to the benefit of those happy chosen few, who enjoy this signal characteristic of divine favour'. He then asks Whitefield to answer the following questions:

I. What are those principles, doctrines, articles of faith, motives, etc. which this extraordinary light reveals; after what manner they come into the mind; and by what mark or character you distinguish them from delusions of fancy, or worse temptations?
II. What are those particular duties you are enabled to perform; which all others must leave undone, till they obtain the same means of performing them, viz. An extraordinary intercourse with the Deity? Or

III. If I am mistaken in my conjectures, 'That if it doth exist, it must exist for such ends or purposes' – be so kind as to mention in a particular and determinate manner for what other uses it is given, to what purposes you apply it, or it applies to you, and for what special ends desirable, which ends could not be obtained without it?

If their sinful natures prevent men from enjoying this blessing, an account of what cannot be known or received without it would alarm them into repentance and rebirth and would therefore be very valuable. Tucker concludes by asking Whitefield to answer the questions in a brief and explicit manner, avoiding generalities.[10]

Although, according to Tucker, Whitefield used his influence to prevent the appearance of the queries in the *Bristol Journal* and refused to reply publicly, he did write him a letter 'wherein he tells me very lordly and laconically, My Motto is, Answer Him Not a Word; applying the expression of Hezekiah against blasphemous Rabshekah, to his own case and mine'. Whitefield added 'that while I continue in this way of thinking he absolutely despairs of meeting me in Heaven'.[11] However, one of Whitefield's supporters undertook the task disdained by his master and it duly appeared in the *Gentleman's Magazine*. The tone was much sharper than might have been expected from the mildness of Tucker's questions, but the writer was obviously reacting to what he probably felt was an implied sneer lying between Tucker's lines. He begins with a personal attack:

> Had not the Bristol Queries been said to be written by the Rev. Mr. T-ck-r, I should have imagin'd, they had come from one, who had no manner and notion of Divine Relation; but as you are a *Reverend Minister*, I must suppose you to be a Christian, tho' you have given great room to think, that you believed nothing of the operations of the Holy Spirit. . . . The most *arrant Deist* could not have gone lower in his notions in this particular, than you have, to the great dishonour of your ministerial character.[12]

This correspondent's actual attempts to cope with the queries did not impress Tucker, whose reply from Oxford, where he was on 'urgent business', was dated 14 June 1739. He begins by trying to explain why his doubts were originally expressed in the form of queries:

> Mr. Whitefield having boasted, that he received extraordinary illuminations, and surprising influxes of the Holy Spirit – That it not only appealed to his understanding, but even over-ruled and forced his will. – That he could no more describe its operations to an unregenerate person, than he could describe colours to a man born blind. – That nevertheless, the best way of conveying his meaning, was to compare them to a flame of fire, hot water, or the motions of the foetus in the womb; these, I say, and many other the like blasphemous and enthusiastical notions, having been propagated with too much success, amongst several well-meaning, but ill-judging people; I thought it my duty as a clergyman, and a Christian, to prevent, as far as was in my power, the spreading of such dangerous principles, which strike at the root of all religion, and make it the jest of those who sit in the seat of the scornful.

He realised that there was no point in arguing with his opponents as to what they fancied they saw and heard. He therefore decided to confine himself to questioning them concerning the visible results. By doing this he hoped either to show that there was no meaning behind their 'unintelligible jargon' or to give them an opportunity of demonstrating in what way they were 'superior to their fellow Christians, who pretend to no more than the ordinary and common assistance of the Holy Ghost'.

Tucker noted that the response he had received was unfortunately in a different spirit. Not only did Whitefield refuse to answer the questions, but, furthermore, Tucker was 'reviled and insulted' in the street by Whitefield's followers as an 'enemy of God and His religion', because of 'Whitefield's pointing at me so often in his prayers, and describing me in his harangues to the populace'. A friend of Whitefield's, a Rev Mr Hutchins, wrote 'with the usual Christian spirit and meekness of the sect he affirms' that 'I had cast a slur upon my gown, – That I ought to quit the ministry, and that I got it by downright falsehood and equivocation'.

Turning to the reply itself, Tucker accuses his opponent of not answering the questions he actually asked. 'My queries are concerning those extraordinary and surprising effusions, or the new birth these people pretend to in particular, and maintain to be absolutely necessary to salvation; and this gentleman is so good as to inform us, what are those ordinary and common assistances of the Holy Spirit, which are communicated to all good Christians in general.' Tucker goes on, as requested by the author, to make clear his own views about regeneration and rebirth, as expressed in a sermon preached at Bristol 'with a view to stop the epidemical enthusiasm'. In sum it is this:

> That there is an ordinary, constant, and regular Operation or Providence of the Deity, concurring with, and aiding our weak endeavours, checking evil thoughts, and inspiring good and virtuous, is a fundamental principle of all religion, natural and revealed.

Orthodox Christians believe that it is 'promised in a greater degree within the pale of the Church, provided they improve their ten talents, proportionably, than to those who are strangers to the Covenant of Grace'. A person thus baptised in the Christian faith is able to call upon divine assistance in progressively casting off his original corruption and having his degenerate faculties restored. 'And this great change, or rather this changing state, commencing at our baptism, and gradually increasing with our endeavours, is, by a figurative way of expression, very frequent in the holy Scriptures, call'd regeneration, or a new birth.'

Along the way, Tucker refers to some of Whitefield's personal behaviour in Bristol. One of his techniques for impressing his listeners was to exclaim, 'If what I say be not strictly true, may all that ever heard me, may you that now hear me, and all that shall hear me hereafter, rise up in judgment against me, and rejoice at my damnation.' He also said that he could produce two cobblers who knew more true Christianity than all the clergy in Bristol put together, and that Butler and other well-known religious writers 'knew nothing of the internal or saving faith'.[13]

The exchange was concluded by *An Answer to Mr. Tucker's Defense of His Queries: In a Second Letter to that Gentleman*, which, along with some of the other material can be found in an early life of Whitefield. In sum, it says that Whitefield preaches no doctrine other than that to be found in Scripture. The writer concludes by asserting,

> I have now, I think, done with you, and would advise you as a friend, to meddle no more with controversy; for that sort of writing seems not to be your talent; you will only entangle and bewilder yourself the more, the further you proceed in it. I will not promise to take any notice of you; because there is no great pleasure in being engaged with one who has not a head turned for the management of a dispute.[14]

No advice has been so thoroughly rejected by anyone! This was only Tucker's opening barrage in a lifetime devoted to controversial writing. As to the identity of the person who so scornfully offered it, the name of John Wesley was early linked with these two defenses of Whitefield, and is so accepted by Wesley's nineteenth-century biographer, Luke Tyerman.[15] Although Wesley was occasionally guilty of indulging in petulant behaviour, such as can be seen in his letters to William Law, it does not seem likely, from his other references to Tucker, that he was the individual in this case. In his Journal of the following year, for example, there is this entry:

> On Good-Friday I was much comforted by Mr. T——'s sermon at All-Saints, which was according to the truth of the Gospel; as well as by the affectionate seriousness wherewith he delivered the holy bread to a very large congregation. May the good Lord fill him with all the life of love, and with all 'spiritual blessings in Christ Jesus'.[16]

Coming from one of the greatest preachers of the eighteenth century this is high praise indeed, and breathes an entirely different spirit from that expressed in the letters to Tucker.

This little controversy, one of the earliest in a flood of pro- and anti-Methodist polemic which kept the presses occupied for many years, is significant in that Tucker seems at this early stage to have put his finger on the most important, if not the only really vital, difference between the Church of England and the Methodist connection. In order to understand this it is necessary to glance at Methodism as it evolved.

Wesley always considered himself a member of the Established Church, even after he began to ordain ministers himself. As long as he lived he insisted that his followers did not differ with Anglican orthodoxy on any essential point. This is possibly arguable, but certainly the differences were sufficiently subtle not to disturb the equanimity of a church which allowed its members considerable leeway in their beliefs. It was the Methodists themselves who departed from the Church of England after Wesley's death. This separation was probably overdue from an organisational viewpoint, but Wesley had good grounds for attempting to remain within the Anglican Church. As H. B. Workman puts it,

> Like St. Francis, John Wesley, the St. Francis of the eighteenth century, did not set out to discover buried truth, but to live out a forgotten life, and to group together into societies those of like mind with himself. Unlike Wyclif, his object was not to overthrow existing dogmas, but to galvanize them into life.[17]

This is echoed by other Methodist writers, such as Dr Henry Bett, who writes,

> The vital things in religion are not, first of all, intellectual issues and a great evangelical revival like Methodism was naturally concerned, in the first place, with the redemptive facts and the redemptive experiences ... the redeeming love of God in Christ, and the work of the Holy Spirit.[18]

Rupert E. Davies, a contemporary historian of Methodism, claims that it originated long before the appearance of the Wesleys. He sees its earliest manifestation as Montanism, which appeared in Phrygia in AD 160 or 170, and then traces it through the Waldensians and Franciscans to the Moravians. He lists a number of characteristics, the most significant of which is the intensely personal experience of conversion and the resultant feeling of redemption through the action of the Holy Spirit.[19]

In sum, the main concern of John Wesley and his followers was really in what Leslie Stephen referred to as the 'physiology of conversion', and it was at precisely this point that Tucker asked his questions. In what practical and observable way did this experience make the recipient a better Christian than one who had not undergone it? How could one distinguish a genuine conversion from some form of emotional convulsion? Should so much emphasis be placed on an occurrence which was so ambiguous in nature? Instead of such a sudden and possibly superficial intuition of salvation, the Church offered the opportunity for a slow but steady growth of spirituality to be achieved with its continuing help and support. Although he did not develop it, Tucker sensed the underlying danger in the position adopted by the Methodists. Once one has accepted the need for an instantaneous conversion of this type, what about those who have not been granted such an experience? As Abbey puts it,

> If the Methodist considered the Churchman 'unconverted', he would be bound by a thousand passages in Wesley's writings to consider that person, however highly he might respect him, either no Christian, with the most awful doom impending upon him, or, at best, a Christian in some miserable 'legal' sense of the word.... The most fundamental differences between the English Church and Methodism were not of a kind to create much controversy, but as causes of alienation were more formidable than many controversies.[20]

With one pass of his wand, Wesley in effect caused the Church of England to disappear like a phantasm, leaving all Englishmen except the Methodists as ripe for conversion as the natives of darkest Africa. However, not even Wesley seemed to have realised the full implications of what he was doing; certainly his opponents in the Church of England did not.

As is so often the fate of sectarian movements, Methodism began to suffer from schism very soon after its birth. Late in 1739 Wesley broke away from the Moravians at the Fetter Lane Society and formed the first official Methodist Society, which met in a building at Moorgate known as the Foundery. In May 1740 he was attacked in a letter by a fellow Methodist, Hulton, and in July the Fetter Lane Moravians forbade Wesley the use of their pulpit. Wesley's sermon on 'Free Grace', published in the summer of 1740, led ultimately to the breach with Whitefield, the separation of Lady Huntingdon's Connexion, and the formation of the Calvinist Methodist Church in Wales by the followers of Howel

Harris. Whitefield wrote an answer, published in March 1741, to Wesley's sermon. The previous month Wesley accused some of the Kingswood group of such misdemeanours as tale-bearing, back-biting, dissembling, lying, scoffing and slandering. This led to the first Methodist expulsion or purge, with the result that Kingswood was thenceforth the headquarters of the Calvinistic branch.

Since these events aroused considerable interest, the Archbishop of Armagh, Primate of all Ireland, desiring further details, requested 'an eminent person, then resident in Bristol, to get him an authentick account of the divisions and quarrels of the Methodists'. This individual, who must have been Bishop Butler, asked Tucker, 'as being a person well acquainted with their principles and proceedings', to draw up an account, which he did, under the title *A Brief History of the Principles of Methodism*, which was published in 1742.[21]

To start with, Tucker traces the various strands out of which Methodism was woven. The first influence was that of William Law, who was referred to by Charles Wesley 'as their schoolmaster to bring them unto Christ'. Law was a High Church non-juror, unable to accept the accession of the Hanoverians, and originally made his name by engaging in controversy with Hoadly, Mandeville and Tindal. He was closely associated with the family of Edward Gibbon for many years, as both tutor and friend. Before he drifted into the mysticism which characterised his later works, he wrote two devotional books which had great influence in their day: *A Serious Call to a Devout and Holy Life* (1728) and *Christian Perfection* (1726). Doctor Johnson referred to the first-named as 'the finest piece of hortatory theology in any language'.[22] Although Law's influence was chiefly owing to his exhortation to *live* Christianity, and to the beauty and simplicity of his own soul, which shone through his words, it was his theology which was to be examined here.

Tucker found it to be a mixture of the Calvinist and Arminian systems, which he then proceeded to sketch briefly. According to Calvinism, 'mankind upon the fall not only lost that grace, in which their original rectitude and perfection consisted, but contracted a positive malignity, or a constitutional propensity to sin and wickedness'. Man remains in a state of perdition until God 'is pleased to endow him with new spiritual powers' and he is born again. In this process man is passive – the impetus must come from God. The Arminian, on the other hand, believes that although human nature is 'much fallen from its first perfection . . . there are some remains of our first paradisiacal state still subsisting; by virtue of which we can cooperate with the Grace of God', the assistance of which, of course, remains necessary. As a result there are 'degrees of regeneration, according to the influence that religion has over our hearts'. Law agrees with the Calvinists in accepting the depravity of man after the fall, but also with the Arminians in supposing that every man has within himself the seeds of regeneration, which can be nourished if he makes the effort.[23]

Tucker went on to claim that Whitefield, 'with a crude and undigested notion of this system in general', preached the need for a new birth. When people thought it 'was a branch of the Calvinistical system revived, and argued with him upon that supposition . . . the poor man was in a maze'. When the Calvinists defended him on the same grounds, he read their books, and 'thus it happened through a blunder on his side, and a mistake of the question on all sides that Mr. Whitefield fell in with the Calvinistical party'. But Whitefield was still confused. The Presbyterians of Pennsylvania put out a pamphlet called *Extract of Sundry Passages Taken out of Mr. Whitefield's Printed Sermons, Journals and Letters together with some Scruples Proposed in Proper Queries Rais'd on Each Remark*, in which Whitefield is taken to task for some of the non-Calvinistic leanings of his ideas. In Tucker's opinion, Whitefield's reply to this showed that he still did not understand the problem. However, except for this residual confusion, Whitefield was a 'thorough paced Calvinist, as his letter in answer to Mr. Wesley's Sermon proves beyond all doubt'.[24]

Tucker then turned to Wesley's spiritual evolution, tracing it from Law, through the Moravians, to his 'conversion' and visit to Herrnhut. Quoting liberally from Wesley's Journal, he placed in juxtaposition statements which appeared to contradict each other, thereby endeavouring to demonstrate that Wesley's 'system' was rather a 'medley' of principles. In order to be fair, however, he summarised Wesley's attempt at 'reconciling these jarring elements, and reducing them into some kind of order and uniformity', although he thought that Wesley had failed in this task. There are three stages in man's spiritual development, according to Wesley.

1. Before Justification: In which state we may be said to be unable to do anything acceptable to God. . . .
2. After Justification. The moment a man comes to Christ, then he is justified, and born again [but in an imperfect sense]; 'He has Christ with him but not Christ in him.' [He can fall again unless he reaches the third stage.]
3. Sanctification; The last and highest state of perfection in this life. . . . Then have they the indwelling of the spirit. [The new man is completely victorious over the old.][25]

The third stage was distinguished from the second by the following: 'Afore time (i.e. when only in a justified state) when an evil thought came in, they look'd up, and it vanished away, but now it does not come in; there being no room for this in a soul which is full of God.'[26] The implication was that perfection is 'attainable, and ought to be attained to by everyone in this life, before he can be received to happiness in the next'. This was the doctrine of Christian, or sinless, perfection, which drew Count von Zinzendorf's fire and was to remain a controversial part of Methodist theology.

> Though the divisions and separations of the Methodists, is a thing which all people of coolness, and a moderate penetration did foresee, and expect would come to pass; yet the breach might not have been made so soon, had not a foreign circumstance . . . brought them to clash with each other much sooner, than they would have done it of themselves. For indeed they had on both sides, such a medley of all sorts of principles (Calvinism, Arminianism, Quakerism, Quietism, Montanism, all thrown together) that each had room enough to please his own fancy, and had enough besides to hold in common with the rest of his brethren. – And thus they might have run on, at least for a longer space of time (and especially had they been persecuted) in a continual round of rapture and inconsistency, without ever discovering whether they agreed, or disagreed with each other.[27]

But the break had come. Whitefield's replacement by Wesley in Bristol had disappointed the Calvinists, which in turn led to Whitefield's letter of complaint about Wesley's preaching against election. The 'more poetical' Wesleys won out with their hymns and, less poetically, their tactics, such as 'securing the property of the Society Room to themselves; by which means they prevented him [Whitefield] from preaching there, to his great disappointment'.[28]

Referring later to the schism with the Moravians in 1739, Tucker defends the logic of the 'still' Moravians, for, if Wesley is right, 'if there are no conditions, or qualifications required previous to justification; if we may as soon be justified, without having attended to the means of Grace (so-called) as by attending to them, to what use or purpose can they further serve?' In other words, if we do not need Scripture, church services, and so forth, to be 'justified', then why have them? Furthermore, if holiness is a consequence of justification and not a condition of it, why try to lead holy lives before we have reached it? Tucker had tried to explain his objections as clearly as possible to the Methodists, but 'either I am very unhappy and obscure in my expressions, or they are strangely prepossessed by a wrong association of ideas, which they could not sever from each other; for so it was, that they seldom understood me, or could be made sensible of my meaning'.[29]

Wesley replied with his *Principles of a Methodist*, near the beginning of which he says, 'I have often wrote on controverted points before; but not with an eye to any particular person. So that this is the first time I have appeared in controversy, properly so called.'[30] Since this is the first occasion on which Wesley answered a particular critic and attempted a summary of his own beliefs, it is odd that Tucker is rarely mentioned in histories of Methodism. Admittedly Wesley's life was long and his writings many, but that he considered Tucker the first opponent worthy of a serious reply is surely of some interest. Bernard Semmel, in a recent book on Methodism, is more generous. He notes that 'events from the 1740's through the 1770's more or less took the turn which Dean Tucker had predicted as early as 1742'. He also notes Tucker's influence on Wesley in economic and political as well as religious matters.[31]

Wesley initiated his career in controversy humbly and in a genuinely Christian spirit: 'I have a brother who is as my own soul. My desire is, in every word I say, to look upon Mr. Tucker as in his place; and to speak no tittle concerning the one in any other spirit, than I would speak concerning the other.' In actual fact he disagrees very little with what Tucker had said. He admits that he believes in justification by faith alone and in sinless perfection, but only on solid scriptural grounds. His quotation of Tucker's version of the three stages he prefaces with the words, 'I desire not a more consistent account of my principles, than he has himself given in the following words.' Wesley did not deny that Law had been the great influence that Tucker had made him out to be, but it is almost certain that he was deceiving himself, because the letters he wrote to Law in 1738, prior to their break, were far too emotional not to appear those of a disciple who felt he had been betrayed by his master. He also claimed that he had seen the difficulties in the Moravian system quite early. He admits that he may have said many things which have already been said by a variety of people, but denies that this has to mean he holds a 'medley of all their principles . . . all thrown together', as charged by Tucker.

He concludes by referring to the summary that Tucker gives of his own position.

> And perhaps, when I shall have receiv'd farther light, I may be convinc'd, that 'Gospel-Holiness (as Mr. Tucker believes) is a necessary qualification, antecedent to justification: And that Christ did not in any degree fulfil the terms of justification in our stead; but having purchased for us sufficient powers and abilities to perform them, then left us to fulfil them ourselves.' This appears to me now to be directly opposite to the Gospel of Christ. But I will endeavour, impartially, to consider, what shall be advanced in defence of it. And may He who knoweth my simpleness teach me His Way, and give me a right judgment in all things![32]

Here the dispute ended. Tucker doubtless retained his beliefs concerning the inadequacy of Methodist theology, and his dislike for the extremer forms of behaviour sometimes displayed by Methodists. But, given his character, there is no doubt that Wesley's moderation must have struck a responsive chord. Some years later he engaged in a friendly correspondence with Howel Harris, leader of the Welsh Calvinist Methodists, and his other religious writings indicate that he was certainly willing to entertain reforms within the Church.

This pamphlet, like his earlier writings on the same subject, is of interest because it points out at the very beginning the chief difficulties of Methodist theology. One is noted by Wesley himself several years later. In the *Conversations* of 1745 we find, 'Q. Does not the truth of the gospel lie very near both to Calvinism and Antinomianism? A. Indeed it does; as it were within a hair's breadth. So that it is altogether foolish and sinful, because we do not quite agree either with one or the other, to run from them as far as we can.'[33] Wesley's attempt to revive the 'old religion', as Leslie Stephen calls it, brought with it the threat of predestination, which Wesley violently opposed. The way to salvation must be open to all. Yet he insisted on justification by faith alone. The other danger was the passive quietism of the 'still' Moravians, the Antinomianism which led to the belief that a person could be saved without being charged with the desire to be holy in deed as well as thought. These problems plus Wesley's doctrine of sinless perfection or sanctification beyond justification, which even many of his followers could not understand, continued to trouble those Methodists who were interested in theology. But, following Wesley's lead, most of the sect were more concerned with action than with hair-splitting. Religion for them was a deeply felt change in their lives – the rebirth – and the practical effects that flowed from it.

3 Early Publications

In the years before his first work on economics appeared, Tucker published a number of other writings on a variety of subjects. Although they are not of great importance in themselves, the stands he took and the arguments he advanced were to remain typical of his thinking throughout his life. The first of these came about as follows:

> In the year 1745, the year of the Rebellion, I wrote a little tract which, with the approbation and by the order of the recorder of Bristol (afterwards Judge Foster) was printed and given away in large numbers.... It was so well received at court, that the Government reprinted and circulated it, together with the Archbishop of York's speech, all over the nation.[1]

This pamphlet, entitled *A Calm Address to All Parties in Religion, Concerning Disaffection to the Present Government*, can be found reprinted as an appendix to part II of the *Reflections on the Naturalization of Foreign Protestants*, published in 1752.

Although, in retrospect, the cause of Bonnie Prince Charlie appears to have been hopeless from the start, many contemporaries had no real idea of how the populace would react should the venture show signs of succeeding. Certainly others, besides Tucker, had come into contact with enough actual and probable Jacobites to be genuinely concerned. Pro-Jacobite forces were preparing to invade England from Dunkirk when the pamphlet appeared, and the eagerness with which the government seized on it indicates the extent of the anxiety.

The argument employed in the tract is typical of Tucker's approach in all his other works. While not averse to calling upon intangibles such as loyalty and the usual moral absolutes, he tends to rely heavily on that more reliable source of human action, self-interest. He lists the probable consequences of a Jacobite success and then says, in effect, 'Is this what you really want? Is this the price you are prepared to pay for permitting a change in regime?'

His first point is that, since the Stuarts claim the throne by hereditary right, as a matter of property, the liberties guaranteed by the present ruling family, which owed its position to Parliamentary sanction, would immediately be threatened by the restoration of the royal prerogative. Secondly, if the Prince succeeded to the throne, it would be owing to the help of the Spanish and French, who would naturally expect something in return – possibly some of the British colonies. Thirdly, since Stuart policy would likely create a substantial number of dissidents, a large army would be required to overawe the people. This would in turn necessitate heavy taxes and an increase in indebtedness, which might lead to a repudiation of the national debt. In a footnote Tucker reminds his readers that in a manifesto, the 'Chevalier', had actually suggested wiping out the public debt, because it was largely contracted in order to keep his family out.[2] Finally, possession of a shaky throne, requiring the perpetual assistance of France, would make the new king little better than a viceroy. To those who argued that he would put British interests first and disappoint his continental allies, Tucker answers, that, if he could be so ungrateful to those to whom he owed so much, what would be the fate of his subjects, whom he regarded as his property? Furthermore, there was no likelihood that France, as much strengthened as Britain would be weakened by his victory, would allow him such latitude.

Having disposed of utilitarian considerations, Tucker turned to the question of duty. Were there any grounds for breaking the contract of 1688, even if the just title of the present ruling family were questioned? The answer is no, for, according to St Paul and the Homilies of the Church of England, as well as the convocation called by the first Stuart king, once a government is *settled*, even if it originated in rebellion, its authority must be accepted. But Tucker saw no reason to doubt the legitimacy of the Hanoverians. A case could be made on their behalf, and had been made, in Ballantyne's *Hereditary Right of King George II Asserted*, according to which the Stuarts were descended from the illegitimate children of King John (the dissolution of whose marriage to Avice of Gloucester was deemed illegal), while King George II was descended from John's sister Maud and her husband the Duke of Bavaria. Tucker did not believe in indefeasible hereditary right, but, for those who did, there it was, albeit a trifle strained!

Just as his defence of obedience to any form of rule once it was firmly established was a foretaste of the ideas in his treatise on Locke published almost forty years later, so his opinions on taxation, as presented for the first time here, were similar to those advanced in his other writings.

It may be further observed, what I do not recollect hath ever yet been particularly taken notice of, that the system of our finances and commerce hath, in some measure, been put on a new footing since the Revolution, to the Nation's great advantage; – though there is still room for very great improvements. For with regard to our finances, it is not so much the consideration of the sum raised, as of the commodity or persons that are to pay it, which should denominate a tax useful or oppressive: – Because a tax producing vast sums, may be laid in such a manner as to promote the publick welfare, by checking those vicious artificial wants, which are prejudicial to a general, lasting, and extensive commerce: And on the other hand, another may be supposed of so fatal a tendency, though its own amount may be but a trifle, as to prevent the circulation of millions, by stopping the machine of commerce in its first motions.[3]

Another work which originated in 1745 was Tucker's sermon preached at the Bristol Royal Infirmary, which sermon he considered important enough to include in his *Six Sermons* of 1772 and the *Seventeen Sermons* of 1776. The contributors to the Infirmary, which had been founded in 1736, gathered together annually for a church service followed by a dinner at a local tavern and further conviviality. 'The affairs of the infirmary were discussed, sometimes with great animation, leading even to broken heads and bloody noses',[4] according to its historian. Nevertheless, a request to preach before this august assembly was regarded as a great honour.

The main burden of Tucker's sermon was that infirmaries should be used for the moral and spiritual improvement of the patients as well as the cure of their physical ailments. The chaplain and the religious tracts provided by the clergy of Bristol were sorely needed, since 'it must be acknowledged [with respect to morals] times were never worse'. Why is it that, as foreigners agree, the common people of England's populous cities were 'the most depraved and licentious wretches upon earth'? His answer: 'Our people are drunk with the cup of liberty.' Their forefathers were serfs and slaves, but because of alterations in the constitution and the increase in the number of electors, brought about by the fall in the value of money, 'even the meanest of the people [are] equally concerned with the greatest, in the choice of representatives'.[5] He takes up a related theme later in the sermon, when he asks why trade is stagnant.

> Why it is really this, that you do not labour as cheap, and are not content to live and fare as hard as the manufacturers in other countries: And consequently their merchants can afford to sell their goods at the market cheaper than ours. . . . For alas! . . . too many there are, who will not accept of work one part of the week, but upon such terms only, as may enable them to live in vice and idleness the rest. . . . In this you are worse, much worse, than the common people of any other nation – Turn ye, turn ye therefore from your evil ways.[6]

Such sentiments may have appealed to the prosperous contributors but were hardly calculated to please everyone. When copies of the sermon were made available to the patients, as was customary, these remarks were attacked in the press, and, according to the Infirmary's historian, Tucker was 'hooted by the boys and the rabble' when he appeared in the streets.[7] In fairness to Tucker, it should be noted that the practice of allowing patients to go off on their own to attend the Sunday service at a neighbouring church was discontinued when it was noticed that often 'on their return they but too clearly exhibited marks of having been to the alehouse instead of the church'. This despite the fact that the infirmary already supplied them with three pints of beer a day. Other signs of the times were the swords worn by medical students with their red cloaks, and the fighting cocks kept in the dispensary by one of the apothecaries.[8]

Tucker's opinion of the lower classes did not change much during his life; in fact, events only tended to confirm it, as we shall see. However, as he made clear in this same sermon, he was, if not a democrat, very much a liberal in the best English tradition. He remained firm in his defence of liberty even at the risk of licentiousness. He refused to consider 'lodging discretionary powers with the magistrate' or 'summary ways of punishing the guilty' and he insisted that the magistrate's powers must be so clearly defined that anyone exceeding them 'may be called to account for invading and encroaching upon the liberties of a free people'. He notes, with approval, that, whereas in most countries there exists a 'perpetual barrier between noble and ignoble blood', in 'these realms of liberty, the very meanest cannot be obliged to comply with many particulars [such as attendance at charity schools], which are even good and profitable for them', without their free consent.[9] He was also not in favour of further extension of one form of punishment then in use, and his remarks indicate how little things have changed: 'For our Houses of Correction, as they are called, are so far from answering the original ends of their institution, that they corrupt more than correct, and harden rather than reform – so as to make the young offender, if sent there, to be threefold more the child of hell than he was before.'[10]

In 1747 Tucker was able to strike another blow at the pretensions of the Stuart supporters, in connection with the supposed power of the royal touch to cure scrofula or the 'King's evil'. In a history of England written by Thomas Carte, a non-juring clergyman whose patrons included many of the leading Jacobites of Oxford, there was an account of how Christopher Lovell, a labourer of Bristol, was sent to Avignon in 1717 to receive the touch of the Old Pretender. On his return apparently cured, the Bristol Jacobites, who had paid his expenses, made sure that the miracle was widely publicised. Carte could speak from personal knowledge, because he claimed to have visited Lovell in 1717 and found him completely cured.

Unfortunately Carte apparently did not know the end of the story, and Tucker undertook to correct that deficiency in a letter to the *London Evening Post* signed 'Amicus Veritatis', which was reprinted in the *Gentleman's Magazine* for January 1748. The truth was that the symptoms of the ailment had shortly reappeared and poor Lovell had died on his way back to Avignon, much to the chagrin of the Jacobites and the glee of the local Whigs.

Tucker's *Two Dissertations* of 1749 were written against Thomas Chubb, the self-educated 'sage of Salisbury', a well-known deist.

Although Chubb had died in 1747, his last writings were published in 1748 in his *Posthumous Works*. In the first volume, *Remarks on the Scriptures*, he supported, with references to specific passages, his contention that much in the Bible was incredible and contradictory. Tucker particularly objected to two of these interpretations.

Dissertation I is concerned with Luke 14: 12–14, in which the faithful are instructed to invite to their tables not their friends, relatives or prosperous neighbours, but 'the poor, the maimed, the lame, the blind'. Chubb's opinion was that this was so irrational that no one bothered to observe it. Tucker hoped to prove that, on the contrary, Christians 'render a better and more perfect obedience to it, according to the true spirit and meaning thereof, than perhaps to many other of his commands'.[11]

His argument was based on the necessity for understanding the precept in the context of its own time: 'The Jews had long been accustomed to think that God was a respecter of persons: This method was intended to show that he was not (p. 16). Furthermore, a 'feast' of the kind referred to was essentially a religious occasion in those days, similar to the Christian *agape* and its derivation, the sacrament of communion. Since all Christians are invited to participate in communion, regardless of class, wealth or physical condition, and since the Church teaches that all are equal in the eyes of God and attempts to inculcate charity and benevolence, Tucker felt that the precept, in its true spiritual sense, was being fully honoured at that time.

The same technique of putting Scripture in its historical setting is used by Tucker in dissertation II. This is concerned with Romans 13:1–4, in which St Paul teaches that 'the powers that be are ordained of God'. Chubb objected to this passage because it seemed to support that unlimited passive obedience and non-resistance which was anathema to Whig defenders of the Glorious Revolution, and also because he felt that man and not God was responsible for the various forms of government. This was the sort of problem that greatly exercised the eighteenth-century mind, and Chubb was too influential for his arguments to go unchallenged.

In this case, the historical setting was one in which the Jews were expecting a temporal messiah and king, a role Jesus refused to play. Because of the political content in their religious outlook, 'they could look upon the Roman Government in no other light, than as an usurpation which they would throw off as soon as ever their Messiah would come to head their armies'. It was the 'want of a just and rightful title' (p. 32), rather than any specific grievances, which motivated them. This distinction is so important that Tucker enlarges upon it in a footnote (p. 33), where he points out that a government may be benevolent or tyrannical regardless of whether or not its title is controverted: 'I desire, therefore, that these two ideas, viz. disputed titles and national grievances, may always be considered as distinct subjects, and never confounded together.'

Because Jews and Christians were, in the early years of Christianity, regarded as one and the same, and because the loyalty of the Jews to the Roman administration was known to be questionable, it was only good sense for Paul to make clear that the Christian attitude towards temporal power was different from that of the Jews. However, because this did not make Paul's position any more acceptable to someone who objected to it in principle, Tucker tried first of all to tackle the question of who was responsible for the political order. 'It is certain, that God himself is the great King and Moral Governor of the Universe. But he doth not preside over this lower world in an immediate and direct manner, as he did formerly over the nation of the Jews.' He has delegated the power to administer rewards and punishments, 'not by a personal nomination, I grant: but by giving men the instinct or inclination to form themselves into societies for their mutual benefit, and by bestowing upon them the use of reason to direct this instinct to its proper end.' When the result 'answers the general end of government, he gives a sanction and authority to it; and constitutes the magistrate his minister and representative to the people for good' (p. 43). Thus, although God is the ultimate source of authority, the specific form that a particular government takes is in the hands of men, and to that extent Tucker agrees with Chubb.

What really concerned both of them was the application of all this to the circumstances of their own day. Whereas Chubb saw St Paul's stand as a possible justification for the Jacobite rejection of the Revolution, Tucker felt that his opponent was confusing the question of rightful title with that of possession of power. How valid, ultimately, was any title? Was that which rested on the

Norman Conquest or the Anglo-Saxon invasion any more justifiable than that based on the Glorious Revolution? 'Thus it evidently appears, that if persons will object to the government founded on the Revolution, as if it wanted a rightful title, they must object to the government preceding it, for the same reason' (p. 50). The real question was whether or not the political order served the public good. 'The powers that be, when they are the ministers of good to the people, are ordained of God. This is the best politicks, as well as true Divinity' (p. 48). This conclusion was to be justified in much more detail in his *Treatise Concerning Civil Government*, written many years later.

Tucker's two other pamphlets relating to social questions appeared in the course of the next few years, in between more substantial publications, and can best be examined here. The first bore a title which may be abbreviated as *An Impartial Inquiry into . . . Low-Priced Liquors*. It was a product of the widespread concern at that time about the evils of excessive gin-drinking. The social cost of cheap spirits was so high that in 1751 the Pelham administration was compelled to introduce legislation which eventually brought the problem under control. Tucker's pamphlet was published the same year but prior to the enactment of the new laws. Characteristically, Tucker tackled the subject in his own special way:

> I think it is incumbent to advertise the candid reader, that he is not to expect in this essay a full and pathetical description of the miseries and destructive consequences occasioned by spirituous liquors. The many tracts and discourses already published, and particularly the last, by the Lord Bishop of Worcester, render any attempt of mine unnecessary. The author's only view, therefore, is to present the impartial reader, with a series of plain answers to the several objections that may be started, and to set forth such facts as seem necessary to be insisted upon, in order to remove every prejudice and obstacle, [which] the partial representation of private interest will attempt to raise.[12]

He does not feel there is any necessity to belabour the obvious: that excessive consumption of liquor is pernicious, is subject to 'the most indisputable proof, *viz.* daily ocular demonstration'. Denunciation is not enough, because certain economic interests benefit from the situation, and it is their defences which must be undermined. Tucker does this by presenting their objections to any reform, and then answering them. An example of this method is objection 1: 'If the use of gin and English spirits is restrained it will cause a very considerable deficiency in revenue.' Among his answers to this objection are that, although a higher duty on spirits will diminish consumption, the larger amount collected on what is sold will help to maintain the total revenue, and, in any case, the revenue from increased consumption of malt, ale and hops will probably make up any loss.

He does a similar job on the other objections, relentlessly closing in on the ever shifting defence-lines of the vested interests. Tucker early realised that, although moral exhortation has its place, there is no substitute for reasoned analysis of the arguments used to oppose needed reforms, in order to clear away the confusion which often prevented action.

An illuminating glimpse of the practices of his time is offered in the Appendix:

> It is a notorious fact, that many of the parish poor have carried their allowance of bread to the gin-shop, and there exchanged the four-penny loaf of bread for three-penny worth of gin. One circumstance relating to this subject may perhaps recur to the memories of several persons, *viz.* that in the late hard winter, the candidates for money, and whole loaves, were vastly more numerous than those for slices of bread, cheese, dressed meat, and good broth; though these latter were intrinsically of greater value: – Nay, they were slighted and despised: And the reason was, because they were not saleable in the gin shop.[13]

The other pamphlet, which came out in 1753 or the previous year, was entitled *An Earnest and Affectionate Address to the Common People of England Concerning Their Usual Recreations on Shrove Tuesday*. This 'recreation' was known as cock-throwing, and consisted of tying a cock to a stake and throwing sticks at it until it was killed. Tucker's sentiments were outlined in the first paragraph.

> Permit me to address myself to you at this season, and to expostulate with you in a loving, friendly manner, concerning the abominable practice of throwing at cocks, and to beseech you to set a good example this year, by leaving off so bad a

custom. I am no enemy, I do assure you, to reasonable and manly recreations. I could wish, that pitching the bar, throwing the sledge, or a weighty stave, leaping and wrestling, and such like sports were more in use. They tend to health and strength; they inspire courage and activity; and would contribute to make us an hardy, stout race of men, such as our forefathers were. But cock-throwing is a most unmanly and cruel diversion, a shame and a reproach to our country, and offensive to God.[14]

He felt it was shocking 'to make the fears, cries, pains, wounds, and agonies of anything that has sense and feeling, the object of one's mirth and diversion', and concluded by saying how unsuitable such behaviour was for the beginning of Lent, a time 'for breaking off all evil practices and sinful dispositions'.

It is worth remembering the sadistic cock-throwers and the irresponsible drunkards of these two pamphlets when one encounters the harsh things Tucker sometimes has to say about the lower orders. It was doubtless people like these that he had in mind when he was making his generalisations.

Finally, there was a pamphlet on foreign policy which appeared in 1755. *The Important Question Concerning Invasions* . . . was reprinted from an article in the *Evening Advertiser*. In it Tucker attacked some prevalent ideas concerning the approaching conflict with France. These were that Britain, as an island, should concentrate on preparation for a sea war only, that a militia should be raised to defend the country in case of invasion, and that British gold should not be wasted on foreign subsidies.

Tucker does not think that a successful invasion could be completely discounted, particularly if the French were free from other entanglements at the time. 'In short, the notion that Great Britain has no concern, and ought to have none with that part of the continent, which is at our very doors, is so very extravagant, and absurd, that it never entered into any man's heart till of late years, and is never vented by any now, but by those who are either the determined enemies of the government, or want to create a disturbance in the administration.'[15] Although Britain's fleets could destroy France's overseas commerce, this would not necessarily bring her to her knees, since she was not completely dependent on foreign trade for her wealth and could, in any case, trade with her continental neighbours.

Early Publications

With respect to militia, Tucker was not convinced by the suggestion that Britain should emulate ancient Rome and modern Switzerland by relying on such a force. Whereas Rome and Switzerland were essentially militaristic societies, Britain's strength depended on commerce, which would be disrupted if men were called away from useful work. He was also worried about the effect of a large body of men in arms on British liberties.

The heart of his pamphlet was a discussion of subsidies. The opponents of the policy believed that England suffered by the export of bullion which it entailed. Tucker's answer was one that he developed further in his economic works of the same period.

> For the whole force of this argument, such as it is, turns upon the supposition that money is wealth: Whereas industry, manufactures, agriculture, mutual and general employment, are the real wealth of a nation; and money is only the sign or certificate of it. . . . But you still reply, the money, the money, the money goes abroad. And in the name of common sense, so let it go; for industry will be sure to bring it back again with increases.[16]

By subsidising France's enemies on the continent, Britain forced that country to maintain larger forces than she would otherwise have done, with a corresponding strain on her resources. Because Britain could borrow at 4 per cent and France had to pay 8 per cent, it was good value for money. 'I do maintain that it is much cheaper to hire 100,000 foreigners to fight by proxy, than it is to take even 20,000 of our own manufacturers and pay-masters, and convert them into soldiers and pay receivers.'[17] Furthermore, since many of those sent abroad to fight would never return, the loss to the country's productive wealth would be even greater.

If Britain had to become involved in a war, that was how Tucker would like to see it waged, but he made it quite clear that he preferred peace. He felt that war, with its disruption of trade, should be avoided, if at all possible, by a commercial nation. This could only be done if Britain recognised that other nations had legitimate interests and was prepared to make the necessary concessions. Such an attitude obviously was not widespread on the eve of the Seven Years' War.

4 The *Essay on Trade*

Tucker's formal entry into the field of study eventually to be known as political economy or economics was made with *A Brief Essay on the Advantages and Disadvantages which Respectively Attend France and Great Britain with Regard to Trade, . . .*, published in 1749. Although it does not represent his last word on the subject, it is worth examining in some detail, not only because it was his first work in economics as such, but also because it was the one for which he was best known in his own day. Both the *Elements of Commerce* and the *Instructions for Travellers*, written later as parts of a never completed 'great work', were only printed for private circulation amongst friends, although an Irish edition of the *Instructions* did appear later.

The short introduction is probably the most significant part of the *Essay*. He begins with a definition of commerce: 'All commerce is founded upon the wants, natural or artificial, real or imaginary, which the people of different countries, or the different classes of inhabitants of the same country, are desirous, in defect of their own single abilities, to supply by mutual intercourse.' Domestic trade is naturally important, but it 'neither increases nor diminishes the publick stock of gold and silver', as does foreign trade. There the goal is a favourable balance expressed in terms of precious metals.[1] As a result of this, Tucker has been seen as a follower of mercantilism in its most unsophisticated form – bullionism, or the belief that real wealth consists of gold and silver acquired at the expense of other countries.[2] However, Tucker moves beyond such excessively simplified notions two pages later, where he says, 'For though a difference in the value of the respective commodities may make some difference in the sum actually paid to balance accounts, yet the general principle, *that labour (not money) is the riches of the people* [emphasis added], will always prove that the advantage is on the side of that nation which has most hands employed in labour.'[3] Ignoring for the present the question raised by the last part of the statement, we have here a recognition of the importance of labour as a source of wealth similar to that given it by Adam Smith.

Tucker goes on to express surprise that, 'the principles of trade therefore being so clear and certain in themselves', they were not better known, and that men of business were so divided as to what they were. The reason, in his opinion, is that men of learning have avoided this 'noble and interesting science' because they think of it as 'dark and crabbed, perplexed with endless difficulties', and fit only for merchants. On the other hand, the merchants, who until then had monopolised the subject, could not agree amongst themselves. Tucker had a simple explanation for this: 'The leading idea, or the point arrived at by every merchant must be, in the nature of things, and in every country, a balance in favour of himself. But it doth not always follow, that this balance is likewise in favour of the nation; much less of other merchants, whose interests may be opposite his own.' Therefore it might be that 'a person of a liberal and learned education, not concerned in trade, is better qualified to engage in the study of it as a science, than a merchant himself: because . . . his mind is freer from the prejudice of self-interest, and therefore more open to conviction in things relating to the general good', even though a merchant may be a better judge of whether what is 'so fair in theory, is feasible in fact'.[4]

Although he does not attach a name to this 'noble science', Tucker clearly recognises that it exists and that it is suitable for investigation by scholars. Unfortunately, his own attempt to explore the subject in an orderly and comprehensive fashion, the 'great work', was not destined to be finished, and any chance that his name would be associated with the founding of economics as an autonomous intellectual discipline was lost. However, the writings that we do have exhibit enough insight into a number of economic problems to give him an honourable place among the forerunners of the Physiocrats and of Adam Smith.[5]

It may be just as well at this point to deal with earlier opinion as to the part played by Tucker in the history of economic thought. With the overwhelming acceptance in the nineteenth century of the rightness of Adam Smith's attack on mercantilism and his justification of *laissez-faire*, any earlier economic writer was bound to be judged by the extent to which his ideas conformed to those of

Smith. Thus, where Tucker was understood to have anticipated Smith's position he was given due credit, but where he appeared to remain faithful to the false gods of mercantilism he was treated with some scorn.[6]

There is no doubt that *The Wealth of Nations* is a useful bench-mark against which to measure the theorising of others and it will be helpful in any assessment of Tucker. However, it must be remembered that the term 'mercantilism', with its pejorative connotations, was created for polemical purposes. Detailed study of pre-Smithian writers has shown that they varied so greatly in their opinions that we do them an injustice by forcing them all into one mould. While it is true that some of them were apologising for special interests, it is also true that most of them were reacting to the problems caused by economic change in their own day, just as Smith himself was doing.

As it turned out, Smith was also laying the foundations for modern theoretical economics when he wrote *The Wealth of Nations*. However, his importance in the history of economic analysis does not alter the fact that, when he made specific policy recommendations on the basis of his own assumptions about the nature of man and the world, the same criteria must apply to him as to his predecessors. For example, although he believed a general policy of non-intervention on the part of the government was the most beneficial one, he was willing to retain the Navigation Acts, on the grounds that, although mercantilist and therefore bad in principle, they did provide Britain with a reservoir of trained seamen in case of war. By giving military preparedness priority over economic efficiency, Smith made the kind of value judgement which others could just as reasonably make in connection with the welfare of factory workers or the protection of any industry regarded as vital to the national interest. Thus, there was not necessarily a tremendous difference in practice between those who accept the dogma of *laissez-faire* and those who did not.

Although Tucker advocated greater freedom in specific areas, he always allotted the government a more active role than did Smith. The reason for this was that he did not believe there was a pre-established harmony between private and public good.[7]

> It is a maxim with traders, and a justifiable one, to get all that can be got in a legal and honest way. And if the laws of their

country do give them the permission of carrying on any particular gainful trade, it is their business, as merchants, to engage in the prosecution of it. – As to the great point of national advantage or disadvantage, this is properly the concern of others, who sit at the helm of government, and consequently whose province it is, to frame the laws and regulations relating to trade in such a manner, as may cause the private interest of the merchant to fall in with the general good of his country.[8]

Tucker condemned specific groups from time to time, but, as the above quote shows, he did not criticise merchants for pursuing their own ends. However, he was not optimistic enough to presume that these ends were necessarily in the public interest. That is why the government must step in and encourage 'the merchant to find his own advantage in labouring for the good of his country', and thus unite individual and social happiness (p. ix).

Tucker concludes the Introduction with an appeal to the landed interest to pay more attention to the subject of trade. The landowners must become aware of the extent to which their fortunes were involved. 'For it is a most certain fact, though not sufficiently attended to, that the landed gentleman is more deeply concerned in the national effects of an advantageous or disadvantageous commerce, than the merchant himself' (p. x). As his capital is fixed in the land and not portable, like that of the merchant, he has the most at stake. 'The more persons there are employed in every branch of business, the more there will be to consume the produce of his estate', and he will prosper accordingly. 'In short, his own interest is connected with the good of the whole' (p. xii). Adam Smith later wrote, in a similar vein, that the interest of the landowner 'is strictly and inseparably connected with the general interest of society'.[9]

Tucker now moves into the main body of his essay, which lists the economic advantages and disadvantages of Britain and France. He nowhere explains why he chose this particular format in which to make his suggestions for improvement. Since Britons writing in the previous century had often held up the Netherlands as an example worthy of emulation, there was nothing unusual in his method; moreover, now that the French had surpassed the Dutch as Britain's most important rivals in trade, there would probably appear to be merit in this kind of comparative analysis.

As Tucker demonstrated later, in his *Instructions to Travellers*, he believed strongly in the usefulness of observing the economies of other countries so that Britain could learn from their successes and their failures. In any case, the *Essay on Trade* caught the public fancy. It went through four editions, was used as the basis for a French work, Plumart d'Angeul's *Remarques sur les avantages et les désavantages de la France et de la Grande Bretagne* . . . of 1754, and was one of the collection of Tucker's books in Adam Smith's library.[10]

Looking first at the advantages of France, he is impressed by the sobriety and industriousness of the common people, who are actively encouraged to marry and have large families. Other advantages include the laws regulating the quality of manufactured goods, the excellent roads and waterways, the strict enforcement of laws against smuggling, and the welcome extended to foreign workers. On the other hand, he finds fault with, among other things, the country's arbitrary government, the large number of unproductive members of religious orders, the oppressive system of taxation, and even the two 'national vices': gaming and fine clothes. Above all, he deplored the fact that France swarmed with impoverished nobles who had nothing but contempt for the bourgeoisie, with the result that the latter abandoned trade as soon as they could buy their way into the nobility.

Tucker then devotes a substantial amount of space to the advantages and disadvantages of Great Britain. The most convenient way to approach them, however, is to move on to a lengthy section entitled *'Certain Proposals for Remedying Many of the Above Mentioned Inconveniences: and Increasing the Trade and Credit of Great Britain'*. This covers the same topics in a context of reform. There are sixteen proposals in all, many of them quite specific and practical in nature. He supports, for example, a system of bonded warehouses, public inspection to improve the quality of export goods, the construction of canals for the expansion of internal trade, a more determined stand against smuggling, and an active policy of encouraging foreigners to visit Britain.

More illustrative of the general nature of Tucker's thought were some of his other suggestions. His first and 'capital' disadvantage of Great Britain was the 'want of subordination in the lower class of people', which was 'attended with dreadful consequences, both in a commercial and a moral view'. Lack of control leads to vice, which 'must be supported, either by an high price for their labour, or by methods still more destructive'. The result is 'poverty and disease; and so they become a loathsome burden to the publick'. The French, on the other hand, were 'sober, frugal, and labourious; they marry and have flocks of children, which they bring up to labour'. His solution is to raise voting qualifications to what they were when the forty-shilling freehold was established in the reign of Henry VI, which he computed to be the equivalent of £20 in 1749, owing to the decline in the value of money. £20 per annum freehold or £200 stock in trade for tradesmen would eliminate those in the electorate who 'run roving after every electioneering'. Freed from the need to oblige these people, the authorities could enforce the laws against idleness and debauchery, and smuggling could be largely suppressed (pp. 36–7). Tucker was not alone here: the first Earl of Shaftesbury and Dean Swift had also advocated changing voting qualifications to reflect the fall in the value of money.[11]

At first glance it would not seem obvious how restricting the franchise would raise the general level of morals, but Tucker saw it as a positive policy. Since, he felt, it would now be an honour to have a vote, the voter would pride himself on his integrity and incorruptibility.

> Likewise a spirit of emulation and industry would be excited; and the privilege of voting would become a laudable inducement to every artificer, (not to get drunk, or to take a paltry bribe, as at present is the case) but to be frugal and saving, in order to raise himself to the degree of a voter. And many artificers might accomplish this by a few years' industry after they are set up. (pp. 50–3)

He also thought that the number of poor would be lessened, the price of labour would be reduced and other desirable effects would flow from this 'reform'. Here, as in so many other places, Tucker is trying to create conditions favourable to individual initiative, a source of energy which could be tapped for the common good.

His second proposal was the establishment, in all the manufacturing towns of Britain, of courts to be called 'guardians of the morals of the manufacturing poor'. To qualify for the court, members had to have no fewer than twenty employees, they had to subscribe two guineas or more a year, and they had to be married in order to set a good example. They should have the power to limit the number of alehouses – not an unreasonable request, since one out of three or four houses in Bristol at that time was a licensed public house; to punish not only persons who arranged cock-fighting and cudgel-playing, but also those who 'bring liquors, cakes, fruit, or any like temptations, to draw people together'; and to expel all those who 'cannot give an account of themselves by what means they subsist', as well as loose women. Most of the powers are of the type now exercised by local authorities. More positively, to encourage good behaviour, the guardians should, in cases where young couples intending marriage had saved £3 or more from their earnings, reward those same couples with another £2 – 4, depending on their behaviour, to be paid a year and a day after their marriage. The sick and those with large families were to be assisted, and the 'remarkably diligent and industrious' were to be rewarded with copies of the Bible and other suitable books, to be stamped in gold letters 'The hand of the Diligent maketh Rich', on one side, and 'To the Praise of them that do well', on the other (pp. 53–7).

There is a footnote to his proposal, part of which has been occasionally quoted.[12] After noting the increasing frequency of complaints about the manufacturing poor – their immorality, the tendency of journeymen to combine 'to extort exorbitant wages', and so on – he mentions a gentleman 'in the clothing way' who had observed 'that in exceeding dear years, when corn and provisions are at an extravagant price, then the work is best and cheapest done: – but that in cheap years, the manufacturers are idle, wages high, and work ill done'. From this the gentleman concluded that high taxes on necessities were not an evil as commonly thought, but were a positive good since they forced the poor to work or starve. Tucker's comment was,

> Some things may certainly be said in favour of this scheme. But an human and compassionate man cannot but be sorry, to see the morals of the poor so very corrupt, as to oblige any one to think of such an expedient. In the mean time, as much may be said against it; and as it would involve the innocent as well as the guilty in the same punishment; perhaps some other expedients would better answer the good end proposed, and not be liable to the same objections. (p. 53n.)

The Essay on Trade

These expedients were the ones he had already suggested – higher voting qualifications, and court guardians – plus a later proposal (no. VII) for encouraging the naturalisation of foreigners, who, by providing competition, would keep the cost of labour down.

The latter was a project which was to exercise Tucker a great deal over the next few years, but the case for immigration is nowhere more clearly and succinctly stated than here. In this proposal he is talking specifically of providing for the naturalisation of foreign Protestants.

> Here again the baleful spirit of self-interest exerts all its powers to oppose so publick and general a benefit, – 'What! must foreigners, and we know not who, come and take the bread out of our mouths?' – An honest Cambro-Briton would have called all Englishmen foreigners, and he knows not who. But waving [*sic*] that, – let me calmly ask, What bread do they eat? –and out of whose mouths? It must be English bread: The corn grew here, – was manufactured, was sold here. And the foreigners, who eat it, earn it by their labour, and pay for it. So far then, we hope there is no offence. The more inhabitants there are to consume the produce of our lands, the better can the farmer and the gentleman pay their shopkeepers and tradesmen, and the more manufactures will they consume in every respect. Let us see therefore, in the next place, out of whose mouths do they take this bread? If they introduce new manufactures, or carry those already established to greater perfection, in that case the publick is greatly benefited, and no individual can be injured. If they employ themselves only in such as are already settled and perfected, they will not defraud the mouths of sober, frugal, and industrious persons, who may work as cheap, and can work as well as foreigners. And therefore should be obliged to do both. It can be, therefore, none but the abandoned, debauched, and dissolute, who would chuse to be idle three or four days in a week, and want to have their wages so high as to support this extravagance, that can make such a complaint. (pp. 84–5)

But, say some, Englishmen are used to living better than foreigners and therefore cannot afford to work as cheaply as they. Tucker expects that buyers in the world market would hardly be persuaded to pay higher prices so that Englishmen can live better.

'For the English must trade, at least upon an equal footing with other nations or not trade at all.' As another example of the weakness of his opponents' arguments, he asks what would have happened if the people of Birmingham had refused to let other Englishmen in, on the grounds that they were foreigners. By following the opposite policy, Birmingham has become one of the most flourishing towns in England, with fewer beggars than the older towns, where the spirit of 'industry, frugality and emulation' is dampened by restrictive practices. He also mentions the stimulation to English manufactures provided by the Huguenots, who were met with the same opposition (p. 87).

Tucker was convinced that England and Wales were under-populated, not to mention Scotland and Ireland. The country had room for more people, but the British themselves were not increasing as they should, owing to their abandoned state and the lack of encouragement for marriage. 'And ten thousand common whores are not so fruitful ... as fifty healthy young married women.' He also blamed the high rate of infant mortality, the drain caused by the sea and the plantations, and the numbers who were killing themselves with gin and other spirits (p. 90).

Yet what had been the result of his efforts to improve this situation? Nothing but abuse. If the arguments presented in detail in his *Reflections on the Expediency of Naturalising Foreign Protestants* (which had appeared before the third edition of the *Essay on Trade*, the edition quoted here) were wrong, were they not at least worth a reasoned refutation? 'But', he sighs, 'it ever was the hard fate of those who have laboured to promote the true interest of their country ... to be vilified and insulted, while living, and never to have real justice done to their characters, till they are dead' (p. 92). His only consolation lay in knowing that he had done his duty.

One may well ask why Tucker was surprised that his suggestion for importing foreigners *specifically* for the purpose of keeping wages down was not greeted with acclaim, especially from those likely to be affected. The answer would seem to be that he did not see the problem in this light. He regarded himself as a compassionate man, and in his private life was extremely generous in helping those who showed any promise. Living in Bristol and therefore very conscious of England's dependence on world trade, he was unusually sensitive to the limited human resources available and the inefficient use made of them. In the early nineteenth century it was assumed that a worker could not earn much more than a subsistence wage, no matter how hard or long he laboured; Tucker, on the other hand, saw men who could subsist in idleness and even dissipation on the proceeds of occasional employment. It seemed to him vital to get these people working full-time and as productively as possible if the country were to remain competitive.

Tucker's programme for increasing productivity by keeping wages as low as possible would at first sight appear to be very reactionary when contrasted with the ideas advanced by Adam Smith, who in a well known passage says,

> The liberal reward of labour, as it encourages the propagation, so it increases the industry of the common people. The wages of labour are the encouragement of industry, which like every other human quality, improves in proportion to the encouragement it receives. . . . Where wages are high accordingly, we shall always find the workmen more active, diligent, and expeditious, than where they are low.

Although he admits that 'some workmen, indeed, when they can earn in four days what will maintain them through the week will be idle the other three', he adds that 'this is by no means the case with the greater part'.[13] However, in his earlier *Lectures* he says that the workers are in a 'despicable condition; their work through half the week is sufficient to maintain them, and through want of education they have no amusement for the other but riot and debauchery. So it may very justly be said that the people who clothe the whole world are in rags themselves'.[14] Even in *The Wealth of Nations* itself, we find that Smith, referring to the possibility of a decrease in the taxes on necessaries, says, 'The labouring poor would thus be enabled to live better, to work *cheaper* [emphasis added], and to send their goods cheaper to market. The cheapness of their goods would increase the demand for them, and consequently for the labours of those who produced them.'[15] The beneficial effects of lower labour costs seemed to him as self-evident as they did to Tucker.

There is no evidence that Tucker wanted the poor to suffer in order that the rich might benefit at their expense. One had to distinguish between two groups within the so-called 'poor'. For the respectable, honest, hard-working, ambitious working man,

Tucker had nothing but praise; this man was out to improve himself and in the process could do nothing but good for the national economy. Tucker's aim was to encourage and reward these people and get others to emulate them. But there was also an element at this level of society which refused to behave as the 'economic man' should; they preferred leisure to work, and that leisure was often spent in a way that was harmful both to the individual and to society. As variations of the domestic system were still dominant in Tucker's day, the worker was not yet subjected to the kind of labour discipline provided later by the factories, and, when business was brisk and wages rose well above subsistence level, he could afford to take time off, if he so desired. Instead of continuing to work and accumulating a surplus for hard times, or for investment in his own looms, the irresponsible individual spent this free time in dissipation, and, when trade was bad, became a burden on the ratepayers. As a clergyman Tucker would be aware of the cost in human terms for the family, and as an economist he would be concerned at the cost to the nation in lost productivity and higher prices. He obviously felt that, in a world where British goods had to be competitive, such behaviour could eventually be ruinous for the country. Therefore his suggested reforms.

Some of them, such as the idea of a court of guardians, are thoroughly distasteful to the liberal mind, but it is interesting to note that practically all Tucker's suggestions have been adopted at one time or another, although sometimes in a more palatable form. Family allowances and other incentives to larger families have, for example, been instituted in a number of countries, although no attempt has been made to reward only those parents distinguished by good behaviour.

Raising the voting qualifications would doubtless be considered a retrograde step. Tucker was certainly no democrat, and his experiences with the lower classes did little to alter his attitude, which was shared by practically the whole educated class of his day, since even the most radical reformers rarely advocated universal manhood suffrage. But the evils he was trying to eliminate should be clearly noted. He believed, as did many nineteenth-century humanitarian liberals, that giving the vote to an ignorant and often debased man was an invitation to demagoguery and corruption. To a poor man, for whom the issues, if there were any, meant nothing, the vote was a salable commodity, available, for money, favours or alcohol, to the highest bidder. This problem can be tackled in various ways, but decreasing the size of the electorate would probably have had little effect, except possibly to make elections cheaper for the candidate. However, Tucker was just as concerned about improving the quality of the electorate as he was about bribery. He obviously hoped that, by making it a reward for responsible behaviour, the vote would be exercised carefully, after due thought had been given to the long-range interests of the country as well as those of the voter.

As for the third answer – that of immigration – we can, since Tucker wrote in greater detail about it elsewhere, defer consideration of it for the moment, except in so far as it involves the question of population. Tucker believed not only that immigration would make Britain more competitive, by increasing efficiency, but also that the resulting increase in the number of inhabitants was desirable in itself. He tackles the subject from another angle in his proposal XVI, on taxation: here he refers to the 'manifold ill consequences that flow from men's living batchelors'. Since this led to immorality, with the result that 'at least ninety-nine in an hundred ... gratify their desires, but so as to add no proper increase to the publick stock of inhabitants, in which the riches and strength of a nation do consist', bachelorhood should be discouraged. Those 10,000 loose women referred to earlier would, if they had been married instead of corrupted, have been capable of producing 'at least one thousand healthy children every year'. In order to make life more difficult for bachelors, he proposed that a number of taxes be trebled for them and doubled for widowers between thirty and fifty who had not fathered any children (pp. 128–32).

Tucker obviously felt that a large and increasing population went hand in hand with advancing prosperity, but, since he was always concerned about the industriousness of the people, there is no reason to believe that he regarded numbers alone as enough. It is notable that he did not utilise one of the standard arguments in favour of a larger populace: the need for a plentiful supply of cannon fodder. Since he was convinced that the bellicosity of his countrymen was responsible for most of their wars, which he regarded as wasteful and unnecessary, he doubtless saw no virtue in encouraging it.

Tucker's proposal III concerns what was to be one of his pet schemes: the union of Ireland with the rest of the British Isles. The advantages were obvious:

> By this mutual benefit, neither kingdom would be looked upon as foreign to the other: But the goods of both would be imported duty-free, or perhaps be considered only as coming coast-wise. The hostile prohibition against wearing, or using the produce of either kingdom, would be repealed; and all that unnatural war between the commerce of the two nations, would be at an end: – which would be attended with these further happy consequences, that many of the necessaries of life would be imported cheaper into England, than they now can be purchased; a great advantage this to the merchant and manufacturer: – and many more of the luxuries, ornaments and delicacies of living, would be exported from hence into Ireland. (pp. 58–9)

In answer to the anticipated objection that English trade would be ruined, he asks how different the Irish, 'some of the best, and most faithful subjects', were from the people of Yorkshire, who had drawn trade away from Gloucestershire. Should their looms therefore be broken? Ireland was admittedly better situated for the West Indies trade, but then so was Bristol in comparison with London. Should the port of Bristol therefore be closed down?

> It would be an endless, and a tedious piece of work, to wade through such gross and palpable absurdities. One thing is plain and obvious, that *self-interest*, the bane of all publick good, is driven to hard shifts, in order to cover such views as she dare not openly avow. (p. 61)

This in essence sums up very briefly also the grounds for his attack on monopolies, which is taken up in more detail below. He was ever suspicious of the way in which interested groups profited at the expense of the general public under cover of specious arguments concerning the national welfare. In this he did not differ from Adam Smith, although he was prepared to use legislation rather than leave it to the 'invisible hand'. He was also practical enough to note that after the union English taxes could gradually be extended to Ireland (proposal IV) so that the English could be relieved of some of their burden (p. 62). This same argument was used by Adam Smith.[16] Ireland is also mentioned in proposal v, which advocated the establishment of wool and silk manufactures on that island as well as in South-West England. Wages were as low in those places as in France, and, since the local people would be involved in the industry, they would be less likely to smuggle wool to France, as they did at that time.

Proposal vi, 'To lay open and extend our narrow and restrained companies; beginning with the Turkey and Hudson's Bay Companies, which hurt the trade of Great Britain more essentially with respect to France, than any other company can do' (p. 65), is the longest and most detailed of all his proposals. In order to be fair, he begins with the arguments on the other side. The first three concern the value to a backward country, such as England at the time of the Hanseatic League, of inviting in more advanced foreigners and giving them a monopoly in return for the economic benefit which flowed from their skills. The fourth is that only in this way could the large sums be raised which had to be expended before a new trade could be made to show a profit. If individual merchants were not prepared to attempt it alone, 'it is but reasonable that those who adventure in a joint stock should be incorporated, and have a privilege excluding all others from interfering in this new branch of commerce, till the adventurers are sufficiently paid for the risks they ran, and the expenses they were at' (p. 67). However, in a footnote he suggests that a fairer method would be 'to allow a sufficient premium or bounty to encourage *all* adventurers, rather than to grant exclusive privileges to a few'. Although both are a charge on the public, the monopoly is the least satisfactory.

The fifth reason is the need in past times to borrow from such groups when individuals did not trust the government. 'But there is a further motive remaining, which, though a very bad and scandalous one, yet it is to be feared, hath had the greatest share in erecting monopolies of all the rest. And that is, in plain, but very expressive English, jobbing.' The charters granted by Charles II were examples of such concessions to the private profit of favoured individuals.

Of all these reasons, in Tucker's opinion, only the fourth, to reward those who have engaged in a trade at excessive risk, had any kind of persuasiveness in his day, but he is convinced that the original proprietors had long since been fully recompensed for their risks. There was also the argument that companies needed to be exclusive so they could support the expense of erecting forts. His answer is that, if forts are really necessary, they should be erected at national expense (p. 76n.).

He then turns to the evils of monopolies:

> In the 1st place, these exclusive companies cannot trade, if they were inclined, upon so easy terms, as private adventurers would do, were the trade laid open. So many directors, super-cargoes, storehouse-keepers, factors, agents, clerks; – and all the pickings of their several dependants: – So many fees, sweetnings, etc. from the manufacturer, or under merchant, that his goods may have the preference to others ... make it impossible for any corporate company to trade upon an equal footing with private adventurers. ... For this reason it has been always found, that if private adventurers shall be permitted to engage in the same trade, they will infallibly carry it away from the company. (pp. 70–1)

As examples, he gives the success of the Bristol and Liverpool merchants in the Africa trade after it was opened up in 1698, and the failure of the Turkey Company when pitted against Marseilles in the Levant trade. The Turkey Company is dealt with at length in a pamphlet he wrote later.

The truth, though, is that the exclusive companies do not *want* to sell cheap; the whole purpose of the charter is for them to be able to sell for more than they otherwise could. 'This is the greatest and most intolerable of all the evils of the monopolies. It is a prostitution of the trade and welfare of the publick, to the merciless ravages of greedy individuals' (pp. 73–4). The effects can be seen even in a free trade where someone with a large capital will drive his competitors out of the field by underselling them at a loss in order to gain a monopoly. But, whereas such an 'engrosser' will eventually retire to enjoy his ill-gotten gains, a company can go on mulcting the public indefinitely.

As a specific case he takes the Hudson's Bay Company, which had been examined before Parliament in 1748. It was shown that the company discouraged colonisation in its 'vast and boundless empire', even in the warmer regions of the south, while the French settlers were moving out and taking trade from the English. He was very critical of the company's forcing the Indians to endure the hardships of the long journey to the Bay rather than building forts further inland to attract more trade. The company defended itself by saying that it took all the furs it could get and (in Tucker's words), 'if more goods were given to the Indians in exchange, they would not bring more beavers; because they are an idle, lazy race of people; and, having no artificial wants to gratify, have no ambition to spur them on to take more pains'. Tucker, of course, disagreed that there were no further wants to be satisfied. Their needs admittedly were different, 'but they want beads, bells, little looking-glasses, rings and such trinkets; (besides many articles of their clothing, bedding, hunting, fishing and fowling) and are as impatient to be gratified in these respects, as we can be in ours' (p. 80).

This leads Tucker to his fundamental criticism of this type of monopoly. The company says that, if it can get all the furs that are available for £5000, why spend £10,000? It is saving the nation £5000. Tucker's answer is a *reductio ad absurdum*: if £5000, why not £1000? If all the kingdom's trade were carried on like this, all the wealth would end up in the hands of the few and the rest would become beggars. 'It is not therefore gold and silver, considered merely in themselves, that can make a kingdom flourish, but the parceling them out in proper shares, by means of the divisions and subdivisions of various trades' (p. 83). The monopolist, by buying at a low price, not only reduced his total sales, although receiving a high profit on them, but also limited his purchases of English goods for use in the trade. Tucker would like to have seen the Indians receive more for their furs. This need not have required an increase in prices, but could have been accomplished by lowering their transportation costs, through the establishment of posts closer to where the Indians did their trapping. Such a move would have encouraged them to bring more furs to market and thus enabled them to purchase more English manufactures. His aim, as always, was to keep as many Englishmen employed as possible, even if this meant a higher price for furs and lower profits for the Hudson's Bay Company. In his words,

> The diminishing of such exports, is in fact the diminishing of our own manufactures, and defrauding the nation of so much labour, whereby the hands employed in those manufactures

must become a rent-charge upon the public – or steal, – or starve, or fly the country. The only limitation which ought to be put upon the quantity of our own manufactures, to be exported, is what the nature of the thing will of itself put upon them; viz. To export no more than is consistent with the reasonable gains and profit of the exporter. If he can afford to export ten thousand pounds worth of English manufactures, where an exclusive company would export but five thousand; it is for the general good of the country that he should do it. And all trade ought to be laid free and open, in order to induce the exporters to rival each other; that the public may obtain this general good by their competitorship. But if they cannot afford to export so much, there is no need to restrain them by laws and penalties, from doing that which their own private interest will suggest to them soon enough. (p. 81n.)

This idea that England could only sell her manufactures abroad if she helped her customers to find the wherewithal to pay for them was destined to enjoy quite a following during the free-trade agitation of the following century.

Tucker's proposal VIII, 'To encourage a trade with our own plantations, in all such articles as shall make for the mutual benefit of the mother country, and her colonies' (p. 92), was essentially a statement of the rationale of the 'old colonial system'. In addition to the need to lessen Britain's dependence on foreign sources for naval stores, Tucker felt that Britain should be prepared to take more of the products of the colonies, especially of the northern ones, in order that they, in turn, would buy more from Britain instead of from other countries. There was another important reason: 'Unless we can supply our colonies with such commodities and manufactures as they want, by way of barter for some of theirs which they can spare, – they will be obliged to raise those things themselves.' There was only one 'just, or practicable' way to discourage the colonies from making for themselves what they could buy from the mother country: 'And that is, by an exchange of commodities to mutual benefit. A mutual benefit is a mutual dependence.' To forestall the possibility of their one day revolting, he emphasises that they must not be driven into a feeling of independence. 'If we would keep them still dependent upon their mother country, and in some respects subservient to her views, and welfare; – let us make it their interest always so to be' (pp. 95–6). In other words, the colonies must be bound to Britain by ties of mutual self-interest; Tucker disavowed any other method from the start.

The practical difficulty was that trade with the northern colonies, especially, was not as profitable to the merchant as that with Denmark, Sweden or Russia, and it was unreasonable to expect him to 'ruin himself to benefit his country'. The answer was to make the plantation trade an advantageous one. He saw four ways of 'turning a trade into a new channel, and stopping up the old one'. These were: additional duties, privileges and exemptions, bounties, and prizes. The last three applied to imports from the colonies could be of great value; higher duties, however, had to be used with caution. They should be raised gradually, because of the danger of retaliation and also to allow the supply to catch up with the increased demand. He anticipated that in a few years Britain could be supplied with such items as hemp, indigo, cochineal, coffee, coconut, pitch and tar from her own colonies. He cited the opposition to the importation of bar iron from the colonies, on which he had written a pamphlet, as an example of the foolishness he was fighting. Not only did Britain, owing to short supply at home, have to import it from a foreign country, Sweden, but, if the colonies were not allowed to export it to the mother country, they were far more likely to carry on the later stages of iron manufacture themselves.

His whole conception of forcing trade into new paths was, of course, typical of mercantilist thought, and completely alien to Adam Smith's belief that trade should be allowed to carve its own channels. The fact that Tucker felt it necessary at this late date to provide arguments for it was a measure of the failure of the government to practise a consistent colonial policy. Although he later changed his mind completely about what should be done with the colonies, Tucker, as we have noted, did not regard them as plantations to be exploited for the sole benefit of the mother country. He ignored, however, the political problems involved in the relation of subserviency that he assumed on the part of the colonies. When it became evident that at least a substantial number of the colonists did not want to continue the old arrangement, he was logical enough to realise that this relationship should be ended. If the colonies did not want to play the kind of complementary role provided for them under the old colonial system, then there was no economic advantage to be gained by retaining them. Thus, although he eventually became a 'free trader' in that sense, there was no change in his fundamental position.

We are left now with only one other proposal, xvi, which concerns taxation. To raise the money required for the bounties, premiums and prizes, for bonded warehouses, and for taking over the responsibility for consuls and forts from the regulated companies, he suggests a number of new taxes on certain 'articles of luxury, vice, or extravagance'. For Tucker, as we have seen, a good tax was distinguished from a bad tax not only by the amount of revenue it raised but also by the extent to which it was socially beneficial. One reform has already been discussed: the increased taxes on bachelors. Another was a tax on menial servants, justified not only because they were hired mainly for show, and their masters could easily afford the tax, but also because society was denied the fruits of their labour. Like Adam Smith, he regarded servants as non-productive members of society. Tucker gives his discussion a characteristic twist when he suggests that women could do many jobs of this type. 'In short, the poorer and middling part of the female sex, are deprived of those employments which properly belong to them, very often to their own utter ruin, and the detriment of society' (p. 134). He had a much higher opinion of the female sex than most of his contemporaries. His hatred of monopoly and special privileges extended to that held by men over women and in this he was far in advance of his day; there is, for example, no reference to this form of discrimination in *The Wealth of Nations*. As for his tax on servants, later in the century it was actually imposed.

There was already a tax on coaches, but Tucker felt that this did not reach a large number of gentlemen who could afford to keep coaches but did not. He therefore desired that it be extended to saddle-horses over five years old, with one horse exempted on the grounds that it was necessary for health or business and not for hunting or racing. Another animal tax could be considered most un-English, but it has been widely adopted in the form of a licence: a tax on dogs of one shilling each per year. He excepted sheep dogs and house dogs but not those used as turnspits, because they could be replaced by mechanical smokejacks. If this meant a diminution of the species, Tucker saw no harm, especially as the danger of bites from mad dogs would be lessened. His fifth tax is positively puritanical: a double turnpike tax on all persons who travel on Sundays. 'A modish and reigning vice this! which ought to receive some check and discountenance from the legislature.' He does not mention the possible effect on church attendance, although this may well have been in the back of his mind!

His philosophy of taxation is summed up at the end of this section. The specific criteria he adopted seem to have been the ability to pay, the discouragement of frivolous or harmful uses of money or time, and the diversion of resources into more productive channels. In the case of bachelorhood, and relatively harmless occupations if they occurred on Sundays, he speaks with a warmth which doubtless reflects personal prejudice as much as it does the welfare of society.

In a footnote discussion of the effects on population of the 'vice, lewdness and debauchery' which appeared so prevalent, especially in London, where bills of mortality indicated that burials exceeded births, he observed, 'What an absurdity, therefore, was it in the author of the *Fable of the Bees*, to say, that private vices are public benefits! It is virtue alone, which can make a nation flourish. And vice of every kind is, either immediately, or in its consequences, injurious to commerce' (p. 128n.) This attack may seem surprising, because of Tucker's recognition of the necessary role played by self-interest in the transactions of commerce. Cannan, in his introduction to *The Wealth of Nations*, traces Smith's concept of the 'invisible hand' back to Mandeville's *Fable*, but noted that Smith disagreed with Mandeville that the acquisitive instincts and the urge to advance one's self at the expense of others should be classified as vices. Tucker obviously agreed. By 'vice' he here seems to be specifically referring to the weaknesses of the flesh, not the businessman's selfish quest for profit, which could have socially useful results.

Tucker concludes the *Essay* by admitting that many of his proposals will be unpopular and that he will be looked upon as a 'projector [of] . . . a race of beings who have something very singular and whimsical in their composition' (p. 141). As to concrete objections, he imagines two. In answer to the criticism that his proposals, although right, are impracticable, he replies that this can only be determined by attempting to carry them out.

with Scotland, opposed as it was by numerous selfish interests. The other objection, that they might replace one set of inconveniences with another, he accepts, because it is obvious that some will suffer in the interest of the general good, but 'the true way of estimating any proposal is, to consider, whether it does remedy more old inconveniences than it introduces new ones'. People are always complaining of immorality and loss of trade. Why then put temptation in the way?

> Now what is the natural tendency of customhouse oaths, election oaths, freedom oaths, etc. etc. but to entice and encourage mankind to be guilty of the foul sin of wilful and deliberate perjury? What are the heavy taxes upon the married state, and exemptions for bachelors, but the like inducements to men to remain single, and to gratify their desires in an unlawful way? What are all the exclusive Companies, all the heavy duties upon importation, and the many statutes for cramping the trade of Ireland, but so many continued attempts to drive away the trade from ourselves to the French, who are not only our rivals, but the most dangerous ones we can have? (pp. 144-45)

Tucker's overall philosophy of trade is put in its simplest form at the very end. If England expected to thrive in foreign trade, it had to produce goods at least as good and at least as cheap as those of countries with whom it competed. Therefore a careful watch had to be kept on the practices of other nations, and, if they innovated successfully, England would have to emulate them. Whether it be a matter of inviting foreigners to settle among them, eliminating exclusive companies, seeing that their workers laboured harder for less, or doing away with import duties to lower prices, Englishmen had to take heed. Other countries in Europe were learning the 'maxims of trade' and by developing their manufactures were competing more fiercely than ever with England, which, as a result, would have to cut costs and improve quality in order to survive.

The *Essay on Trade* moved a long way towards complete freedom of trade, and in his later works Tucker went even further, but he never relinquished the belief that intervention by the State in the economy could be a positive good rather than an occasionally unavoidable evil. As a result, he was never accepted as a member in good standing of the doctrinaire *laissez-faire* school, which dominated economics in the years after the publication of *The Wealth of Nations*.

5 The Naturalisation Question

Tucker's next works were concerned with one proposal of the number that he had made in the *Essay on Trade*, that which concerned the naturalisation of foreigners. First the question of the naturalisation of foreign Protestants and then that of Jews became burning issues of the day. All the latent prejudices of the populace were aroused and used for party purposes by those who wished ill of the government. A bill to naturalise foreign Protestants had been introduced in 1747 by Robert Nugent, an MP who was later to represent Bristol and to be closely associated with Tucker. The Pelham administration supported the bill until the City made known its opposition. Since the help of financiers such as Sir John Barnard was needed in reducing the interest-rate on the national debt, the bill was dropped, but, once the interest-rate change was completed, Nugent reintroduced it, in 1751. There was support from many of the Bristol merchants and, of course, Tucker, who had already spoken out on the question in his *Essay on Trade*. They sent forward two petitions in favour of the bill, although Bristol was also responsible for a petition opposing it. However, the opposition among the ordinary people, who saw an influx of foreigners as a threat to their jobs, was vehement, and, when news arrived, on 18 April 1751, that the third reading had been postponed for the third time (and the bill effectively killed), there was great rejoicing, which included the burning of Tucker in effigy.[1]

Tucker's reaction to this was the *Reflections on the Expediency of a Law for the Naturalisation of Foreign Protestants*, which appeared in two parts, the first in 1751 and the second the following year. Part 1 was subtitled *Containing Historical Remarks on the Disposition and Behaviour of the Natives of This Island, in Regard to Foreigners; Occasioned by the Rejection of the Late Naturalisation Bill*. The Preface is instructive as to the reception given the *Essay on Trade*. Since it is something in the nature of an apologia for at least ten years of Tucker's life's work, it is worth quoting at length.

As the author of the following treatise has already appeared in public on a subject of commerce, and undergone some censures for engaging in enquiries, seemingly beside his profession; he begs leave to offer some reasons for his interfering in these matters, and, at the same time, to vindicate himself from the supposition of having deserved the ill treatment he has met with. If it shall appear then, that he has not been wanting in his endeavours to discharge his clerical duties punctually, as he hopes it would appear, if enquiry were made in his parish (in which, though large and populous, he performs all the offices of his function himself, according to the best of his abilities:) If, in this particular, he is not found neglectful, and these enquiries, which he prosecutes at his leisure hours, are not, in their tendency, inconsistent with piety to God, and good offices to man, – he flatters himself, that as long as he follows these studies, without neglecting his other engagements, and delivers his opinion in an inoffensive manner, he shall be excused in the judgment of all candid persons, tho' the warmth of party zeal, or the resentment of those, whose interest clashes with that of the publick, may excite them to vilify and insult him. It has been thought excusable for a clergyman to write on subjects of amusement, or on curious points of learning; and therefore, it may not be reckoned absurd in a clergyman, to form a judgment (and deliver it modestly) on subjects, by which, not only national wealth and prosperity, and the external blessings of life are increased; but, by which, industry, frugality, and sobriety are promoted, – and promoted too, by protecting persecuted and conscientious Christians.[2]

It is a clergyman's duty to do all he can to suggest means whereby the general standards of morality can be improved or impediments in the way of better behaviour removed. In connection with the latter, he refers to his own efforts directed against two great sources of 'wilful and corrupt perjury': the oaths used at customs houses and those for making freemen of towns. In order to become a freeman of London or Bristol, for example, it was necessary to swear not to 'know' a foreigner or have any dealings with one without informing the chamberlain, nor could one take as an apprentice the child of an alien. It is important to realise that the term 'foreigner' was meant to be applied not only to genuine aliens, but also to any Englishmen not 'free' of the corporation concerned. Naturally such an oath was honoured more in the breach than the observance; until the wording of these oaths was changed, men were under the 'sad necessity of destroying their commerce, or preserving it by a continual profanation of the sacred name of God'.[3] Since commerce was part of human relations and therefore ethics, it was desirable that clergymen should take an interest in it, especially if they could, at the same time, make suggestions which would add to the trade and prosperity of the realm.

The body of part 1 is taken up with a history of England's treatment of foreigners based on acts passed in the reigns of various monarchs, some of whom resisted the opposition of vested interests and native prejudices, and others of whom succumbed. Tucker emphasises the inveterate antipathy the ordinary Englishman had towards foreigners, and the way in which this was used to engross trade to their own benefit by monopolists, especially those of London, who practised the same techniques against their rivals in the outports. As one example out of many, Queen Elizabeth was credited in Tucker's day with the great development of the woollen industry during her reign, but he felt that the one really responsible was the Duke of Alva, who by his persecution drove thousands of skilled workers out of Flanders because they were Protestants. There is no reason to believe, says Tucker, that they would have been any more welcome than their predecessors if it had not been for a desire to strengthen the Protestant party at home. Petitions against foreigners were renewed in the next reign, and by a commission dated 5 June 1622 James I expressed the hope that 'after these troubles shall be overblown, they [the French Protestants] shall return into their own country again'.[4]

In Queen Anne's reign Tucker saw 'a mixture of four distinct principles in the opposition made to the naturalizing of foreign Protestants, viz. The inbred national aversion – The narrow monopolizing views of short sighted tradesmen – Superstitious fears about the church in danger – And the latent schemes of the disaffected party; each of which had their respective influences, and disposed different persons to unite in one common point' (p. 53). Bringing the Church into the argument was a new development, which Tucker heartily condemned.

The Naturalisation Question 73

As to religion, I hope I may be allowed in my turn to say, that when anything is proposed for the importation of nutmegs, or the curing of herrings, it is very strange, that some people should immediately take it into their heads to raise an outcry, that the Church is in Danger. I really think, the Church of England comes the nearest to perfection, of any since the Apostles days; and under that persuasion, I confess it appears to me a most injurious treatment, to be always representing her to be in a crazy, tottering condition, ready to fall, and never out of danger. The Church of Christ is described by our Lord Himself, as founded upon a rock; and nothing, I am persuaded, will be able to shake the foundation of the Church of England, but the unworthy and unchristian behaviour of its own members.

(pp. 57–8)

Tucker saw no danger from the arrival of large numbers of Calvinists and Lutherans. Lutheran missionaries were actually supported in the East Indies by the Society for Promoting Christian Knowledge.

He pointed out how France naturalised foreign Catholics (especially from the British Isles), how Spain was planning to naturalise 200,000 foreign Catholics, and how even the King of Prussia was using foreigners to build up his country and enlarge his army. Pennsylvania had been so enriched by the thousands of Germans who had emigrated there that land prices there had tripled. French Huguenots were welcomed in other lands with exemptions, loans at low interest, free land, and the King of Prussia even had agents out to provide free transportation. Of the 800,000 who left France during the reign of Louis XIV, England had not received 5 per cent. At the same time a welcome was extended to 'cooks, fidlers, dancers, singers, etc. etc. . . . who come expressly to debauch our morals, increase our expences, lessen our industry, impoverish our country, introduce new luxuries, and do everything that is prejudicial to our well-being, as members both of church and state' (p. 72).

The body of part 1 bears the subtitle *Important Queries*. It is prefaced by a short discourse on the persecution of Protestants by the Church of Rome. Tucker is afraid that the English might be misled by the mild treatment of the Catholics in England into thinking that Protestants in Catholic countries were afforded the same consideration. The laws in England were directed against the Catholics as a political faction rather than a religious sect. As long as they behaved themselves the laws were not enforced. Such, unfortunately, was not the case in Catholic states.[5]

Having appealed to the sympathy of the English people, Tucker now turns to their self-interest. In forty-eight pages consisting solely of questions, he makes an exhaustive brief in favour of immigration and the value of a larger population in general. Seldom can the subject have had a more thorough airing. Its main interest for us, however, probably lies in the incidental discussion of economic and political topics.

The first query throws more light on Tucker's attitude towards the common people: 'Whether popular prejudices are to be considered the test of truth? Whether there have not been the most violent oppositions against Christian forbearance and toleration in each part of the United Kingdom . . . and against almost every publick-spirited undertaking, and useful invention, when first attempted?' (pp. 1–2). The contributions to English prosperity made by the despised foreigners are the subject of another query: 'Whether we do not originally owe all our knowledge in the several manufactures of cloths, stuffs, serges, druggets, silks, velvet, ribbands, laces, cottons, linens, paper, hats, iron, steel, copper, brass, etc. to the instruction of foreigners?' (p. 2) This leads in turn to the question of whether foreigners did not have further contributions to make. Areas in which they excelled the English included various types of paper, silks, embroideries, laces, dyeing, as well as tapestries, carving, gilding, coach-making, and the arts in general.

Tucker recognised that the existence of unemployment in England at that time was the major argument against immigration. Where would the jobs for foreigners come from when they could not be found for natives? It is interesting in this connection that the word 'unemployment' does not appear in the index of *The Wealth of Nations*. Smith's only reference to the subject is when he notes the ease with which 100,000 soldiers and sailors, discharged at the end of the Seven Years' War, were absorbed into the work force.[6] He admits they may have 'suffered some inconvenience', but for Smith, as for his classical successors, full employment seems to have been assumed. Tucker's approach to this problem involved the concept of the 'circulation of labour', which he re-

The Naturalisation Question 75

gards as important as the circulation of money. If this circulation is clogged, or, as it would be put today, if labour is not sufficiently mobile, unemployment may be the result. He does not discuss it in any detail, but obviously thinks that monopolies have an adverse effect, and he also notes that unemployment forces people to leave thinly populated places for more populous ones, the inference being that a larger population creates work, rather than the reverse.

Then he raises the significant question, 'Whether the artificial wants of mankind, properly circumstanced, and under due regulations, are not the great master-spring of the machine of commerce?' (p. 10). In a footnote he points out that man's natural wants are few and can be satisfied in a primitive society:

> But as such a state would be little different from that of brutes, most of those moral obligations which now constitute social virtue, or relative duty, would have been unknown. – If therefore it was the wisdom of Providence, that there should be relations and subordinations in society, the artificial wants of mankind will ever be found to be relative to their stations; and the better any person discharges the duties of that sphere of life he belongs to, the more he will be enabled to contribute to the present happiness of society, by promoting a regular and permanent circulation of industry and labour, through the several ranks he is connected with. (p. 10n.)

He does not develop this theme here, nor does he give examples. But the implication seems to be that, by living up to the standards expected of his station, by purchasing the luxuries as well as the necessities of life, the well-off individual contributes to the growth of trade. Thus we have hints of the idea of conspicuous consumption, and, although the development of *new* artificial wants, which seems to be the mainspring of our modern economy, is not mentioned, it would follow from Tucker's line of reasoning. However, and this may account for the vagueness of his language and the emphasis on 'moral obligations', which at first sight appear to have little to do with artificial wants, there is a narrow line between the elegancies of a civilised life and the degeneration of these wants into 'vice, intemperance, and extravagance', which tend to obstruct rather than assist the machine of commerce. This leads us back to the well-worn theme summed up in the question 'Whether gaming and debauchery, poverty, idleness, and disease, can, in the main, create any employment, but for two sorts of occupations, the Hangman, and the Sexton?' Gin-drinking is an artificial want, but obviously not the kind that Tucker desired to encourage. This was true for commercial reasons as much as moral ones, since the wants of gin-drinkers are not of 'so extensive or commercial a nature, as those of sober, frugal, and industrious people' (p. 11). The connection between commerce and morality is never far from Tucker's mind.

With reference to unemployment, the question to be asked when there is a disagreement over commercial policy should always be the same: 'Which scheme tends to find a constant employ for most hands at home, and to export most labour abroad?' (p. 12). Tucker recognises that certain trades will have too many hands at a given time because, for example, of the fluctuations of fashion. But he doubts 'whether it is possible . . . for all trades and professions to be overstocked' for any lengthy period (p. 13). Another way of looking at it was this: would the unemployment rate be reduced any more by halving the population than it would be increased by doubling the population? Each individual added or subtracted is a potential customer as well as a potential competitor, a consumer as well as a producer.

Tucker, as we have already seen, supports the value of a large population. He quotes both Sir Josiah Child and Sir William Petty against the idea that a nation can be too populous.

> What are the riches of a country? – Land? Money? or Labour? What is the value of land, but in proportion to the numbers of people? What is money, but a common measure, tally or counter, to set forth or denominate the price of labour in the several transfers of it? If labour is the true riches, and money only the sign or tally, is not that country the wealthiest, which has the most labour? And hath not that country the most labour, which hath the most people to create mutual employment for each other? (p. 19)

The last sentence gives a rationale for a large population. Implicit in it is a kind of multiplier effect. The interaction of large numbers of people itself creates additional employment and prosperity.

To support his argument he compares the single province of Holland with the county of Devon. Half as large, it supported ten times the population and possessed twenty times the wealth. In his enthusiasm for population Tucker asks, 'Was a country thinly inhabited ever rich? – Was a populous country ever poor?' (p. 19). The answer would, of course, have to be 'Yes'. Even in his own day, the Dutch, to whom he constantly refers, could hardly be considered typical, any more than the Japanese are at present. However, he had earlier asked, more cautiously, whether the most populous nations are not the strongest, *other things being equal* (p. 17). His exhortations against vice and idleness, and his emphasis on the new trades the immigrants would bring with them indicate that he realised that something more than additional bodies was necessary: they had to be skilled, hard-working and driven by a desire to advance themselves.

Of course, they would compete with native labour, but Tucker outflanks that objection.

> If there will and must be rivals either at home or abroad, – which is the most detrimental to a kingdom? – To have competition at home? or to be outrivalled abroad? Was a nation ever hurt by competitions at home? . . . What is the publick good? Is it not, for the most part, the result of emulation among the members of the same society? And what would become of industry, temperance, frugality, and the desire of excellence, if there were no emulation? Which is best for the Publick, – To have emulations among tradesmen and manufacturers, or combinations? (p. 33)

Thus, whereas competition at home was good – since, although some individuals might temporarily have to suffer, other individuals and the nation as a whole would gain – competition from abroad was an unmitigated evil, because everyone at home would lose. Adam Smith would say that, as consumers, the public would benefit from cheap imports, but he is silent on the question of whether the nation would not be better off if these goods were made just as cheaply at home through the importation of skilled workers instead of the goods. In fact, he does not touch on the topic of immigration at all.

Those who thought, like Tucker, that England was under-populated, often opposed the drain of manpower to the colonies by pointing out the harm that had been done to Spain by the exodus to Spanish America. Tucker questions whether Spain would have been depopulated if she had kept the manufactures for her colonies to herself instead of letting the English, Dutch, French and others take them over from her. He refers to proposal VIII in the *Essay on Trade*, which concerned the proper division of functions between mother country and colonies. If this were adhered to, England would not really lose by emigration to the colonies, because she would still retain the colonists as customers. He believed that two doors should be kept open: those who for whatever reason wanted to leave England should be encouraged to settle in the colonies rather than move to a foreign land where they would be completely lost, and immigrants should be encouraged to settle in England.

Concerning the suggestion that only impoverished foreigners would be likely to come, Tucker asks, 'Is that objection that we shall swarm with foreign beggars', consistent with the other, 'that foreigners will come over to underwork the natives, and take the bread out of their mouths' (p. 39). On the contrary, it is usually the industrious who go to the trouble of emigrating to a place where they have to learn a new language and customs. As for the possible threat to religion, he asks,

> Are not the English noted throughout Europe at this day for breaching heterodox systems and Latitudinarian opinions? And is there any country, where the grand and fundamental articles of both natural and revealed religion are attacked in so outrageous a manner as they are in England? Is there therefore any danger that we should be corrupted in our principles by the introduction of foreigners? (p. 44)

The answer surely is 'No'; the foreign Protestants, because of their flight from persecution, were likely to form a bulwark of British freedom.

The *Reflections* aroused sufficient interest to be translated into French by Turgot and published under the title *Questions importantes sur le commerce* in 1755. Like d'Angeul's *Remarques*, mentioned previously, it was known in France before the appearance of the major Physiocratic writings.

It also received high praise from another unexpected quarter. In the spring of 1752, Tucker received a copy of *National Thoughts by a Landowner* (second, corrected edition, 1751) from its anonymous author. He acknowledged the gift in a letter sent via the printer, and in this letter said that he was happy to find that he and the author were in agreement on most issues. He did take exception to the latter's attack on the bounty on the export of corn, although he admitted to being impressed by his arguments.[7] It was not long before Tucker learned that the author was Charles, third Viscount Townshend (1700–64), the father of Charles Townshend of American taxation fame. In a letter he wrote to Tucker on 2 April, identifying himself, he again defended his position on the corn bounty, saying that it was folly to subsidise foreigners by permitting them to feed their workers more cheaply than could the British themselves. Now that he knew who his correspondent was, Tucker adopted a more suitably respectful tone to his next letter, but, although his support for the bounty began to waver, he still felt that the home market was too small to maintain a price level high enough for the producer. It is in this letter, incidentally, that he first mentions the *Elements of Commerce* and its origins.

Townshend's reply contained further arguments against the bounty and protection in general. The extent to which free trade was in the air is indicated by his reference to 'the many absurd laws we have' and the need for their repeal. Later in April Tucker finally capitulated, thanking Townshend for removing his prejudices and convincing him that 'bounties cannot be of any national service to a manufacture which is passed its infancy'. Townshend replied in an equally handsome fashion, declaring that Tucker's *Reflections on Naturalisation* was the best pamphlet he had ever read, and that the *Essay on Trade* revealed a grasp of the subject which was far beyond his own. Other topics are discussed in this short exchange of letters, but there is nothing so striking as this illustration of how Tucker's mind could be changed if the arguments were convincing enough.

The naturalisation question did not die away with the failure of Nugent's bill; it was shortly revived in another form. As early as 1746, some of the Spanish and Portuguese Jews in the country had set up a committee to lobby on behalf of a Jewish naturalisation bill. Nugent had only refused to add a suitable clause to his 1751 bill because of the difficulties it already faced. Early in 1753 they tried again, and were successful in obtaining the support of the leading members of the government, although the bill which was introduced was not made a government measure. The reasons for the support given by the Pelhams, Hardwicke and Halifax appear to have been the financial help provided by wealthy Jews in the recent war, their record as staunch Hanoverian Whigs, and the general Whig commitment to the principle behind the bill.

Unlike its predecessor of 1751, it was speedily passed into law as the Jewish Naturalisation Act of 1753, although it has always been known by historians as the Jew Bill. This time opposition was slow in developing, but it kept mounting after the bill had been passed, in late May, and was so successful that the government had to back down. When a repeal bill received the royal assent, on 20 December, rejoicing was widespread.

The full story of how a seemingly innocuous piece of legislation could arouse such passions is told by Thomas W. Perry in his study of the affair,[8] which demonstrates the way in which the commercial self-interest of leading London merchants, the easily aroused religious and racial prejudice of the populace, and anxieties related to the prospect of an election in the near future combined to produce an explosive mixture which was too much for the coalition of captious Whig factions upon which the ministry depended.

In the battle of words which raged during the period between passage and repeal, Tucker had more than a few of his own to contribute. In fact, his *Letter to a Friend Concerning Naturalization* and its successor the *Second Letter* were two of the major works written in defence of the Jew Bill, and the first was one of two pamphlets which were distributed in thousands throughout the country with government backing.

In the *Letter to a Friend*, Tucker analyses the significance of the naturalisation process itself and in the *Second Letter* he puts the treatment of the Jews into historical perspective, much as he had done for the Protestants. However, with the latter he had never discussed the naturalisation process itself: he had been concerned with overcoming the objections to a policy of encouraging immigration. But in his *Letter to a Friend* he attempts to show the irrelevance of most of the hue and cry which had been raised over the issue, once its narrow legal implications were closely examined.

Under the topic of what naturalisation is not, he demonstrates that, without benefit of a naturalisation bill, a foreigner could acquire right of parish settlement 'by service, apprenticeship, or renting a tenement of a certain value, in the same manner as such rights are obtained by English-born subjects: And a female foreigner may gain a parish settlement by marriage.' In fact, a foreigner, if unable to work, was eligible for parish relief wherever he happened to be living; his rights were equal to those of native-born subjects in this respect. Furthermore, foreign beggars could not be sent home in the same way that English ones could be returned to their own parish. Freedom of a city or corporation was not granted by naturalisation, but could be granted without it. Finally, 'a naturalization bill never can qualify a person to be employed in any office, or trust, civil or military; a naturalized foreigner never can receive any grants from the Crown directly, or indirectly; he never can be a member of the Privy Council, or of either House of Parliament'.[9]

The question then arises, what *does* a naturalisation bill do? The answer was that by it foreigners who had the money were allowed to purchase lands and carry on trade in England. Even the first privilege could be obtained without naturalisation, by a letter of denization from the Crown, which, however, 'cannot convey the right to demand the freedom of the Turkey, the Russia, and some other exclusive companies' (p. 7). What a naturalisation bill did, in essence, was to free the foreigner from the burden of the alien duty, which Tucker describes as follows:

> When an alien, or foreigner, though residing in England, and navigating his ships according to the law, engages in merchandise, he is burdened and plagued, particularly in the port of London, with an innumerable set of fees, duties, perquisites, pickings and squeezings, in order to distress and discourage him.

A foreigner, no matter how much he might do for the economy of the country, had to pay these additional fees 'and be subject to be teized in a thousand instances', or, if he were dishonest, as all this additional expense was likely to make him, he would have a sympathetic freeman make a false entry covering the merchandise in his own name. This kind of practice was a source of deep concern to Tucker, because of his own position.

The alien duty, for Tucker, is the crux of the matter. The only people who would gain by the exclusion of Jews and others were those who were going to be exposed to competition from them: namely, his usual villains, the monopolists, particularly of London. No one else in the country would be affected, because there was nothing to stop poor foreigners from entering the country and practising their crafts and trades in any of the free towns. Those who wanted to maintain their protected position put forth arguments designed to scare each section of the populace. The country gentleman was told that he would have to face an increased poor rate. For the tradesmen, a picture was painted of thousands of competitors taking away his customers. Labourers were frightened by the spectre of starvation. And even Christians allowed their religion to be perverted by prejudices against Jews. In sum:

> Religion was only the pretence; – but monopoly the *noli me tangere*, and the real cause of the clamours. – If the Jews had been content with getting rich as stock-jobbers, as brokers, or in any other capacity but as merchants, all would have been well; . . . But when one or two alien Jews wanted to get footing within the precincts of an exclusive company, and to trade directly to Turkey, without going round about by Leghorn, then Heaven and Earth were to be conjured, every thing sacred to be invoked; O Religion! O Liberty! O my country! And all for what? Why truly to prevent these wicked Jews from exporting English manufactures in the most advantageous way, and importing raw materials for the farther employment of our people. (pp. 20–1)

He concludes by proposing a series of regulations which would treat resident foreigners as natives except for the right to vote and to obtain the patronage of ecclesiastical endowments.

This analysis of the forces which brought about the repeal of the Jew Bill appears to be very close to the truth. In Perry's words, 'the primary purpose of the Bill was to make possible the naturalization not of prospective immigrants, but rather of foreign-born Jews already resident in England', for whom the most immediate benefit would be freedom from the alien duties.[10] The fear of increased competition this aroused was obviously behind the first petition against the bill, drawn up by a group of London merchants. However, a second petition, from the Common Council of the City of London, quickly escalated the threat into one against Christianity and the Constitution, thus obscuring both the limited objectives of the bill and the self-serving motives of those who opposed it, much to the chagrin of the ministry and the disgust of Tucker.

The *Second Letter* concerns a point raised in its predecessor: that of the legal rights of natural-born Jews to purchase lands. Many, influenced by the propaganda of the 'disaffected' party, which was preparing for the next election, believed that this was not possible, 'nay, that all their goods and possessions lie at the meer mercy of the crown'.[11] In order to combat this idea, Tucker sketches the history of the Jews in England. Because they fitted into none of the three traditional classes of mediaeval society – the military, the servile and the freemen of the towns – they had to be considered 'immediate dependents of the crown, and wholly protected by the royal prerogative' (p. 11). In this sense they could be considered the property of the King. But that was 500 years before, and no one could claim that the King's prerogative was now the same as it had been then, especially since the Glorious Revolution. To buttress his case Tucker quotes the opinions of a number of eminent lawyers, all to the effect that a natural-born Jew could purchase lands. However the Country party had actually proposed that the estates of all such Jews in England (estimated at £5 million) could be confiscated at the royal pleasure. Tucker exclaims at the audacity of people who would abridge an Englishman's traditional rights and enhance the royal prerogative on such flimsy grounds.

He is surprised that those who were so concerned about the privilege of the Jews to own land ignored the fact that they held £2 million in government funds. That no outcry had been raised, he suggests cynically, was owing to the fact that those whose prejudices could easily be aroused knew nothing of stocks and therefore could not be reached this way.

He does admit the truth of his opponents' accusations about the 'excessive usury and monstrous extortion of Jews in former times', but this was only because 'our princes used them as sponges, to suck up the treasure of the nation; and then when they had a mind to squeeze them dry, they let loose the popular odium and fury upon them'. This, in turn, was owing to the system.

> For it must be observed, that both Church and State had in those times enacted several foolish absurd laws, that no Christian should lend money upon interest, grossly mistaking the meaning of the Scriptures on that head. The necessary consequence of which was, that the Jews had the monopoly of money in their own hands, and could make a prey of the kingdom at their pleasure just as our exclusive companies do now. (pp. 36–7)

Despite Tucker's best efforts, which included, in addition to the above, a satirical reply in the press to a charge that Jews crucified infants, the demand for repeal continued to mount and the bill's supporters lost heart. Philip Yorke, the eldest son of Lord Chancellor Hardwicke, penned the following words to Thomas Birch, who had sent him a copy of Tucker's latest pamphlet:

> The domestic politics of this summer will make but a contemptible figure in history, which can afford nothing else than the art employed by faction to swell a most inoffensive Bill into a national grievance, and the success with which the weak and credulous have been deluded into the grossest of absurdities, more deeply imbibed, I fear, than the ingenuity and reasoning of Mr. Tucker can remove.[12]

Tucker received much personal abuse for his role in the affair, which culminated in his being called Josiah ben Tucker ben Judas Iscariot.[13]

The opposition to the Jew Bill in the City was not unrelated to another controversy in which Tucker was involved. This concerned the monopoly possessed by the Turkey or Levant Company in the eastern Mediterranean trade, which monopoly came under attack earlier in the same year. An attempt in 1744 to open the trade had failed by three votes in the House of Lords, largely because it provided for the admission of Jews to the trade. Since Jewish brokers already acted as intermediaries between the English merchants and the Turks, it was widely feared that any Jews engaged in the trade would have an immediate advantage over the Christian merchants. This apprehension was revived when another, more successful move to open the trade was made just before the Jew Bill was introduced. Tucker's contribution took the form of a pamphlet called *Reflections on the Expediency of Opening the Trade to Turkey*. In it he expanded on his previous criticisms of foreign-trade monopolies.

The aims of an exclusive company can never coincide with the welfare of the publick; inasmuch as monopolists, established by law, are thereby secured from rivals; so that their particular interests consist in selling as dear as they can; whereas the interest of private adventurers is to sell as cheap as possible, in order to get custom by rivalling each other. Thus the public is benefited by emulation, as it promotes the circulation of labour and universal plenty; – but is hurt by monopolists, who are a check to industry, to the circulation of labour at home, and the exportation of it abroad; and whose only view, whatever may be pretended, is to sacrifice the general interest of the kingdom to that of a few individuals. The Turkey Company is a monopoly, in every sense, – as no private member is allowed to fit out a ship when he pleases, or to export and import what quantities of goods he would chuse, – as the trade is confined to the single expensive port of London, – as the freedom of the company is limited to merchants by profession, and has been obstructed under frivolous pretences, – and as the members themselves are fettered with by-laws.[14]

To make matters worse, the Turkey Company had lost a substantial portion of the trade to the merchants of Marseilles, who were able to provide a lighter and lower-priced cloth made in Languedoc. Tucker argues that, since English interest, insurance and freight rates were lower and some types of labour cheaper, English goods should have been more competitive, and he was convinced they would be if the monopoly were ended. He had no doubt that in such circumstances English manufacturers could rival the French cloth. The Company was equally vulnerable to criticism on the import side of its trade, since Turkish goods handled by foreign merchants and transhipped at Leghorn were sold for less in England than goods brought direct by the Company.

In his Appendix to the second edition, he discusses the impact of the pamphlet. Money was raised to support the opening of the trade and petitions were sent. The monopolists reacted by vilifying Tucker's 'little treatise, which had raised such a national spirit against them' – one of them calling it 'a lie from beginning to end' (p. 21). When they claimed that it was no monopoly, the free-traders printed the report of a committee of the House of Commons made in 1744, which showed that it was. In 1718 the Company had even put an embargo on the trade for 2½ years, advancing as its reason 'That cloth may be bought the cheaper at home and sell the dearer abroad; and that [raw] silk may be bought the cheaper abroad and sell the dearer at home', to which Tucker's response was, 'A noble remedy truly! and a most infallible presentation against those two great national evils, wealth and industry!' (p. 24). It was from this period that Tucker dated the greater successes of the French as well as the Dutch in this trade.

Unfortunately for Tucker and his friends, the Act of 1753 did not go as far as they wanted. It did allow any British subject to obtain the freedom of the company on payment of £20, thus opening the way for merchants of the outports. But those who took advantage of this opportunity showed no interest in pressing for further reforms, 'it being too just a remark that the person who cries the loudest for opening the door, in order that himself may enter in, is sometimes the readiest to shut it against those who would come after him' (p. 32). Here Tucker puts his finger on one of the major reasons for the longevity of monopolies. In any case, the admission of the outports had little effect; dramatic improvement in the Turkey trade did not come until the end of the century, when Britain's cheap cotton textiles swept all before them.

While Tucker's role in all three controversies was important, it was not unique. He can be seen as one of the best known of what Perry calls 'a school of protoliberal pamphleteers'[15] who opposed the restrictionist and exclusionist attitudes held by those with a vested interest in the economic *status quo*. That most of these writers were Whig partisans is not surprising, since, as he noted, 'Henry Pelham himself was on record as favoring, at least in principle, not only a general naturalisation but also "the repeal [of] every law, tending to establish a monopoly, in any quarter of the realm"'.[16] A bill was even introduced in the House of Lords in early 1753 to end all restrictions on the freedom to practise a trade, but protests from the City Liverymen were sufficient to stifle it. This, together with the fate suffered by the legislation on behalf of which Tucker had written, indicates that the time was not yet ripe for this kind of reform. Over the next few years Tucker became more and more convinced of this depressing truth, with unfortunate results for his 'great work'.

6 The 'Great Work'

In answer to an invitation from Lord Townshend to visit him in London, Tucker wrote on 5 April 1752 that he would probably make the trip the following winter 'if I can finish a task which is now set me; *viz.* to write a treatise upon the principles of commerce for the use of the Prince of Wales, and to be entitled, *The Elements of Commerce and Theory of Taxes*'.[1] This is the first reference to a project which never came to fruition.

Further details may be found in the preface to Tucker's *Four Tracts*, first published in 1774. Tract 1 was a fragment of what he called 'a greater work'.

> This work was undertaken at the desire of Dr. Hayter, then Lord Bishop of Norwich and Preceptor to the Prince of Wales, his present Majesty. His Lordship's design was to put into the hands of his royal pupil such a treatise as would convey both clear and comprehensive ideas on the subject of national commerce, freed from the narrow conceptions of ignorant, or the sinister views of crafty and designing men; and my honoured friend and reverend Diocesan, the late Lord Bishop of Bristol, Dr. Conybeare, was pleased to recommend me as a person not altogether unqualified to write on such a subject. I therefore entered upon the work with all imaginable alacrity, and intended to entitle my performance *The Elements of Commerce and the Theory of Taxes*. But I had not made a great progress before I discovered that such a work was by no means proper to be sheltered under the protection of a royal personage, on account of the many jealousies to which it was liable, and the cavils which might be raised against it. In fact, I soon found that there was scarcely a step I could take, but would bring to light some glaring absurdity which length of time had rendered sacred, and which the multitude would have been taught to contend for as if their all was at stake: scarce a proposal could I make for

introducing a free, generous and impartial system of commerce, as would have excited loud clamours and fierce opposition; and, therefore, as the herd of mock patriots are ever on the watch to seize all opportunities of inflaming the populace by misrepresentations, and false alarms; and as the people are too apt to swallow every idle tale of this sort, I determined to give no occasion to those who continually seek occasion. In short, as I perceived I could not serve my Prince, by a liberal and unrestrained discussion of the points relative to these matters, I deemed it the better part to decline the undertaking, rather than do any thing under the sanction of his patronage, which might disserve him in the eyes of others: For these reasons I laid the scheme aside; and if ever I should resume, and complete it, the work shall appear without any patronage, protection, or dedication whatever.[2]

However, *The Elements of Commerce and Theory of Taxes* did actually appear in 1755, but it consisted only of part I and a portion of part II out of the five parts included in the outline provided at the end of this version. Furthermore, only a limited number of advance copies were printed, to be distributed amongst Tucker's friends for their comments. With the exception of several other selections, which appeared later, this was as far as he got.

Although we have Tucker's reasons for not publishing it under its original patronage, they do not explain why he eventually dropped the project completely. Two reasons emerge in his correspondence with Lord Kames. One was the outbreak of the Seven Years' War in 1756 and its effect on public opinion. In 1761, when the nation was 'frantic with military glory', he wrote, 'War, conquests and colonies are our present military system and mine is just the opposite. Were I to publish at this juncture, the best treatment I could receive is to be taken for a knave or a madman.'[3] In addition to this, after 1758 he was Dean of Gloucester, with all the work that new position entailed. Writing again to Kames, in 1764, he said, 'But with regard to my great work, the fact is, that I am not ready for publication were I ever so willing; nor can I say when I shall be, for the avocations belonging to my new office of Dean are too many and too important to be omitted.'[4]

One other factor, which he did not mention, is perhaps a weariness with the scheme itself. If he had been driven by the need to get his ideas down on paper, he doubtless could have done so, whether he felt it was expedient to publish or not. He was essentially a topical writer, stimulated to take up his pen by the disputes of the day. His move to Gloucester coincided with the change in the political climate caused by the accession of George III, and it was not until the American troubles began that he was again drawn into the kind of controversy which suited his temperament.

Whatever the reasons were for his not completing it, he did have sixty or seventy copies of the first part of it, some of the second and an outline of the rest printed with wide margins for the comments of his friends. It is obvious that he intended the final work to be a systematic study of what is today called economics, and that in his own mind he was breaking new ground. 'It is to be observed', he informs the reader in the Advertisement, 'that the principles laid down in the ensuing treatise, are, for the most part, general and universal; viz. such as would suit (with very little alteration) any kingdom, state or climate whatever', and he adds that 'as his manner of treating this subject is entirely *new*, he is obliged to be the more explicit in setting it forth'.[5]

The title of his preface, 'A Preliminary Discourse, Setting Forth the Natural Disposition or Instinctive Inclination of Mankind towards Commerce', sounds remarkably like the 'propensity to truck, barter, and exchange' which is discussed in the second chapter of *The Wealth of Nations*. Tucker begins with an analysis of human nature: 'Man hath the appetites of an animal, – the temper and affections of a social being, – and the understanding of a rational agent' (p. 55). Considered only as an animal, man is a very inferior one: he is not provided with a natural covering but has to make his own, and in his quest for food and shelter he usually needs the help of others. However, his inadequacies are really an advantage, since they encourage an improvement which is not possible for animals such as birds, whose first nest is as good as their last. Furthermore, as a mere animal man would be levelled and degraded to such an extent 'that the social relations of high and low, rich and poor, benefactor and receiver, governor and governed, learned and illiterate, would be absolutely unknown' (p. 56). A social hierarchy was for Tucker not an evil but a positive good, providing a framework within which emulation can operate and the individual is motivated to improve his lot.

Making full allowance for the evidence of complex social relationships found in the animal world, Tucker sees them as different in quality from the 'social and benevolent affections' of mankind. The gratification of these instincts is as necessary to man as the satisfaction of his hunger. The social intercourse that results brings to light differences in ability among human beings which are exploited for the benefit of all 'by dividing the general labour into different branches' (p. 57). This is the origin of commerce. It will be remembered that Adam Smith begins his book with a chapter entitled 'Of the Division of Labour'.

For Tucker, society functions not only to satisfy our animal needs but also to create new, artificial wants, which are related to our particular place in society. 'And as our present secular happiness appears to arise from the enjoyment of superior wealth, power, honour, pleasure, or preferment, self-love, the great mover of created beings, determines each individual to aspire after these social goods, and to use the most probable means of obtaining them' (p. 58). Adam Smith refers to self-love in a slightly different context in his second chapter. Although the individual human needs the help of others, any appeal for that assistance must be based on the other's self-love: 'It is not from the benevolence of the butcher, the brewer, or the baker that we expect our dinner, but from their regard to their own interest. We address ourselves not to their humanity but to their self-love . . . .'[6]

However, Tucker characteristically sees self-love as a potentially destructive force which must be subject to control. This is where man's third characteristic, reason, enters the scene. What is its role?

> Not surely to extinguish self-love; that is impossible: And it might be questioned whether it would be right to attempt even to diminish it. For all arts and sciences, and the very being of government and commerce, depend upon the right exertion of this vigorous and active principle. And were it once restrained, or greatly weakened, human nature would make but feeble efforts towards any thing great or good. Nay, in such a case, the social temper itself would want a spur; and all the benevolent affections being destitute of their proper incitement, would be very feeble and languid in their operations. Consequently, the main point to be aimed at, is neither to extinguish nor enfeeble self-love, but to give it a direction, that it may promote the

> public interest by pursuing its own! And then the spirit of monopoly will operate for the good of the whole. And if this is the proper business of reason, consider'd in the abstract; the reason or public wisdom of a state, or community is particularly called upon to pursue such a plan.... Divert therefore the pursuits of self-love from vicious or improper objects, to those that are commendable and virtuous; grant no privileges to indolence and ignorance; give no assistance to the ingrossing schemes of monopolists; but raise a general emulation among all ranks and professions in things relating to the public good; and let superior industry and skill, integrity and virtue, receive all your encouragement, because they alone deserve it. (p. 59)

Although Tucker expresses these ideas more than once, he nowhere does so more clearly. Man's self-love is the driving force behind his actions both good and bad. Benevolence counteracts some of the excesses but must be aided by reason, which foresees the long-term results and steers man's actions into those channels which really lead to happiness and genuine satisfaction. Whatever reason does for the individual, it must also be enabled to do for society as a whole.

> The passion of self-love therefore must be taken hold of by some method or other; and so trained and guided in its operations, that its activity may never be mischievous but always productive of the public welfare. When things are brought to that pass, the consequence will be, that every individual (whether he intends it or not) will be promoting the good of his country, and of mankind in general, while he is pursuing his own private interest. (p. 61)

The first sentence reflects no faith in the benign intervention of Smith's 'invisible hand', but the final outcome, as expressed in the second sentence, is identical. Compare Smith's words in *The Wealth of Nations*: 'By pursuing his own interest he [the individual] frequently promotes that of the society more effectually than when he really intends to promote it.'[7]

There are two ways of directing self-interest: a penal law, which works by fear, or what Tucker calls a 'judicious polity', which operates by encouragement. 'The one is to deter the multitude from offending, the other to lead them by their own free choice to virtuous industry.' The latter, which avoids the 'appearance of restraint or compulsion', is obviously preferable. He uses the analogy of a road: 'Thus a traveller may be said to choose that road, which the public hath laid out for him, when he finds that the by-roads are deep, intricate, and disagreeable, and the other straight, easy, safe, and good: – He prefers the public road, not because he is compelled by any penal statute, but because he finds his own advantage in his compliance, and cannot find it any other way' (p. 62). Politics must be designed so as to make socially desirable behaviour profitable as well as virtuous.

The question that now has to be answered is this: What is the public good towards which self-interest must be directed? Tucker's answer is that 'the good of any state doth plainly arise from the increase, employment, and morals of its subjects, because a numerous, industrious, and virtuous people cannot fail of plenty and content at home, of respect and influence abroad' (p. 63). His first 'polities', as he calls his suggested reforms, are thus concerned with increasing the number of people. Although he would seem to labour the point, it is true that Great Britain was able to absorb a much-increased population and it is also true that there were still those, against whom Tucker felt impelled to argue, who believed that, because of the large number of poor, Britain was overpopulated. After producing examples showing that heavily populated states are more prosperous than sparsely inhabited ones, Tucker goes on to specific suggestions, all intended to encourage marriage and particularly to discourage bachelorhood. It never seems to have occurred to him that some people are unsuited to marriage or might have difficulty in finding anyone willing to marry them. In any case, Tucker took the position that, since a larger population was desirable, everyone should get married or suffer the consequences. These were to be as follows.

First, 'No persons shall either elect, or be elected to any post of honour or profit, throughout the kingdom, but those who are, or have been married.' The same was to apply to non-elective posts of honour.

Secondly, the age of majority was to be raised from twenty-one to twenty-five unless the individual was married. Tucker felt that twenty-one was too low in any case and was responsible for eldest sons' squandering their inheritances.

Thirdly, the statute requiring seven years' apprenticeship was to be repealed for married men but not for single ones. This reflects an important opinion of Tucker's, shared by Smith, that a long apprenticeship was not necessary, as a person either had talent for a trade or he did not. He notes that it was 'very remarkable, that not only all new inventions, but almost all the improvements in the arts and sciences were the discoveries of those who had not served a regular apprenticeship to the business'. Rather than withdraw the requirement completely, he would use it to encourage marriage and thus, as always, 'to draw good out of evil'.

Fourthly, married men should be free to set up trade anywhere without fee – again, a selective relaxation of a prohibition of which Tucker disapproved in principle. In order to make this reform more acceptable to the citizens and businesses, he would let them retain the exclusive privilege of hanging out signs and displaying their goods in the open.

Fifthly married men should be free to reside wherever they pleased, 'provided some substantial person (an inhabitant of the parish to which they came) shall give five pounds security to the overseers of the poor, or the proper officers that such shall not be chargeable to the parish for three calendar months after their arrival' (p. 70). This leads Tucker into an attack on the whole parish-settlement system, which he regarded as an absurdity. But, as before, rather than undertaking the uphill task of doing away with it completely, he hoped to undermine it by lifting its burden from the shoulders of at least a portion of the population – namely, the married men.

His sixth suggestion is of special interest: 'That men shall not be allowed to work at, to set up, or carry on certain trades which properly belong to women, – unless they marry and so may be considered as assistants to their wives.' Here again he demonstrates that characteristic consideration for the interests of women most unusual in his age.

Seventhly, 'It is proposed, that all men for the first twelve calendar months after marriage, shall be exempted from serving any offices they shall please to decline; also be freed from paying all personal duties and taxes whatsoever.' This he defends on the ground that it is 'a part of that admirable polity which Moses introduced by divine command into the Hebrews' constitution;

The 'Great Work' 95

whereby the little territory of Palestine (not much larger than the principality of Wales) became the most populous and the best cultivated country on the face of the globe' (p. 73). Tucker is led here into a lengthy historical digression on the question of divorce. He supports divorce for adultery only, but suggests that an act of Parliament should not be necessary for remarriage. An inferior court could be allowed this jurisdiction.

Here is Tucker, although showing some incidental good sense, at his most meddlesome. While prepared to free the populace from the stultifying restrictions of the apprenticeship system and the parish settlement, he was prepared to penalise them for refusing to marry, which is surely one of the most basic freedoms of all. It may be socially useful to encourage marriage and certainly the taxation system should not penalise the married state as it sometimes does, but to take away the bachelor's franchise is an example of how Tucker's vein of common-sense ran out in the enthusiasm of the moment. But if it is true that even genius can at times be responsible for producing complete nonsense, then Tucker, with a wife seventeen years older than himself, may perhaps be forgiven a rather testy attitude towards the joys of bachelorhood. For that matter, his interest in population increase may also have had some psychological connection with the fact that he was never able to have children of his own.

In chapter 2 he provides 'A Polity for the Admission of Wealthy and Industrious Foreigners', which covers familiar ground. His main concern is that all the fuss made over naturalisation bills has convinced foreigners that they will not be welcome in England. He therefore makes two suggestions: first, that the Board of Trade should widely advertise the true nature of English laws, which actually laid few limitations on the rights of foreigners; and, secondly, that these restrictions should be removed as soon as possible. In his suggestions for the titles of the necessary bills Tucker shows an awareness of the need for public relations:

> Nay, such is the force of a proper title, that if the late Jew Bill itself had been called, *A Bill to prevent the Jews from profaning the Christian sacraments*, (which was the real tendency of the bill) instead of, – *A Bill to enable the Parliament to naturalize foreign Jews*, all would have been well; and the zeal for Old England! and Christianity for ever! would have been still asleep!

Thus *'An Act for encouraging the exportation of English manufactures and the importation of raw materials'* could have a clause repealing the alien duty, and the difficulties about a foreigner holding an estate in fee could be eliminated by *'An Act to abridge or limit the prerogatives of the crown in certain cases'*, which Tucker points out 'carries the air of popularity, and would be received with greediness' (p. 87).

Chapter 3 refers briefly to the provision of marriage portions to encourage matrimony – a favourite scheme of Tucker's – again with the purpose of increasing the population.

Part II contains 'Polities for the Extension and Improvement of Commerce'. He is at pains again to stress the close relationship between the landed and commercial interests. 'All commercial employment may be divided into two kinds, husbandry and manufacture; the immediate object of the one being to provide food and of the other to procure raiment and dwelling: And from the concurrence of these three every other trade, calling, or profession derives its origin and support' (p. 91). It is therefore wrong to regard agriculture and manufacture as enemies of one another; their prosperity is linked.

Tucker suggests first that large estates should be divided rather than passed on whole to the eldest son. Like Adam Smith, he believed that primogeniture and entail had been necessary in feudal times but had outlived their usefulness. He does not go so far as to suggest that land, like movable goods, should be equally divided amongst all the children, but he compromised by suggesting that one half should go to the eldest son, with the remainder being divided amongst the other children. Thus, if 20,000 acres is left to ten children, the eldest would get 11,000 and the rest a thousand each. Through this compromise 'the corporative dignity of the family would be decently preserved, and the mansion house might still remain in the possession of the eldest branch', but younger sons would receive a better start in life. Dependent on their eldest brother and too well-born to engage in certain trades, they frequently became 'miserable in themselves and the pests of society' (p. 95). Also Tucker felt that the resulting smaller estates would be more intensively cultivated. He realised that there was a limit to subdivision and suggested that the inheritor of a small estate should marry a wealthy woman to pay off his younger brothers rather than break his land into uneconomically small parcels. All this would apply only to those who died intestate: he would not interfere with the right of anyone to leave his property as he saw fit, although he thought his scheme might become a popular alternative.

Next is 'A Polity for Inclosing Commons and Common Fields'. Tucker examines various objections, the most important of which is the adverse effect on poor people. It is his opinion that the enclosure and improvement of commons and waste lands would, on the contrary, create more employment and have a beneficial effect on the poor, provided, of course, that they were adequately compensated for any loss of privileges. The benefits of making enclosure easier and cheaper to obtain would be 'more valuable than a thousand victories by land or sea' (p. 104). Why should nations engage in wars of conquest when so much land at home remained unimproved and uncultivated?

Tucker goes on to propose not only further draining of fens and swamps but also actively encouraging the inhabitants of such regions to build their houses on stilts. He believed that the 'noxious vapours' rarely rise more than ten feet; therefore, if the first floor of living quarters were placed at sixteen feet above ground, life would be much healthier for those who dwelt in such locations. In Venice the first several floors were used for storage and the people who lived higher up were not noted for being specially unhealthy, considering the unfavourable location of the city. He would encourage such buildings by various tax and other exemptions.

Another polity which must have been close to Tucker's heart was one for changing tithes into glebes. He regards tithes as undesirable taxes, which penalise the industrious, and, because of the temptation to cheat, the clergyman either had to accept perhaps half of his rightful income or be perpetually engaged in quarrels and litigation, which detracted from his proper role in the community. Tithes should be replaced by income-producing glebe lands, which could eventually be compacted so that each living would be self-sufficient.

The purpose of the next polity is to create 'a plenty of timber'. Because of increased demand, England's timber reserves were being rapidly depleted, and the operation of self-interest was failing to make up the loss. The obvious reason for its not functioning in this area was the length of time required for the growth of trees as opposed to other crops. Therefore Tucker recommended that every landowner be required to plant twenty acres out of every 400 he owned, under pain of doubled land, window and local taxes. It is surprising that in this case, where governments in recent times have tended to use the carrot, Tucker resorts to the stick. He admits that it carries an 'air of force and compulsion', but defends himself as follows: 'For the expense of making such a plantation would be inconsiderable in itself; and as it would fall on persons of respectable landed property, it could scarcely be felt. . . . The rich cannot be said to be hurt by such a law; because it would only spur them on to do those things, which they ought to have done without compulsion' (p. 124).

There then follows a section calling for the registration of title deeds of houses and estates. There were no sound arguments against such a register, but this had not prevented successful opposition from those who were unsure of their titles. He suggests, that rather than upset the *status quo* completely, registration should in future be required in connection with marriage settlements, sales and mortgages.

The next chapter is devoted to 'Certain Polities for the Increase and Improvement of Manufactures'. As always, his aim is 'to remove those obstructions which impede the industrious and useful operation of self-love, and to set mankind free'. At this point he uses a medical metaphor:

> Hence therefore the physician to the body politic may learn to imitate the conduct of the physician to the body natural, in removing these disorders which a bad habit, or a wrong treatment hath brought upon the constitution; and then leave the rest to nature, who best can do her own work. For after the constitution is restored to the use and exercises of its proper faculties and natural power, it would be as wrong to multiply laws relating to commerce, as it would be to be for ever prescribing physic. (p. 126)

This would have appealed to Quesnay, who was physician as well as Physiocrat and used an organic analogy in his *Tableau économique*, which was privately printed in 1758.

Tucker had always been against special privileges, but section 1 of chapter 2, 'A Polity for Opening Such Exclusive Companies, as Relate Principally to our Home-trade, or Domestic Commerce',

The 'Great Work' 99

considers the arguments in more detail. He notes that limitations on the freedom of the individual which would cause outrage if imposed by the Crown are accepted and even honoured when exercised through charters and corporations. This is truly surprising, 'for surely nothing can be plainer, than that every man hath a right by nature to subsist himself, by his own labour and industry, in any way that is compatible with the good of the whole; for this is the only limitation that should take place'. Among the arguments used to justify the existence of these incorporated societies was that of maintaining standards. Tucker's answer is interesting in light of what he had earlier said in favour of quality control: 'The very notion of keeping manufacturers up to a standard is absurd and ridiculous: for different nations, countries, climates, different ages, sexes, and statuses, different times and seasons of the year, different customs and caprices, and consequently different prices require different sorts of goods.' He is contemptuous of claims to self-policing made by these organisations.

> But suppose they should have some concealed fault or blemish, then, I ask, are the Wardens and Masters of the companies the proper persons for detecting these frauds? Will these men, who have their own wares to sell, will they impeach themselves for making bad ones? – or indeed will they impeach a Brother of the Craft, who may soon be in office, and will surely retaliate the favour to them? – No; the thing is incredible and absurd: And fact it is, that there have been more bad goods manufactured and vended, especially for foreign markets, by such as have borne offices in exclusive companies, than by any other set of men whatever. (p. 131)

With reference to the excuse that they were necessary to encourage 'ingenious artists' to settle in England, Tucker touches on the problems of the 'infant industry'. Unlike Smith, he accepts that new trades may have to be nursed in their infancy, but he suggests that paying bounties and premiums to all is a much better method to attain the objective than is an exclusive charter. Not only is monopoly avoided and competition encouraged, but also, as the new industry becomes stronger, the bounties and premiums can gradually be withdrawn. As an example he notes the change in the whaling industry when the Greenland Company's monopoly was removed and a bounty offered instead. From almost nothing it expanded within a few years to the level where no fewer than eighty ships were fitted out. He also asks why it was that Birmingham rather than Worcester had all the trade in that area, despite the latter's natural advantages, if the reason was not that Worcester had exclusive charters and Birmingham had none.

A third defence of exclusive companies was that, if there were free entry, too many would engage in the trade. Tucker's main reply to this shows clearly his *laissez-faire* tendencies and links with the classical school.

> Granting, that a trade may be accidentally overstocked with numbers; – when that is the case, the best and safest way is to let the evil alone, and then it will infallibly cure itself. For in process of time, some of these persons will go to other trades; and, as the trade is out of repute, there will not so many young recruits be bred up to it. Thus the occupation that was once overstocked, will soon be reduced to a medium, and may in its turn want hands again; the consequence of which may probably be, that it will be again overstocked: For such is the rotation of human affairs, dearness begets cheapness, and cheapness dearness. But if you should take any other course than what is here mentioned, which is in fact the course of nature, and of Providence, like summer and winter in the natural world, your attempts will not only be frustrated, but by endeavouring to remove one seeming evil, and temporary inconvenience, you will certainly introduce a thousand real ones, which will grow more dangerous, and inveterate by length of time. (pp. 134-5)

Could Adam Smith have put it any better himself? However, like Smith, Tucker does not favour action so drastic as to cause a painful disruption of established trade: 'And therefore, far from endeavouring to take these pretended privileges away at once, let us rather undermine them by degrees, and by that means render the people themselves weary of their chains' (p. 136).

The particular method he adopts has already been mentioned: namely, to allow married men full freedom to practise any mechanic trade, and to keep shops 'within glass windows', by means of legislation with a non-controversial and philanthropic

The 'Great Work'

title, such as 'An Act for the more effectual incouragement of marriage among industrious people'. Tucker, of course, foresees objections, the most significant of which would be: why not apply this to other trades and professions? His answer is that it would not be socially beneficial in certain cases, such as the following.

1. Occupations such as that of alehouse-keepers, of whom it could be said that 'the more industrious they are, so much the less industry there will be among other people'.
2. Those professions which 'ought to be subject to a license, or examination before they practise, because the injury done by unskilful practitioners may be irreparable and fatal' – the obvious example being the medical profession. Adam Smith was more consistent, if possibly less humane here, when he opposed licensing requirements for doctors, on grounds that some quacks might have more talent for medicine than graduates of medical schools, and that the patient would benefit from the competition amongst them.
3. Professions such as law and divinity which also require some proof of proficiency before being practised or taught. 'For in regard to divinity, it is absurd to suppose that the persons to be taught, are the proper judge of the abilities and learning of the teachers' – an opinion that would not be accepted in at least some quarters today. As for lawyers, because of the element of trust involved, 'as many securities should be taken by the public, both of their integrity, and abilities in their profession, as the nature of the case will bear'.

Tucker has another argument for limiting the numbers in the professions, which was echoed with some vehemence by Adam Smith – i.e. their unproductive character. As these people 'live by the labour of others, the increase of their numbers would be so far from adding to the public stock of wealth, that it would greatly diminish it in every view' (pp. 138–9). The other orders must first increase before a larger number of clergymen, lawyers and physicians can be supported.

Tucker concludes this section with another rousing exhortation, which, taken by itself, sets him firmly in the camp of Adam Smith.

> Put therefore your commercial affairs into that method, which is planned by Providence itself; and then all will go well. As to our

present numerous and contradictory laws concerning the quality and price of goods, hours of working, hire of journeymen and labourers, high wages, oppressive combinations, etc. etc. they are only the poor efforts of after-thought to prevent the ill effects of original blunders. And as they frequently do more harm than good, if attempted to be executed, our old legislators may be very justly compared to an unskilful physician, first stopping up one sore, and then another, instead of correcting the original malady, from whence all proceeded. (pp. 139–40)

This could be considered a manifesto against the evils of mercantilism, which are discussed at greater length in section II of chapter 2, where he favours the opening of foreign trade. Here again we are on familiar ground. The first argument he attacks is that they have to pay for the forts and their garrisons along the coasts. There is no evidence that these are necessary, except to provide additional perquisites for company officials and their dependants. Merchants of other countries have flourished without forts, but, if a company feels that forts are required for its operations, then let it pay for them without pretending that the nation is benefiting at the same time.

Another defence of exclusive companies which Tucker quickly rejects is that they 'sell dear, and buy cheap'. Keeping the price of British manufactures artificially high will not encourage their sale in quantity, and he doubts that the raw materials they purchase cheaply abroad are such bargains when sold in Britain. However, by paying less abroad these companies were credited by their defenders with reducing Britain's trade deficit and therefore the export of bullion, especially to the East. His answer:

If this bullion or coin, is carried out to purchase raw materials, for the employment of our people, the trade is good and beneficial to the state, because it creates industry and promotes labour. For industry and labour are the only real riches; money being merely the ticket or sign belonging to them; and the use of money is to certify, that the person possessing that piece of coin, hath likewise been in possession of a certain quantity of labour, which he hath transferred into other hands and now retains the sign of it. – Money therefore being nothing more than a certificate of labour, it necessarily follows that national industry will always command as many of these certificates i.e., as much gold

The 'Great Work'

and silver, as are wanted for these purpose. For if Great Britain had industry, and another country money, the industry of the one will soon extract the money of the other, in spite of every law, penalty, and prohibition that can be framed.

Furthermore, if we were to assume that in an industrious country all the gold and silver were to vanish overnight, 'the inhabitants would then devise some other ticket or counter for the exchange of mutual industry, and the circulation of labour among one another' (p. 146). He thus moves firmly away from an oversimplified bullionism, but he does not show any inclination to explore the role that the movement of money across national borders could have on the domestic economy of the countries concerned, or the relationship between the quantity of money and prices – a relationship examined by Cantillon earlier and by Hume in the same period.

Despite his rejection of naïve bullionism, Tucker is not satisfied with the situation whereby the East India Company made up the deficit in its trade by shipping bullion to the Indies. Here he has to cross swords with Montesquieu, who said that the Indians had no need for and did not want European goods (*De l'esprit des lois*, book XXI, ch. 1). Tucker, 'with all due respect to the genius of so great a man', believes that no people are so different from Westerners as not to be drawn to some at least of the great variety of attractive goods produced in Europe. His answer to Montesquieu is that people will buy if the goods are cheap enough, but that, because of the monopolistic prices charged by the East India Company, they were not cheap enough.

The 'pretence' that only exclusive companies with their large resources can avoid the maltreatment which would be the lot of the lone adventurer is treated by Tucker as another version of that used to support forts. He cites many historical examples of trade's being successfully conducted without the necessity for overawing local rulers.

Finally there is the argument that such companies must be worthwhile since so many countries had chartered them. In this connection Tucker calls on 'that truly great and honest patriot John De Wit' who, in *De Wit's True Interest and Political Maxims of Holland* (1702), chapter 19, wrote that in the beginning the Dutch East and West India Companies were given their privileges because Spain made it very difficult for the individual adventurer to prosper alone, but that as the years went by and the threat of Spain receded, these reasons no longer applied and the companies became more and more a hindrance. The interests of the company and those of the Dutch people thus diverged, to the detriment of the latter.

Turning from the general to the specific, Tucker takes a critical look at the Turkey Company and then the Hudson's Bay Company. In connection with the latter, Tucker makes a suggestion which was remarkably prophetic. He proposes first that the British should buy the Company's territory, as it 'is particularly adapted by nature for the reception of a British colony'. This was down in 1870, when it became the North-West Territories of Canada. Secondly, he suggests that Scottish Highlanders should be used as settlers. 'Their Highland dress, their diet, their dwellings, genius, imployments and diversions – all bespeak them the fittest people in the world for such an undertaking' (p. 172). Just fifty-seven years later, in 1812, Lord Selkirk, who had bought control of the Hudson's Bay Company, was to send parties of crofters to the junction of the Red and Assiniboine rivers, where Winnipeg now stands, to establish the first settlement in western Canada.

Another possible use for this 'English Siberia' was as a suitable destination for the transportation of convicts, but this time he was in the wrong hemisphere, for it was the less inhospitable shores of Botany Bay that were destined to be used for this purpose in the next century.

Tucker concludes section II with a lengthy appendix containing historical evidence concerning the origin of monopolies. First he quotes from the debates of the forty-third year of the reign of Queen Elizabeth, which showed the popular opposition which built up at that time against domestic monopolies and resulted in the cancellation of many of the patents. Then he refers to a document drawn up by Sir Edwin Sandys in the third year of James I, entitled 'Instruction Touching the Bill for a Free Trade'. Tucker thus lays no claims to originality in his attack on monopolies. He goes back beyond earlier writers, often given credit for free-trade ideas, to show how 'stale and hackneyed' were the apologies for monopoly which Sandys undertook to refute 150 years before Tucker's time. His reward, and that of the other

The 'Great Work' 105

supporters of this bill to abolish the Company of Merchant Adventurers, was to be thrown into prison, and James went on to establish new monopolies. Such was life in 'good old England', a phrase Tucker occasionally used when driven to sarcasm by criticisms of the Hanoverian present. He strongly believed that the power of monopoly had declined during the rule of this 'patriot family' (p. 213).

The *Elements* included at the end a table of contents outlining the rest of the 'great work' (pp. 214–19). If the major concern of economics is considered to be theory rather than policy, then Tucker did not quite make the leap. Listed here are more 'polities' or prescriptions for improvement, many of which he advocated in his other writings. One wishes, however, that he had expanded his ideas on money. What were his 'reasons for increasing the quantity of metal money', and how did he propose to change 'a considerable part of the dead national debt into circulating certificates or paper money'? The latter sounds very much like a form of the monetisation of the national debt which has played so large a part in increasing the money supply in modern times. There seems no doubt that Tucker was just as much an expansionist in monetary affairs as he was in population growth and productivity.

Section IV of part V, 'General Directions for Travellers, etc.', was the only major part of his outline to receive further development. It emerged two years later as *Instructions for Travellers*, privately printed in 1757. Although published in Dublin in 1758, it was, like the *Elements*, not widely known. Its background is explained in the Advertisement.

> The following pages are part of the work, which the author of *The Elements of Commerce and Theory of Taxes*, proposed to offer to public consideration. The subject of them is of great importance, though not the next in order according to the original plan. This alteration is owing to the request, or rather command (for such it ought to be esteemed) of a person equally eminent for his great learning and public spirit, as for his rank and quality; who being advanced beyond the usual age of man, was desirous of seeing the *Instructions for Travellers* before the rest of the work could be completed. And as the general plan will receive a particular illustration by it, the author humbly hopes, that this anticipation will not be disagreeable to the rest of his

worthy friends. The breadth of the margin is the same with the former: And the press is still to be considered only as a more expeditious amanuensis. Due thanks are returned by the author for the corrections and amendments already received; and he earnestly solicits continuance and increase of these favours.[8]

Subtitled *A Plan for Improving the Moral and Political Theory of Trade and Taxes, by Means of Travelling*, it is the same kind of exercise in comparative study for the purpose of national improvement as the *Essay on Trade*. Needless to say, it allows Tucker to ride all his favourite hobby-horses. However, along the way he makes a number of perceptive comments, several of which have found their way into books about the eighteenth-century economic life of Great Britain, and which reveal Tucker in one of his most useful roles: – as an observer of above-average acuteness.

He begins by recommending foreign travel, but not for the usual reasons it was undertaken. His traveller

> must dedicate his principal studies towards tracing such secret, though powerful effects and consequences, as are produced by the various systems of religion, government and commerce in the world: He must observe, how these systems operate on different people, on the same people in different periods, *viz*. Whether they enlarge, or contract the active powers in human nature, and whether they make those powers become useful or pernicious to society. (p. 4)

But first he must acquire sufficient knowledge to make such judgements. Tucker recommends that the student should learn what to look for by first touring his own country under suitable guidance. He had his stepson Richard Woodward, do just that.[9]

But he required, first of all, a good liberal education and the perusal of a number of works he had selected as most suitable for the purpose. These are listed under various headings, the first of which, naturally, was religion. Because he felt that half-formed minds were extremely susceptible either to being put off all religion by 'the impudent tricks and forgeries of the Church of Rome', or to becoming a convert through her 'snares', he recommended several devotional works, including Seed's *Sermons*, which contained the philosophy of Bishop Butler's *Analogy* in a more palatable form than the original. His comments here are of interest because this is the only occasion on which he refers by name to the man who must have been, more than any other, his spiritual mentor:

> As to Bishop Butler himself, he certainly pursues a method, the fittest in the world to put to silence the superficial, licentious extravagances of modern times; were his manner of writing a little more pleasing and alluring. For by demonstrating, that there is a system actually carrying on by the Author of the Universe, both in the natural and moral world, he confutes the sceptics on one extreme; and by proving how imperfectly this system is yet comprehended by us, he checks that arrogance, and self-sufficiency on the other, which are too natural to young minds just tinctured with a smattering of knowledge.   (p. 6)

In government he recommends Burlamaqui and Montesquieu, as well as several lesser-known authors on constitutional law. In economics, the only one of his predecessors mentioned 'as a commercial writer of the first note' is Sir Josiah Child.

> And then at a respectful distance after him, the *Remarks on the Advantages and Disadvantages of France and Great Britain in regard to Trade* may be no improper book: *viz.* because it exhibits a comparative view of the commerce of both kingdoms, and enters deeper into the inconveniences or obstructions attending the French government, regarding trade, than any author whatever. This tract is in a great measure a translation of my *Essay on Trade*, and other commercial pieces. But as the author is a native of France, viz. The Marquiss D'Angeul (though appearing under the borrowed name of an Englishman, Sir John Nicholls) he was capable of making great improvements on my plan; and being likewise employed in the Finances, he could speak to the difficulties and discouragements attending trade in that kingdom, with more experiences and certainty than a stranger was capable of doing.

An author could scarcely be more generous than to recommend someone else's version of his work in preference to his own, but Tucker rarely showed personal pettiness. It was the propagation of what he considered the right ideas, rather than the enhancement of his own ego, that motivated him. This quality is also illustrated by the book he suggested as the most suitable explanation of the special position occupied by the Church of England: William Warburton's *Alliance between Church and State*. Warburton, who was destined to be Tucker's superior in Gloucester, never liked him and made little effort to conceal his feelings.

Tucker's plan is to ask about England the sort of question which should be asked about the country the traveller visits, and then provide the kind of answer expected. For example, here is his first question under the general heading 'Natural Causes': 'Is the soil of England naturally good and fertile, or barren and sterile? Is it a shallow, or a deep mould? inclinable to sand, or clay? And what seems to be the most noted produce of the country?' (p. 11). A typical answer is that he gives to the second question, about the climate:

> The air is moist, the sky subject to be cloudy; and the climate remarkably mild, as to the extremes of heat, and cold: But the country cannot be pronounced so very healthy as some others abroad. The prevalent distempers are such as proceed from obstructed perspirations, *viz*. scurvies, colds, coughs: And in consequence thereof, and of the smoak of sea coal, asthmas and consumptions: Colds and coughs usually come on, when the chills of Autumn lock up the perspirable matter, which used to pass in summer. (p. 11)

Although medical science has advanced beyond the 'perspiration' theory, the English climate does not appear to have altered noticeably.

Given Tucker's particular bent, it is not surprising that after several general questions he is already asking what 'improvements' may be made in such things as water-carriage or conservation. Typical of a theme that haunted him for years is the following part of an answer:

> Moreover were a great part of the wastes on the south coasts from Kent to Cornwall to be parcelled out into small shares, suppose ten or twenty acres, as portions to virtuous young women remarkable for their diligence in spinning certain

quantities of wool, flax, or cotton, provided they married labourers or farmers; this circumstance alone would render that country, which now looks like a desolate wilderness, as populous and industrious as a bee-hive. (pp. 13–14)

As this work is discursive by nature, there is no need to go through it in detail. We shall content ourselves with the odd striking idea or observation. One of the first is what must be among the most unique arguments ever made in favour of a large population. As part of the answer to a question concerning the types and quantities of manures applied to the soil Tucker says,

> Only let it be always remembered that the more populous any country is, the more manure and soil will be made by the inhabitants: So that large towns and populous villages do not only furnish a market for the produce of the country round about, and thereby pay for the labour, and excite the emulation of the husbandman, but also supply him with dung, rags, horn-shavings, ashes, soot, etc., etc., to load his carriages back, in order to fructify his grounds for fresh crops. So little cause is there to fear, that a country can be too populous! (p. 16)

Considering the problems of waste-disposal and pollution that face the modern world, it is too bad that Tucker's simple solution (which might be called the 'manure theory of population') has not, for the most part, proved economically feasible – at least in the developed world.

In answer to the question, 'What machines are used to abridge the process of manufacture, so that one person can do the work of many?', Tucker notes,

> Few countries are equal, perhaps none excel the English in the numbers and contrivance of their machines to abridge labour.... When we consider that at Birmingham, Wolverhampton, Sheffield, and other manufacturing places, almost every master manufacturer hath a new invention of his own, and is daily improving on those of others; we may aver with some confidence, that those parts of England in which these things are to be seen, exhibit a species of practical mechanics scarce to be paralleled in any part of the world. (pp. 20–1)

Tucker seems to have been more clearly aware of the significance of labour-saving machinery than Adam Smith, who, writing twenty years later, at the dawn of the official 'Industrial Revolution', was still talking as if the division of labour alone was the key to productivity. Although he mentioned machinery briefly, there is no indication that he was as impressed as Tucker was by the potentialities of devices such as the steam engine, which is given here as an example of English ingenuity.

Tucker also referred to a question much talked of by Smith: the economic and social effects of increased efficiency.

> In regard to the other part of the query, *viz.* what is the consequence of this abridgment of labour, both regarding the price of the goods, and the numbers of persons imployed? The answer is short and full, *viz.* That the price of goods is thereby prodigiously lowered from what otherwise it must have been; and that a much greater number of hands are employed. The first of these is a position universally assented to; but the other, though nothing more than a corollary of the former, is looked upon by the majority of mankind, and even by some persons of great name and character, as a monstrous paradox. We must therefore endeavour to clear away these prejudices step by step. And the first step is that cheapness, *caeteris paribus*, is an inducement to buy, – and that many buyers cause a great demand, – and that a great demand brings on a great consumption; – which great consumption must necessarily employ a vast variety of hands, whether the original material is considered, or the number and repair of machines, or the materials out of which those machines are made, or the persons necessarily employed in tending and conducting them: Not to mention those branches of the manufacture, package, porterage, stationary articles, and bookkeeping, etc., etc., which must inevitably be performed by human labour. (pp. 21–2)

Here is an acute understanding of the accumulating benefits of technical innovation, together with an appreciation of the way in which it stimulated the service industries. He gives as examples the effects of machines in making wheaten bread the 'common food of the kingdom' instead of a luxury. As an author he was especially conscious of the way in which printing machinery had

The 'Great Work'

made cheap reading matter available, whilst giving employment to a large number of people.

> But examples are endless; and surely enough has been said to convince any reasonable man, though even the great author of *L'Esprit des Loix* should once be of a different mind, that that system of machines which so greatly reduces the price of labour, as to enable the generality of people to become purchasers of the goods, will in the end, *though not immediately* [emphasis added], employ more hands in the manufacture, than could possibly have found employment, had no such machines been invented.

Tucker was thus prepared to admit that the beneficial results took time, although he did not go into the disruptive possibilities of this lag, probably because of his expansionist's optimism about available opportunities.

It was too early for any great concern to have developed over the use of child labour. Tucker notes with approval how a child could be used to assist a man operating a button-stamping machine.

> By these means the operator can stamp at least double the number, which he could otherwise have done.... And his gettings may be from 14d to 18d and the child's from a penny to 2d per day for doing the same quantity of work, which must have required double the sum had the man alone been employed; this single circumstance saves about 80, or near 100 per cent, at the same time that it trains up children to an habit of industry, almost as soon as they can speak. And hence it is, that the Bijoux d'Angleterre or the Birmingham Toys, are rendered so exceedingly cheap as to astonish all Europe; and that the Roman Catholic countries are supplied with such vast quantities of crucifixes, Agnus Dei's, etc. from England.   (p. 23)

The same applies to jobs suitable for the strength of women. He notes that the proportion of women to men on the parish 'pay-bill' in Birmingham is much less than in Bristol or London, where the same opportunities for useful employment were not available for them.

Like Smith, Tucker had doubts about the capitalist system of organisation as opposed to the independent master. They were both looking backward rather than forward here, but one can hardly blame them. Tucker gives a perceptive comparison between human relations in the woollen industry of Yorkshire and those in the rival industry in the West Country. The domestic system existed in both areas, but it was at a more primitive, idyllic level in Yorkshire, where a greater degree of independence was maintained by the spinner, weavers, dyers, and so on.

> Their journeymen likewise, if they have any, being so little removed from the degree and condition of their masters, and so likely to set up for themselves by the industry and frugality of a few years, have no conception that they are embarked in an interest opposite to that of their masters, or that they are called upon to enter into clubs and combinations against them. Thus it is, that the working people are generally moral, sober, and industrious; that the goods are well-made, and exceedingly cheap; and that a riot or a mob is a thing hardly known among them. (p. 24)

In Gloucestershire, Wiltshire and Somerset there existed a more advanced version of this form of enterprise, which was much closer to the factory system.

> One person, with a great stock and large credit, buys the wool, pays for the spinning, weaving, milling, dying, shearing, dressing, etc., etc. That is, he is the master of the whole manufacture from first to last, and perhaps employs a thousand persons under him. This is the clothier, whom all the rest are to look upon as their paymaster. But will they not also sometimes look upon him as their tyrant? And as great numbers of them work together in the same shop, will they not have it more in their power to vitiate and corrupt each other, to cabal and associate against their masters, and to break out in mobs and riots upon every little occasion? The event hath fully shewed, and is now shewing, that these conjectures are too frequently supported by facts. Besides, as the master is placed so high above the condition of the journeymen, both their conditions approach much nearer that of a planter and slave in our American colonies, than might be expected in such a country as England; and the vices

The 'Great Work' 113

and tempers belonging to each condition are of the same kind, only in an inferior degree. The master, for example, however well-disposed in himself, is naturally tempted by his situation to be proud and overbearing, to consider his people as the scum of the earth, whom he has a right to squeeze whenever he can; because they ought to be kept low, and not to rise up in competition with their superiors. The journeymen on the contrary, are equally tempted by their situation, to envy the high station, and superior fortunes of their masters; and to envy them the more, in proportion as they find themselves deprived of the hopes of advancing themselves to the same degree by any stretch of industry, or superior skill. Hence their self-love takes a wrong turn, destructive to themselves, and others. They think it no crime to get as much wages, and to do as little for it as they possibly can, to lie and cheat, and do any other bad thing; provided it is only against their master, whom they look upon as their common enemy, with whom no faith is kept. The motives to industry, frugality, and sobriety are all subverted by this one consideration, *viz*, that they shall always be chained to the same oar, and never be but journeymen. Therefore their only happiness is to get drunk, and to make life pass away with as little thought as possible. (pp. 24–5)

Here we have a concise summary of the evolution of the two major classes of modern times, the capitalists and the proletariat, the theme of class struggle, the barrenness and alienation of the factory worker's existence, and the attitudes which have permeated the English working class to the present day. It is a remarkable statement of the factors that were to play such an important part in economic history over the next two centuries, and which were to lead to the rise of socialism, communism, and for that matter all the other 'isms', which were attempts to deal with the strains built into the new arrangements.

There is nothing in *The Wealth of Nations* with which to compare it. Adam Smith, although he exposed the working of the various parts of the economy in much greater detail, nowhere displays the almost prophetic grasp of the forces which were to dominate the future, as Tucker does in this passage. Typically, however, Smith sharpens the conceptual tool, inherited from Locke and others, which was to be used to shape future attitudes: the labour theory of value, with its explosive corollary, the surplus-value theory of exploitation. Whether or not this was a useful direction in which to move is another question. Tucker himself would certainly not have followed the path of either the classical economists or Marx. His cardinal belief in self-love would have precluded Marx's sharp division between the exploiting capitalists and the exploited worker. For Tucker, the workman was just as likely to exploit his employer, by not doing an honest day's work if he could get away with it. On the other hand, as we have noted before, he did not belong to the deterministic 'gloomy science' school either. He believed in intervention, where necessary, to encourage the workman through an appeal to his self-interest, to escape from his rut by emulation. His position was closer to that advocated later by Proudhon and widely accepted by Americans: that is, to encourage the individual to move up into the middle class instead of resigning himself to being a permanent member of the working class.

Tucker by no means approved of the picture he had drawn, and obviously would have been horrified by the 'dark, Satanic mills' which were to make it the pattern for Victorian England. Influenced by the fact that the woollen trade was declining in the West and flourishing in Yorkshire, he drew the conclusion that the system adopted in his area was to blame. 'The real surprise would be to discover that such causes did not produce such effects: And if ever the manufacturers in the north should adopt the bad policy of the west, and vice versa, things will come round again' (p. 25). In the event, he was wrong. The factory system, for hard practical reasons, was to become predominant and the Jeffersonian dream of sturdy independent craftsmen and yeomen farmers was to become as illusory in America, where it had far more chance of success, as it was in England, where Tucker seems to have shared such a dream in a less egalitarian form.

However, despite its inequalities, eighteenth-century England was already more advanced than other European countries in providing its ordinary citizens with a variety of cheap and useful goods, as Tucker pointed out:

That is, they [the kingdom's manufactures] are more adapted for the demands of peasants and mechanics, in order to appear in warm circumstances; – for farmers, freeholders, tradesmen and manufacturers [artisans] in middling life; – and for wholesale dealers, merchants, and all persons of landed estates, to appear in genteel life; than for the magnificence of palaces, and the cabinets of princes. Thus it is, according to the very spirit of our constitution, that the English of these several denominations have better conveniencies in their houses, and affect to have more in quantity of clean, neat furniture, and a greater variety (such as carpets, screens, window curtains, chamber bells, polished brass locks, fenders, etc., etc. (things hardly known abroad among persons of such rank) than are to be found in any country in Europe, Holland excepted. Moreover, as the demand is great and continual, the numbers of workmen and their greater experience excite the higher emulation, and cause them to excel the mechanics of other countries in these sorts of manufactures. (p. 26)

He thus noted the importance of a large home market in sustaining a competitive export market. He estimated that the value of the household goods of a peasant or mechanic in England at that time would be three times that of one in France.

There is another statement of Tucker's *laissez-faire* principles in answer to the question 'What good laws regarding commerce and manufactures are now in force?' He answers that there are few positive laws in England for that purpose and little necessity for them. 'For let the legislature but take care not to make *bad laws*, and then as to *good ones*, they will make themselves: that is, the self-love and self-interest of each individual will prompt him to seek ways of gain, trades and occupations of life, as by serving himself, will promote the public welfare at the same time.' Laws which punished a vendor for misrepresenting his merchandise were not regarded by Tucker as laws of commerce. Of the latter he was prepared to see bounties and other support given to 'infant' industries. But this support should not be continued indefinitely; after a reasonable number of years the 'commercial child' must be weaned, that it may not develop 'a lazy habit of leaning continually on the leading strings' (pp. 31–2).

However, there were still a large number of bad laws in existence, among which were: all laws and exclusive privileges relating to internal commerce, especially the Statute of Apprentices; all exclusive charters concerning foreign trade; statutes concerning pauper settlements; regulations governing the manufacturing standards of goods; and laws intended to fix wages.

> Absurd and preposterous it must surely appear, for a third person to attempt to fix the price between buyer and seller, without their own consents: for if either the journeyman will not sell his labour at the fixed or statutable price, or the master will not give it, of what use are a thousand regulating laws? Nay, how indeed can any stated regulations be so contrived, as to make due and reasonable allowance for plenty or scarcity of work, cheapness or dearness of provisions, difference of living in town or country, firing, house-rent, etc., etc., also for the goodness or badness of workmanship, the different degrees or skill or despatch of the workman, the unequal goodness of materials to work upon, state of the manufacture, and the demand, or stagnation at home or abroad? (pp. 34–5)

With regard to taxes, we know Tucker's general criteria for a good one. Here he discusses them individually. The salt tax had 'no shadow of an argument to plead on its behalf', since salt was 'an absolute necessity of life, administering to no pride, vanity, or excess whatever'. The duty on coals was similarly bad. Those on soap and candles were of mixed value. The large candles which were used by the wealthy for display should be taxed, but not the small ones required by the poor. The tax on olive oil was attacked because it was used in making Castile soap. As the usual tallow soap was not suitable for hot climates, the West Indies had to import Castile soap from foreigners, when it could easily be made in England, if this were not discouraged.

As for new taxes, we catch a glimpse of the amusements of the time as seen through the eyes of a disapproving Tucker:

> Taxes ought to be laid on dogs, on saddle-horses, when exceeding two in number; on livery servants, on all places of public resort and diversion, such as public rooms, music-gardens, play-houses, etc., also on booths and stands for country wakes, cricket matches, and horse racing, stages for mountebanks, cudgel playing, etc., moreover on five places, and ball courts, billiard tables, shuffle boards, skittle alleys, bowling-greens, and cock-pits: – Also capitation taxes should

The 'Great Work'

be levied on itinerant players, lottery-men, shew-men, jugglers, ballad singers, and indeed on all others of whatever class or denomination, whose very trades and professions have a natural tendency, and whose personal interest it is to make other people profuse, extravagant and idle. Lastly, the stamp duty might very properly be extended to take in printed songs, novels, romances, music, plays, and such like articles of mere amusement, to be stampt in the same manner as almanacks now are. (pp. 42-3)

Turning to constitutional matters, Tucker's answer to a general question concerning the effects of the English constitution upon the behaviour of the people is worth quoting in full because it not only indicates the reasons for his anti-democratic proclivities but also offers a picture of eighteenth-century English political life, as seen by a contemporary, that conflicts with that held by many people who judge it by the standards of a later age.

The general result is – An independence of the lower and middling people in regard to the Great, – but a dependence of the Great upon them. And from the clashing or mixture of these two opposite principles, arises that medley, or contradiction of characters so remarkable in the English nation. The people are independent, because they have nothing to fear, and very little to hope from the power of the great; but the great are rendered dependent upon them; because without the assistance or approbation of the people, they cannot be considerable either in the Senate, or out of it; they cannot either be ministers themselves, or raise an effectual opposition to the ministry of others. Hence it is, that the bulk of the people are always appealed to in every dispute; and being thus erected into sovereign arbitrators, they act without disguise, and indeed without reserve; so that both the good and bad qualities in human nature, appear bolder and more prominent in the inhabitants of England, than in those of any other country. For if the people are good, they are remarkably so; but if they are bad, they will take no pains to conceal their vices. Their unbounded generosity, frankness of disposition, great sincerity, and above all, their glowing spirit of patriotism, are proofs of the former; and the surliness, brutality, and daring, declared venality and prostitution of many among them, are too sad instances of the latter. In other countries, the mass of the people know nothing of state affairs; being things indeed dangerous to be meddled with: and therefore they are simple and credulous, believing what is told them, and inquiring no farther. – But in England, every creature is a politician; and has formed in his own mind the best system both for peace and war. He dislikes the ministry, because he is no minister himself; and therefore reckons up all their failings, and a great many more than ever belonged to them: and if things go on unsuccessfully, he is sure to impute it to the fault, rather than the misfortune of the administration; because it is natural to a free people to be suspicious of their governors; but he never distrusts his own opinion, or imagines another may see farther, or know better than himself. Thus it is, that the English populace are too deeply versed in politics, – and yet too little; too deeply to obey with readiness and cheerfulness; and too little, to make a wise and prudent choice for themselves. On the other hand, the Great, finding no other way to the honours and emoluments of the State, and the gratification of their ambition, but through the labyrinths of popularity, take the shortest and the surest road they can find, to arrive at them; that is, they apply to the passions and foibles of the people, rather than inform their reason, or enlighten their judgments. For the mass of mankind are much sooner cajoled, than instructed. Flattery is pleasing, instruction disagreeable and forbidding. Therefore a candidate at an election, is servile and fawning to an astonishing degree: he consults the humours, tempers, caprices, follies, nay the vices of the voting mob, their friends and acquaintance; and suits his own behaviour accordingly. Nothing is too abject for him to stoop to, no lye so absurd, no party distinction so ridiculous, that he will not by himself, or his agents, make use of on that occasion. And while the mental part of these unhappy people is thus continually inflamed with noise and nonsense; their brutal and animal part is gorged and intoxicated with gluttony and drunkenness. – But if the candidate is out-done by his antagonist in these disguised methods of bribery and corruption; if he is inferior to the other in the arts of political lying, popular declamation, carousing, and huzzaing: then he has recourse, as the last shift, to the tempting influence of pecuniary bribes; and so corrupts the heart, where he cannot corrupt the

The 'Great Work'

understanding. Thus it is, that many of the nobility and gentry in England, are too frequently found to have certain meanesses and basenesses in their conduct, which are seldom to be met with in other countries among persons of the same elevated rank and station. And yet, as a great deal must still depend upon the reputation of a good character, and as it is impossible, that popular deception should last long, or serve in all cases; the very same motives of popularity, which lead them to do much evil in some instances, operate as powerfully towards doing great good in others. Hence that diffusive charity, great liberality, and condescension, so conspicuous in persons of fortune in this country; hence those noble instances of public beneficence for the relief of the poor, in times of scarcity and general distress; hence also that rivalship and emulation in some of the members of the legislature, to patronize a public-spirited scheme, and to take the lead in doing the most signal service to their country. In short, this independency, and this dependency create such a mixture of good and bad effects, both in the inferior, and superior stations, that it is difficult to say which of them at present doth preponderate, and whether the balance at the foot of the account can be placed to the doing more benefit, or more harm to society. – But it is to be hoped and earnestly wished, that some method or other may be happily hit upon to produce the same, or more good, and yet avoid the evil.   (pp. 43–5)

Tucker continues his sociological analysis with a discussion of social mobility, which, despite the inequalities of the era, was one of its most notable features.

As the spirit and bent of the constitution so strongly points towards liberty and independency, the consequence is, that every profession and occupation is deemed honourable and eligible in proportion as it can attain this great end. And hence it is, that the military service so much coveted in other countries, as the most honourable, is not entitled to a very great respect in this; *viz.* because it creates a dependency, instead of promoting an independency; hence also the true reason why trades, even mechanic trades, are no disgrace, provided they produce riches; because riches in every free country necessarily make the possessors independent. . . . And certain it is, that though the low bred mechanic may not always meet with respect equal to his large and acquired fortune; yet, if he gives his son a liberal and accomplished education, – the birth and calling of the father are sunk in the son, and the son is reputed, if his carriage is suitable, a gentleman in all companies, though without serving in the army, without patent, pedigree, or creation. In one word, trade begets wealth, and wealth independence: but the assistance of learning and education must be called in, in order to set off, and embellish them both. (pp. 45–6)

But, of course, the gentry and nobility were still very apparent in the English social hierarchy. One of their characteristics attracted Tucker's interest: the love they had of living in the country. He sees it as another example of self-interest at work, at least in the beginning, although it had become an agreeable habit.

To explain this, let it be observed that a country residence is necessary to create a country interest: For, was the great man never to see, to converse with, or reside among his country neighbours, he would soon find, that another of much less property would eclipse him in influence and power, and that the independent Britons would give their votes to that candidate who studied most to please them. (p. 46)

Once having established a country residence where they spent the summer (winter being for Parliament) it was only natural that they should vie with each other in the beautification of their estates.

The next section is devoted to the effects of religion on the life of a country, including such topics as toleration, oath-taking, holidays and religious education. Finally, Tucker looks at ways of determining the relative wealth or poverty of each region. Important clues are provided by the condition of the inns, the number of wagons on the roads, overcrowded housing, and whether rents are paid in money or in produce. The most significant factors are the price of land and the interest rate. For example, because the English enjoyed lower interest rates than the French, they could accept a lower profit, undersell their competitors and still pay higher wages.

Tucker concludes by apologising for any mistakes he may have made owing to the fact that he was exploring untrodden ground, and claims that 'the manner of doing this, it must be acknowledged, is intirely new'. R. J. White, noting Tucker's attempt to make the 'grand tour' serve a useful purpose, comments,

> Evidently, the *beau ideal* of Dean Tucker would have been a political economist, a utilitarian, and something of a bore. Arthur Young, while he was never a bore, was to fulfill most of his demands. Young's *Travels in France*, on the eve of the Revolution, answers most of the questions outlined by the Dean. The Suffolk farmer was the type of 'the man with the notebook' and he was only the greatest of a multitude who travelled for information about existing conditions.[10]

There is one more fragment of the 'great work' which may be conveniently discussed here, although it did not appear until 1763. This is *The Case of Going to War*, which was reprinted as tract II of *Four Tracts*, in 1774.[11] It bears the subtitle, 'Chapter III Prevention of Wars', and, since he says on the first page that 'as the nature of my argument leads me to set forth several means of rendering a country populous, certainly the prevention of wars, as one of the capital means cannot be omitted', it seems obvious that this was originally meant to be a chapter in part I of the *Elements of Commerce and Theory of Taxes*, which is entitled 'Certain Polities for Increasing the Number of People'. It had a chapter 3, 'Other Polities for Increasing the Number of People', which is little more than a page of references to polities for encouraging marriage and good morals, which he intended to discuss in parts II and III. Significantly, there is not reference to war in it, so this new attitude must have been a result of the excitement engendered by the Seven Years' War, which was just ending when this tract was first published.

The theme is laid bare in the first paragraph: 'Did the difficulty in this argument consist in the dubiousness of the fact, "Whether wars were destructive to mankind or not", that difficulty would not long subsist; for, if ocular demonstration can be allowed to be proof, it is but too manifest, that both the conquering, and conquered countries, are prodigious losers by them.' But such are the 'bewitching, tho' empty sounds of conquest and glory', that there is only a slight hope of dissuading mankind from this activity (pp. 9–10). Reading these words 200 years and millions of casualties later, one can only label them an understatement. However, Tucker proceeds to try, at least, to do the impossible.

> Among barbarians war was an acceptable and honourable activity. But at present, we who chuse to call ourselves civilized nations, generally affect a more ceremonious parade, and many pretences. Complaints are first made of some injury received, some right violated, some incroachment, detention, or usurpation; and none will acknowledge themselves the aggressors; nay, a solemn appeal is made to heaven for the truth of each assertion; and the final avenger of the oppressed and searcher of all hearts, is called upon to maintain the righteous cause and to punish the wrong-doer.

The real motives are 'on one side if not both, a thirst of glory, a lust of dominion, the cabals of statesmen, or the revenous appetites of individuals for power or plunder, for wealth without industry, and greatness without merit' (p. 12).

The aims of the rulers and their subjects are not far different:

> As far as reknown is concerned, their views are alike, for heroism is the wish and envy of all mankind; – and to be a nation of heroes, under the conduct of an heroic leader, is regarded, both by prince and people, as the summit of all earthly happiness. It is really astonishing to think with what applause and eclat the memoirs of such inhuman monsters are transmitted down in all the pomp of prose and verse, to distant generations.

The people are so dazzled that they are prepared to sacrifice everything for 'this idol, glory'. Furthermore, 'the greatest conquerors abroad have proved the heaviest tyrants at home', but as Tucker notes wryly, 'victory, like charity, covereth a multitude of sins' (pp. 13–14).

Was man, then, designed by nature to make war? Perhaps the earth would otherwise become overpopulated, or possibly one nation could only prosper by impoverishing another. Tucker refuses to accept such reasoning. If the rulers of England or France can govern their territories without the necessity of internal war, then surely God intended the whole world to enjoy the blessings of peace.

The 'Great Work'   123

As for the practical objects of war, Tucker names three: more territory, more subjects or more revenue. For him, territory in itself is almost meaningless. He quotes with approval one of Bishop Berkeley's *Queries*: 'May not a man be the proprietor of twenty square miles in North America, and yet be in want of a dinner?' Land, to be worth anything, must be cultivated, and cultivation requires people. But, if more people is the goal, 'a scheme, which consists in the destruction of the human species, is a very strange one indeed to be proposed for their increase and multiplication' (p. 18). On the other hand, to acquire a land already densely populated is hardly worth the trouble, because of the continuing cost of military occupation.

But what about individuals – surely they acquire riches in the form of booty? Tucker grants this, but points out that, 'in proportion as this heroical spirit and thirst for glory have diffused themselves among his countrymen, in the same proportion the spirit of industry hath sunk and died away; every necessary, and every comfort and elegance of life are grown dearer than before' (p. 21). As an example he chose ancient Rome, tracing its fortunes from the early days of the sturdy frugal farmer and militiaman to the continual war which professionalised the army, made Rome more and more dependent on loot, and turned the populace into a brutalised propertyless rabble. Similarly, the wars of the previous 200 years in Europe had benefited no one. If the rulers had put into improving their own lands the same effort that they had expended in attempting to seize that of others, they would have had a greater claim to greatness than a Caesar or an Alexander.

Providence has created a world in which climates, soils, and products vary and each part can benefit most by trading its specialties for those of other parts. Even Norwich and Manchester, similar as they are in latitude and soil, have produced entirely different kinds of textiles.

Now, had Norwich and Manchester been the capitals of two neighbouring kingdoms ... each would have prognosticated, that the flourishing state of one portended the downfall of the other; each would have had their respective complaints, uttered in the most doleful accents, concerning their own loss of trade, and of the formidable progress of their rivals; and, if the respective governments were in any degree popular, each would have had a set of patriots and orators closing their inflammatory harangues with a *delenda est Carthago*. (p. 33)

Tucker was obviously referring again to the opposition which destroyed the peaceful policy of Walpole, whom he defends in a footnote:

> The Wealth of this Nation – that amazing wealth which has been so profusely squandered away in the two last general and devouring wars, is principally owing to the wise regulations of that able minister Sir Robert Walpole. Justice to his character and gratitude to his memory, demand this tribute of acknowledgement to be paid him when dead, which was shamefully denied him while alive. (p. 37n.)

Tucker provides a list of the kinds of people he blames for the warlike policies pursued by his country. The first is the 'Mock-patriot and furious anti-courtier'. He shows how this type first attacks a standing army of any reasonable size, then stirs up the bellicosity of the people so that they enter a war for which they are ill-prepared, then uses the early failures to bring down the government, then how, after taking over, he 'adopts those measures he formerly condemned, reaps the benefit of the preparations and plans of his predecessors, and, in the natural course of things, very probably gains some advantages'. The war continues with an 'expense ten times as great, and ... forces twenty times as numerous as were complained of before' (p. 42). Campaign follows campaign, with the enemy still holding out until an unpopular peace is finally made and the cycle starts again with a new set of patriots. If this sounds like the career of William Pitt the elder, it is no coincidence.

The 'hungry pamphleteer' who writes against the ministry in order to be bought off is next on Tucker's list. It is he who whips up the public against both the government and the enemy. 'Near a-kin to this man is that other monster of modern times, who is perpetually exclaiming against a peace, *viz*. the broker and the gambler of Change-Alley.' By spreading unfounded rumours of defeat or victory, he manipulates the market, 'and by these flagitious means the wretch, who perhaps the other day came up to London in the waggon to be an under-clerk or a message boy in a warehouse, acquires such a fortune as sets him on a par with the greatest nobles of the land' (p. 47). These people are helped by the news-writers, who, because of the freedom of the press, flourish in England as nowhere else. 'In fact these people may be truly said to *trade in blood*: For a war is their harvest; and a Gazette Extraordinary produces a crop of an hundred fold: How then can it be supposed, that they can ever become friends of peace?' Yet their influence is enormous, for their opinions are accepted unquestioningly 'by thousands, almost by millions as the standard of right and wrong'. The country, Tucker avers, is 'as much news-mad and news-ridden now, as ever it was Popery-mad and priest-ridden, in the days of our forefathers' (p. 49).

The eighteenth-century 'merchants of death' and other suppliers did not escape condemnation. Jobbers and contractors 'and every other agent, who has the fingering of the public money, may be said to constitute a distinct brood of vultures, who pray upon their own species, and fatten upon human gore' (pp. 49–50). The attitudes of other merchants he considers more complex. General trade benefits by peace, but prices do not fluctuate as much as in war when more opportunities occur for growing suddenly rich by speculation, prizes, smuggling and provisioning contracts. Many merchants could therefore be numbered among the warmongers. But the other classes of artisans and manufacturers should not be led astray by their stories of benefits to be gained. The acquisition of Canada, they were told, would bring down the price of furs so much that every man would have a beaver hat and every woman a fur, and the sale of woollens would be greatly expanded. In fact, after having possession of Canada for a few years, the prices of furs and hats were higher than ever and fewer woollens had been sold than would have been bought by soldiers and sailors lost in the conquest. The same applied to Guadeloupe and Martinique (which obviously had not been returned when Tucker wrote). Sugar, coffee, chocolate, and so on, had all been supposed to come down in price but had not, yet taxes to pay for the fighting were higher than ever.

Finally, the officers of the army and navy, as would be expected, favoured war, since it was their bread and butter. However, they were at least open and honest in their position. Tucker concludes,

> Some few perhaps, a very few indeed, may be struck with the force of these truths, and yield their minds to conviction: – Poss-

ibly in a long course of time their numbers may increase; – and possibly, at least the tide may turn; so that our posterity may regard the present madness of going to war for the sake of trade, riches, or dominions, with the same eye of astonishment and pity, that we do the madness of our forefathers in fighting under the banner of the peaceful cross to recover the Holy Land. (pp. 58–9)

If they did, Tucker reckoned, it would be by a process of repeated losses and disappointments rather than by cool reflection. Although Tucker was not alone in his pacificism, the climate of opinion against which he was struggling is indicated by the fact that even such an enlightened individual as Adam Smith regarded war as the 'noblest of all arts'. In 1790 he actually added a section to his *Theory of Moral Sentiments* praising the military virtues. However, Tucker's words were not completely unheeded. Turgot translated the tract into French, and Jeremy Bentham, in his discussion of a plan for universal and perpetual peace, acknowledged that Tucker, with his attempt 'to persuade the world of the inutility of war', was one of the 'original writers' who had preceded him in the endeavour.[12]

Although it was not part of the projected 'great work', Tucker made one more contribution to economics, though this did not see the light of day until 1774, when it was published as tract 1 of the *Four Tracts*. Its title is 'The Great Question Resolved, Whether a Rich Country Can Stand a Competitor with a Poor Country (of Equal Natural Advantages) in Raising of Provision, and Cheapness of Manufactures? – With Suitable References and Deductions'. In his Preface to the collection Tucker says, 'The piece itself rose from a correspondence in the year 1758, with a gentleman of North-Britain, eminently distinguished in the republic of letters. Tho' I cannot boast that I had the honour of making the gentleman a *declared* convert, yet I can say, and prove likewise, that in his publications since our correspondence, he has wrote, and reasoned, as if he were a convert.'[13] The 'gentleman of North-Britain' was David Hume. In his essay 'Of Money' one of the *Political Discourses* published in 1752, Hume had expressed the belief that the lower price of labour and provisions in poor countries would attract manufactures from rich countries, which would eventually lose their wealth to the formerly poor countries.

The 'Great Work'

Tucker disagreed, and expressed his objections through the medium of his correspondent Lord Kames, who was a friend of Hume's. This pamphlet, published many years later, represents his side of the controversy.

Tucker begins, 'It has been a notion universally received, that trade and manufactures, if left a full liberty, will always descend from a richer to a poorer state; somewhat in the same manner as a stream of water falls from higher to lower grounds', with, of course, the corollary that the process can reverse itself when the rich nation has become poorer.

> The reasons usually assigned for the migration, or rather circulation of industry and commerce are the following, *viz*. In rich countries, where money is plentiful, a greater quantity thereof is given for all the articles of food, raiment, and dwelling: Whereas in poor countries, where money is scarce, a lesser quantity of it is made to serve in procuring the like necessities of life, and in paying the wages of the shepherd, the plowman, the artificer, and manufacturer.   (pp. 17–18)

Goods will thus be cheaper, will undersell those of wealthier countries, and will ultimately cause a redistribution of wealth. The conclusion must be that goods from richer countries cannot be sold in poorer ones. Tucker thinks that if this were true every poor country would be considered a natural enemy of every rich one, which would be obliged to make war on the poorer one to destroy this threat to its welfare. As this is not the case in reality, doubts must be raised about the theory. As a clergyman, Tucker cannot see that Providence would organise the world in such flagrant opposition to the 'fundamental principle of universal benevolence' (p. 20), but he reinforces this rather frail argument by examining what would happen in several different hypothetical situations. He supposes that two adjacent countries, such as England and Scotland, are equal in all respects except that England has twenty million pounds and Scotland only two million. The following question then arises:

> How came England to acquire this great surplus of wealth? And by what means was it accumulated? – If in the way of idleness, it certainly cannot retain it long; and England will again

become poor; ... But if by a course of regular and universal industry, the same means, which obtained the wealth at first, will, if pursued, certainly preserve it, and even add thereto....

(pp. 21–2)

In the first case, if England has acquired its wealth 'in the way of national idleness', either by discovering gold and silver mines, by successful piracy, or by any other method involving very few productive workers, then it would be likely to suffer the same fate as befell Spain after the discovery of the New World. The easily acquired gold and silver encouraged idleness and luxury at the expense of industry. Once the flow of wealth slowed, such a nation faced abject poverty. In these circumstances, Hume's pessimistic conclusions would be justified.

However, a different situation arises if the additional wealth is acquired by 'general industry'. Assuming that the Scots had only £2 million to the £20 million of the English, but were in other respects, including population, equal, one would expect, according to the popular theory, that low wages and low prices in the north would give the hypothetical Scotland an advantage. Not so, says Tucker. First of all, 'as the richer country hath acquired its superior wealth by a general application, and long habits of industry, it is therefore in actual possession of an established trade and credit, large correspondences, experienced agents and factors, commodious shops, workhouses, magazines, etc., also a great variety of the best tools and implements in the various kinds of manufactures, and engines for abridging labour', better communications, trained craftsmen, more advanced agriculture, and so on (p. 30). The poor country has yet to acquire all these advantages.

Furthermore, the wealthier country, because of its long experience in innovating, is better able to invent more new devices. Tucker was an optimist about future possibilities in this direction.

> The importance of this will appear the greater, when we consider that no man can pretend to set bounds to the progress that may yet be made both in agriculture and manufactures; for who can take upon him to affirm, that our children cannot as far exceed us as we have exceeded our Gothic forefathers? And is it not much more natural and reasonable to suppose, that we are

rather at the beginning only, and just got within the threshold, than that we are arrived at the *ne plus ultra* of useful discoveries? (p. 31)

This means that the poorer country even if it moves ahead will tend to remain a 'respectful distance' behind the richer one.

The necessity for large amounts of capital to undertake great works which may not bring any returns for years means that the poor country will also have difficulty in attempting this kind of project. Another very significant advantage of the rich country is that its higher wages and the resulting encouragement for ambition will tend to attract the more enterprising individuals away from the less fortunate state. Although they were given equal population for the sake of argument, the magnetic pull of the more prosperous country would soon alter the balance in its favour.

The next reason is that familiar friend, the division of labour. The tremendous demand for goods in the richer country would encourage specialisation, so that, although wages might be higher, the goods would be produced at lower cost. Competition would be far more active there also, with the same effect. Finally, the plentiful supply of money would mean lower interest rates in the wealthy country, with all the benefits that that would bring in the stimulation of trade.

The argument that goods would be dearer in a rich country takes the following form, according to Tucker: 'The more labour, the more wages: – the more wages, the more money; – the more money paid for making them, the dearer the goods must come to market.' The price level would thus be proportional to the wage level. But the reverse is actually truer. 'For it may be laid down as a general proposition which very seldom fails, that operose, or complicated manufactures are cheapest in rich countries; – and raw materials in poor ones' (pp. 36–7). For example, cattle-raising requires little labour and thus cattle and its by-products are cheaper in poor countries. But, when leather and horn appear in the form of shoes and ink-horns, one finds English-made ones being sold in Scotland, rather than *vice versa*. Timber was cheaper in a poor country, but furniture in a rich one. The most astonishing case was that of Sweden, considered at that time a poor country. Its iron paid a large export duty to leave the country, freight to England, where it was fabricated, freight back to

Sweden, a high import duty, and yet the Swedes had lost money in every attempt they had made to rival English goods.

The lesson Tucker draws from all this is that the only true riches are those acquired by diligence and used to promote further industry. War, for example, whether followed by victory or defeat, 'can never prevent another country from being more industrious than you are' (p. 41). If England is ever ruined, it would only be owing to a decline in the industriousness of its people. On the other hand, Scotland might very well benefit from having a prosperous England next door. The English could help their neighbours in various ways: 'By lending them money at moderate interest, – by embarking in partnership with them in such undertakings as require large stocks and long credits, – by supplying them with models and instructors, – exciting their emulation, and directing their operations with that judgment and good order which are only learnt by use and experience' (p. 42).

In a Postscript Tucker deals with several objections to his arguments. Although he does not say so, these objections originated with Hume. In a letter to Lord Kames back in 1758, Hume wrote, 'I am very much obliged to you for allowing me a reading of Mr. Tucker's papers; in all that gentleman's productions, which have come to my hand, I can perceive a profound knowledge of the theory of commerce, joined to an enlarged acquaintance with its practice; and I own I have received both pleasure and instruction from the perusal of them'.[14] Hume then raised the points which Tucker attempted to answer in his Postscript.

The first objection is that, if Tucker were right, riches could be increased *ad infinitum*, 'which is a proposition too extravagant to be admitted'. Tucker's answer is that he did not say *that*: he merely claimed that it was not possible to set limits to progress. He does not consider himself metaphysician enough to comprehend the meaning of infinity.

Secondly, if what he said were true, 'one nation might engross the trade of the whole world and beggar all the rest', which would result in the kind of monopoly he always attacked (pp. 49–50). Tucker's reply is that he does not foresee such an eventuality, because the poor nation can, by suitable legislation, always encourage industry; it can make use of any special advantages it enjoys in soil, climate or the genius of its people; and, finally, it can benefit by the presence of the lucrative market offered by its rich neighbours. Superior wealth may be more evident in certain manufactures than in others. He offers the example of linen manufacture, which had advanced further in Ireland and Scotland than in England, and confirms his earlier assertions by noting that, though rents and prices had doubled or even trebled in those localities since the beginning of the century, their linens were not only better but also cheaper than they were earlier.

The third and fourth objections are really parts of a cyclical philosophy of history: that a poor country will take over from a richer one, because 'all human things have the seeds of decay within themselves: – great empires, great cities, great commerce, all of these receive a cheque, not from accidental events, but from necessary principles' (p. 55). Tucker's answer to the first part is that, while the poor country were moving slowly ahead, its prices would also be rising and its supposed advantages would disappear. Furthermore, he refuses to accept the biological analogy in the fourth objection.

> It is taken for granted, that as all animals by having the seeds of decay within themselves, must die sooner or later, therefore political or commercial institutions are subject to the like fate, and on the same principles. Now this remains to be proved; for the parallel doth not hold in all respects; and tho' it be true that the body politic *may* come to an end, as well as the body national, there is no physical necessity that it *must*.

The body politic may succumb to old age like the physical, but, on the other hand, 'the diseases of the body politic are not absolutely incurable; because care and caution, and proper remedies will produce those effects in one case, which it would be impossible for them to produce in another' (pp. 55–6).

These answers are similar to those originally put forward in Tucker's letter to Kames, replying to that of Hume. In it he pays his respectful compliments to Mr Hume, with thanks for his ingenious animadversions', which he found 'plausible' but falling 'short of conviction'. He does expand one point which is only hinted at in his pamphlet. Referring to the possibility that the poor countries would always be undersold, he says, significantly,

It is true likewise, that all of them have it in their power to load the manufactures of the rich country, upon entering their territories, with such high duties, as shall turn the scale in favour of their own manufactures; or of the manufactures of some other nation, whose progress in trade they have less cause to fear or envy. Thus it is in my poor apprehension, that the rich may be prevented from swallowing up the poor; at the same time, and by the same methods, that the poor are stimulated and excited to emulate the rich.[15]

In an article on the Hume–Tucker debate, Bernard Semmel notes that in his pamphlet 'Tucker anticipated, at many points, the nineteenth-century classical view of the international free trade economy', and that in his 'private rebuttal' quoted above he 'anticipated the programme which was to be put forward by economists of less developed countries who sought to combat British industrial predominance, men such as Hamilton, List, and Carey'.[16]

In the event, Tucker's arguments certainly influenced Hume, who largely reversed his position when he wrote 'Of the Jealousy of Trade', which appeared in later editions of his *Essays*. Writing to Dr Birch in 1760, Tucker, who had not seen a copy of the new essay, asked if his name had been mentioned by Hume, adding plaintively, 'If he has not, he acted unworthily, for I made him a convert to the doctrine he now espouses.'[17] Hume, in fact, had not given him any credit, but that did not affect their friendship. To have altered the views of the mighty Hume was probably satisfaction enough. All in all, we must agree with W. E. Clark, who considered *The Great Question* 'the most suggestive of Tucker's minor works'.[18]

7 Political Activities

Under the Septennial Act, a general election had to take place in 1754. Since Tucker began to play an important part in politics at this time, it is desirable to sketch in the setting for his activities. Outside of the City of London and Westminster, Bristol was the only city in the land with over 5000 electors. The franchise was open to all freemen of the city and could be acquired by birth, purchase, apprenticeship, or marriage to the daughter of a freeman. Voters also had to be natural-born subjects, Protestants, not in receipt of alms or poor relief over the previous twelve months, and over twenty-one years of age. As noted, freedom could be purchased and this was an important source of income for the Common Council, which had a special committee to handle it. In April 1754, 986 new freemen were created, with both parties engaging in the activity. In theory, an elector was not entitled to exercise his franchise until he had been a freeman for one year, but this and other tiresome restrictions appear to have been overlooked in the heat of the contest. The reform-minded Oldfield, writing in the early nineteenth century, said about Bristol,

> This city also labours under the intolerable grievance of having its right of election so complicated, and so exposed to fraud and imposition, as to render it abundantly impossible for them to accomplish a fair choice of their representatives. This right being in the freeholders and freemen, and the latter qualification extending to freemen's sons and to the husbands of freemen's daughters, it is not unusual for a number of persons to be brought here at an election to personate the sons of freemen, whose absence may afford an opportunity of substituting a proxy; and others to swear themselves the sons of parents to whom they have no other affinity than of recording their names on the same parchment, in the indenture of admission. Freemen's daughters have also been married for the express purpose

of qualifying their husbands to vote, and the husband selected for the occasion, after fulfilling the purpose of the marriage, appears to have provided, by anticipation, against the evils that might arise from the inconvenience of having a bad partner, by discovering that the marriage had no validity, from the circumstance of his having a *former wife* living.[1]

Although Bristol had been represented by Whigs earlier in the century, when Tucker arrived on the scene both seats had been held by the Tories for fourteen years. It was the decision of both of these members to retire in 1754 which opened up fresh opportunities for political action in the city. Each party had a local organisation through which its supporters could work. The Steadfast Society, which met at the White Lion Tavern, was founded in December 1737 by the leading Tory merchants. It made its wishes known by drawing up instructions and preparing petitions opposing, for example, the naturalisation of foreign Protestants and a street-lighting bill promoted by the town corporation. The Whig organisation was called the Union Club and it used the Bush Tavern. The date of its formation is not known, but it held an annual dinner on 1 August to which it invited important politicians. In the words of P. E. Underdown, 'Besides undertaking the task of organizing the electoral interests of the Whig party in Bristol, the Union Club also advised the Government on the distribution of local patronage, kept the Whig member of Parliament for the city informed on the state of local opinion, and attempted to marshal it in support of the Government whenever any opposition appeared likely to develop.'[2] By 1754 Tucker had become its political adviser. As the Corporation had a Whig majority in this period and the Society of Merchant Adventurers seems to have had a similar coloration, the success of Tory candidates is somewhat surprising, but, judging from Tucker's experience, it would appear to have been owing to factionalism among the Whigs.

Since one of the principal sources of information about the Bristol elections of 1754 and 1756 is Tucker's correspondence, a brief glance at its origins is advisable. The story is told in his letters to two men: Thomas Birch (1705–66) and Nathaniel Forster (1718–57). Like Tucker, both were clergymen and doctors of divinity. Another thing they had in common was the friendship of the family of the Lord Chancellor. The *Dictionary of National Biography* article on Birch notes that 'Being a diligent student of English history and a firm supporter of the whig doctrines in church and state, he basked in the patronage of the Hardwicke family.' Forster was also indebted to them for the various livings which he, like Birch and Tucker, received over the years. Another characteristic they shared was their scholarship. Forster published learned works on the classical and biblical languages: in fact, his death at the early age of thirty-nine was laid at the door of 'excessive study'. Birch became not only, like Forster, a Fellow of the Royal Society, but also, from 1752 until 1762, its Secretary, and wrote its history in four volumes. He was responsible for a number of other works, including a life of Archbishop Tillotson, but he was not noted for a sparkling style. Johnson is quoted as having said, 'Tom Birch is as brisk as a bee in conversation, but no sooner does he take a pen in his hand then it becomes a torpedo to him and numbs all his faculties.'[3]

Although Tucker's earliest extant letters to both men were written in 1752, these were obviously not the first ones. How he met Dr Birch is not known, but his acquaintance with Dr Forster is easily explained through the latter's connection with Bishop Butler. The great theologian actually died in the arms of Forster, who was his domestic chaplain at the time, and he and Tucker were joint executors of the Bishop's estate. In fact, the first letter in the Forster collection refers to the inscription Tucker was having done for Butler's memorial. However, regardless of the circumstances in which they originated, both friendships flourished, and, as far as Tucker was concerned, they provided a much needed contact with the great world, from which he was to some extent excluded by his geographical location. Birch was, as we have noted, Secretary of the Royal Society, and Forster was, at this time, at Lambeth Palace, as one of the chaplains to Dr Herring, Archbishop of Canterbury. Tucker's letters show that he used both of his friends to keep in touch with the Yorke family, including Hardwicke and his sons Philip (the eldest) and Charles – all of whom, as part of the Lord Chancellor's circle, had to be cultivated. They were Tucker's link with the Whig leadership and the government; through them he passed on information as to the state of affairs at Bristol and sought in return their reaction to it, as well as news about what was happening in the capital.

Birch and Forster were useful in other respects also. Tucker had direct dealings with several London printers and also with the periodical press, but he often sent his writings to at least one of his friends first. If it were merely a fugitive polemic, he would ask them to check it for errors and then place it in a newspaper such as the *General Evening Post*. For more substantial works he usually requested an opinion, suggestions for changes or even a decision as to whether it should be published at all. He often wanted them to show it to others and obtain their reaction also. Occasionally, in order to save time, he would ask them to pick up the proofs, correct them and return them to the printers. When he was extremely doubtful about the reception of one of his works, he had it privately printed with large margins, for circulation amongst his friends for their comments. As we have seen, the *Elements of Commerce* never got beyond this stage.

Finally, Tucker also looked after the interests of Forster, who had a prebendal stall at Bristol, and much of their correspondence is taken up with the collection of rents and fees and the handling of these funds. There were also many passages in both sets of letters devoted to the question of ecclesiastical preferment, which consumed so much time and energy in those days.

Although the first reference in the election does not occur until 21 March 1754, when Tucker wrote to Birch, 'Mr. Nugent is declared this day by the Whiggs: And the Tories resolve, together with some others not yet named, upon Sir John Philipps',[4] a number of significant events had already occurred. As early as May 1753, the Steadfast Society had set up a committee to prepare for the election, and in December the Union Club had suggested a meeting with their opponents for the purpose of avoiding a contest. After several joint meetings had been held, the Union Club, in early March, suggested the names of Nugent and Lord Barrington. The Steadfast Society rejected both and offered three alternative names for one of the seats while reserving to itself the right to choose the other candidate. Without waiting for a reply from the Whigs, it went ahead and nominated Sir John Philipps, Bart. The Whigs, meanwhile, decided against all three choices and remained faithful to Mr Nugent. The Steadfast Society then felt free to seek another candidate. As the one it chose, Richard Beckford, was absent in Jamaica, it sent a deputation to London to seek the approval of his brother, Alderman William Beckford.

This was obtained and, at a public meeting on 28 March, Philipps and Beckford were formally nominated.

Things had not gone so smoothly for the Whigs. Tucker had already entered the fray with the first of a series of broadsides which we shall discuss later, but he was not satisfied with the performance of his own party. As he wrote to Birch at the end of March,

> The mob is all of our side, great numbers of the low and middling tradesmen of theirs; but if proper care had been taken at first, I am persuaded the Whiggs would have got the day by a thousand majority. As it is, I believe we are pretty sure of carrying it, tho the Tories were suffered (notwithstanding all my entreaties and remonstrances to the leading Whiggs for the six months past) to canvass the whole city almost twice over before a Whigg would stir. Little divisions and separate interests are the bane of the Whigg cause in Bristol. The Presbyterians would not give up their favourite Lord Barrington, tho he himself had the generosity, prudence and good sense to disswade them from thinking of such a project.[5]

Worse was to come. Several days later he wrote,

> Surely there is some fatality attending the management of the Whiggs in Bristol. For after we had drove the enemy from every battery and almost compelled them to quit the field [this refers to his propaganda campaign] a deputation was sent, who met Mr. Nugent at Marlborough on his way to Bristol, to propose terms to him as to the proportion of the expense. One would have thought it was impossible but that those points had been previously settled and concerted long before: Yet so it was, it seems that nothing had been done: And when the parties met, they differed; Mr. Nugent expecting, as he had been made to believe, that nothing more was expected from him than the credit of his name, leaving the rest to their generosity; and they proposing that he should bear half the expences.

Nugent had returned to London and a deputation of four now had been sent after him to propose new terms. The outcome was not known when Tucker wrote. He concluded,

My present situation grows irksome to me, as I find myself connected with a set of men, who have neither heads nor hearts. They cannot manage themselves, and will not take advice from others. The city of Bristol must appear in a very strange light to those who are ignorant of our situation. And yet to my certain knowledge ¾ of the people of property are Whiggs . . . .[6]

Nugent was persuaded to run after being offered up to £10,000 towards defraying the cost of his election. There was, however, more to it than that. Probably unknown to Tucker, Nugent wanted something tangible from the government as well. The Newcastle correspondence contains the record of this negotiation. Writing on 19 March, the Duke reported that Nugent 'declines undertaking Bristol unless he can have such employment before the election'.[7] Nugent was considered important enough to get his way and he was duly appointed a lord of the Treasury.[8]

The Whig candidate was a man about whom contradictory opinions have been held and it is difficult to render a final verdict.[9] Robert Nugent was born in Carlanstown, County Westmeath, in 1709 of an old and notable Irish family. He got off to a bad start in the eyes of many when he abandoned his cousin Clare after making her pregnant in 1730. She followed him to London, but he was adamant in his refusal to marry her. Instead he married Lady Emilia Plunkett, daughter of the Earl of Fingall. She died the following year in childbirth. It was only then, and upon her deathbed urging, that he returned to Ireland and offered to marry his cousin, but another marriage had been arranged and his offer was spurned.

Since both of his marriages were to extremely wealthy women, his motives were considered suspect by his contemporaries, even though he had a private income of £1500. However, that rather pales in comparison with what his second wife brought him in 1736. She was Anne Craggs, daughter of the Postmaster General, who was involved in the South Sea Bubble. Not only did she inherit from her father and her brother, Secretary Craggs, but, in addition, she had married well twice before. The result of all this was that Nugent received along with his bride a fortune of about £100,000 in cash and property, which included the estate of Gosfield Hall in Essex and the borough of St Mawes in Cornwall. The latter provided him with a seat in Parliament, which he first

Political Activities 139

occupied in 1741. Thus began a career in the House of Commons which lasted until 1748.

Once in Parliament, he followed a path not calculated to endear him to those who respect faithfulness to both friends and principles. He started out in the circle of the Prince of Wales, becoming comptroller of the Prince's household and loaning him substantial sums of money, which, although never repaid, must have been a good investment, judging by the places and titles he later received. After the Prince's death, he turned to the Pelhams and became a loyal supporter of the Duke of Newcastle, at least until the latter fell from power, when Nugent attached himself to Bute. This tendency to support the ministry, no matter who was in power, which Nugent was to demonstrate until the end of his career, accentuated that unsavoury reputation for opportunism which he had already acquired in private life. In any case, his rewards for being what Sir Lewis Namier called 'a notorious time-server'[10] were considerable. In addition to becoming a lord of the Treasury, he received the Irish titles of Viscount Clare in 1767 and Earl Nugent in 1776.

Nugent and his wife got along well, at least in public, and many of the leading figures of the day were happy to be entertained at Gosfield Hall. Alexander Pope and Oliver Goldsmith were numbered among their friends. Nugent not only cultivated poets but also was one himself, in a minor way. His best-known piece, the *Ode to William Pulteney*, was admired by Gibbon and Horace Walpole. He was also a good companion, jovial and exuberant, and given to occasional practical jokes.

In politics too, Nugent can be looked at in a more favourable light. Despite his dexterity in avoiding time spent in unprofitable opposition, the *History of Parliament* concludes that he 'at no time hesitated to speak his mind or incur ministerial displeasure'.[11] He was by no means a party hack and in fact was surprisingly consistent throughout his career on certain issues. These included support for the removal of restraints on trade with Ireland, legislation intended to improve the lot of the poor, and any measures which he thought would benefit trade. Indeed, it was the concern he had already shown for the last, while still representing St Mawes, which first attracted the attention of the Bristol Whigs. Once elected from Bristol, he took his duties seriously and was an effective spokesman for the mercantile interests of Bristol until the

American Revolution. Tucker may be considered a prejudiced witness, but his defence of Nugent's conduct in a pamphlet written in 1776, when Nugent had lost his support in Bristol, nevertheless makes a convincing case for his efforts on that city's behalf.[12] Furthermore, whatever opinion may be held about the content of Nugent's speeches, he cannot be accused of shirking his Parliamentary responsibilities. There was not one issue of importance over a period of forty years on which he did not speak. As far as Tucker is concerned, Nugent and he were of one mind on many subjects, even when there was no possible reason for Tucker to echo Nugent rather than *vice versa*, and Nugent certainly did not forget Tucker when it came to pressing for some recognition of his efforts.

Those efforts had already started. Even before Nugent had been chosen, Tucker was on the offensive against the Tory favourite, Sir John Philipps. In order to discredit their opponent, both sides speedily surrendered to the temptation to blacken his reputation by any means at hand. Neither side seemed to be over-fastidious about the smear technique. The Tories tried to make use of the fact that Nugent was a convert from Catholicism (he returned to the fold just before his death). However, they were already on the defensive, because Tucker had found a far more useful chink in Sir John's armour. The Jacobite label was still an effective means of frightening off some electors, and Tucker felt there was enough evidence to make the charge credible. As soon as Philipps was selected by the Tories, Tucker wrote to Birch asking for confirmation of several vague recollections concerning him.[13] This apparently arrived, for Birch was thanked in another letter.[14] Tucker deployed the evidence in several of the series of addresses to the electors which appeared as broadsides and in the Bristol press.[15] A trick which Tucker seemed to like was to argue apparently for the other side against his own, in order to make the other position appear perverse, such as he did in the one entitled *Reasons against Chusing Mr. Nugent*. His most interesting effort against Philipps took the form of a 'papal bull'.[16] Here it is in full:

Great News from Rome!
Being
The Pope's Bull in favour of the High-Flyer, against N——t, the Heretic.

Translated into English for the benefit of the Gentlemen of the W. L—n C—b.

Leo Episcopus, Servus Servorum Dei, in perpetuam Rei Memoriam, etc.

Whereas one R———d N———t, hath these many years, apostasized from the Roman Catholic faith, and is become a convert to that pestilent heresy, called, the doctrine of the Church of England, still persisting in his rebellion against us, and giving no signs of returning to Obedience: – And whereas, there is, as we are informed, a certain high-flying Sea S———t [Sergeant – see below] set up against him, who has proved his obedience to us, and his loyalty to the House of S———t, by wearing Plaid Dresses and White Roses on the 10th of June; (the birthday of our beloved son, James the IIId.) also by endeavouring to prosecute those incorrigible heretics who associated in the year 1745, in defense of the Protestant religion . . . We therefore in order to assist the cause of the said loyal and catholic high-flying Sea S———t, and to oppose that Arch-heretic N———t, 'DO grant full powers to all our friends, open and secret, to abuse, asperse, blacken, and revile the said N———t, and all his adherents, in all ways they can possibly invent . . . and to promote the interest of our hopeful high-flying Sea S———t, by every method, that either fraud, violence, or malice can suggest.

We do therefore decreee, and by these presents declare, that all persons well-affected to this good and catholic cause, may freely, and without scruple or remorse, be guilty of the crimes of bribery and corruption, or lying, swearing and forswearing, or any other that may be judged necessary for the carrying on this laudable design; – Inasmuch as we do absolve them, by our plenitude of power, from any obligation of gratitude, duty or conscience, and do dispense with all oaths and engagements, however plainly specified . . . solemnly and frequently repeated . . . or strongly insisted on in that heretical book call'd the BIBLE.

Moreover, we freely grant unto all that shall eminently distinguish themselves in the promotion of this catholic cause, the release of a thousand years from PURGATORY: and for the great encouragement of their zeal, we do hereby assure them upon our infallible word, that we will immediately transfer all the merit of that great English high-flying Saint Doctor S———ll

[Henry Sacheverall, impeached in 1709, for violent preaching in the High Church cause], for their sole use and benefit.

Lastly, to express the uncommon regard we have for our dear Sea S———t, and to prosper his cause, we send him this our Papal Bull and benediction, together with a precious relic, which we greatly value, viz. A Night Cap of Saint Sach———ll, of sovereign use to save his head.

Dated at the VATICAN, our Papal Palace in ROME, etc. etc.

This contains most of the charges which were also levied against Philipps in the other pieces. The one most harped upon was that the Tory favourite, who came from Wales, where he had been Mayor of Haverfordwest and MP for Carmarthen in the 1740s,[17] belonged to a group known as the 'Ancient and Honourable Society of Sea Sergeants' (he had been President of it in 1752), which was suspected of having Jacobite sympathies. Little is known of it except that it was the South Wales counterpart of the better-known Jacobite 'Cycle' Society of North Wales. Its badge was the eight-pointed Jacobite star, with a dolphin in the centre.[18] Another charge was that he had appeared in a plaid waistcoat or breeches in Bristol shortly after the 1745 affair. Not only did this indicate Jacobite sympathies, but, in addition, wearing the tartan had actually been outlawed by Lord Hardwicke following the rebellion.

The document also refers to another action of Philipps which could be called into question. In 1745 a number of persons went around from door to door in the capital attempting to persuade people to enter into an association in defence of the Hanoverian settlement. They were interested not only in obtaining expression of loyalty *per se*, but in keeping an eye out for suspicious strangers who might have subversive intentions. When the fuss died down, Philipps had tried to get the Westminster Grand Jury to prosecute some of the associators, but had failed.

Finally, although they are not mentioned in the 'papal bull', there were several other minor accusations, the most significant of which was probably that Philipps had been friendly with one David Morgan, who had been executed as a rebel in 1745, and who was alleged to have been a Sea Sergeant. Morgan was a middle-class lawyer with strong Jacobite sympathies who joined the Prince at Preston. When Charles was persuaded to turn back,

Morgan, who thought it was a mistake, said he would be hanged before he would go to Scotland. He was captured shortly thereafter and was eventually hanged on Kennington Common.[19]

These charges apparently were quite effective, since the Tories felt compelled to answer them. In one of their broadsides against the Whigs and 'their Jew chaplain', the Sea Sergeants are described as a society 'composed of gentle men of first rank and fortune who meet at a seaport for a week of innocent mirth'. That Philipps ever wore plaid was denied, as was the claim that David Morgan was a Sea Sergeant. It was true that Sir John had attempted to prosecute some of the associators, but only on the grounds that they had tried to extort money under this guise. Tucker's answer to the latter was that the Westminster Grand Jury obviously did not agree, and that the Lord Chancellor himself had said at the trial of the rebel lords that the associations were legal. Tucker apparently did not bother to answer the other claims, although he did say in a letter to Birch that 'the truth seems to be that he [Morgan] was once a Sea-Sergeant and was afterwards expelled from the society, least he should betray them, a practice he had been guilty of more than once'. Sir John had visited him at Newgate before he was hanged.[20]

Tucker, naturally, did not confine his attentions to Philipps. The previously mentioned *Reasons against Chusing Mr. Nugent* was, of course, a list of reasons for choosing him. These included his support of the bill to encourage the settlement of wealthy foreign Protestants, his prevention of the importation of French wine in bottles, his work in opening the Turkey trade, his opposition to the East India Company and Hudson's Bay Company monopolies, and his special efforts on behalf of the interests of Bristol. Amongst these hard-headed economic arguments was a curious non-economic one. Number 7 was: 'Mr. Nugent warmly opposed the Marriage Act, and is determined next session to do the same: . . . therefore all who would have partners for life of their own chusing, ought to reject him with disdain.' In the margin of the copy sent to Birch, Tucker wrote, 'Added by another hand since the first publication.' It could have been embarrassing for him as it stood, since this act was pushed through by Lord Hardwicke against strenuous opposition from Nugent and Charles Townshend, among others. The Marriage Act provided that, except in the case of Jews, Quakers and members of the royal family, a marriage was invalid unless performed by an Anglican clergyman, after banns had been published or a licence obtained. By requiring a waiting period and the consent of a parent or guardian in the case of minors, it tackled the problem of clandestine marriages. Since Tucker had submitted a model register for the records, there is no reason to believe that he did not heartily approve, but here was a case where the exigencies of politics made any ammunition useful.

The initial success of Tucker's campaign against Philipps was marred by Whig indecision over Nugent, as noted in one of his letters quoted above. However, by 13 April Tucker felt able to express complete confidence in the Whig candidate's success. This was a few days after Nugent had arrived in Bristol. In a letter enclosing a copy of a Bristol paper describing the reception Tucker wrote, 'The Acct. of the reception of Mr. Nugent is a little exaggerated as to the numbers; – tho upon the whole the appearance was very elegant and striking. I was desired to plan out the procession and to fit the mottoes; and then some other persons made additions to it. It was a full hour in passing by.'[21]

The newspaper devoted a satisfactory amount of space to the event:

> On Monday last we had the pleasure of seeing our worthy candidate Mr. Nugent, whose politeness and affability exceeded all expectation: The gentlemen, merchants, and citizens in his interest, assembled themselves in our great square, to the number (by the best account) of 3000 persons, who made a gay and splendid appearance upon the joyful occasion of welcoming their candidate to town.
>
> The procession began from the square to Templegate, where they met Mr. Nugent; who alighting from his coach, saluted some of the principal citizens, and then returned with them to the great square, from thence to the Key, where the ships were beautifully decorated with their colours flying, and guns firing as they pass'd amidst the loud acclamations of the citizens. He then went over the Draw-Bridge, and round the College-Green; from thence the procession moved to the Council House, where Mr. Nugent address'd the Mayor and Aldermen.

The burden of the address was that he had always done his best for Bristol and would continue to do so. The Mayor's reply was brief

Political Activities 145

and to the point: Bristol's prosperity rested on *trade*, in case Nugent had any doubts about what would be expected of him. The procession then continued on to the Exchange, where it ended with another short speech by Nugent. The writer thought the procession so striking that he felt it would be unfair to omit a detailed description:

> It was as follows: *First Division*, a Band of Musick of French Horns, Hautboys, Bassoons, playing Long Live Great George our King! *Second Division*, the Bottlemakers carrying bottles on poles, with inscriptions, No French Bottles! Nugent for Ever! and followed by the white glass-makers. *Third Division*, the Weavers and Woolcombers, dress'd in Holland shirts, and woollen perukes of various colours, curiously made, carrying white rods in their hands tipp'd with wool, and an ensign of party-coloured unwrought wool carried before them, and inscriptions on poles, Open Trade to Turkey! English manufactories! *Fourth Division*, The Hatters with furs on poles, and inscriptions, No Monopolies! Hudson's Bay open'd! *Fifth Division*, Six poles with elephants teeth, and inscriptions, Trade to Africa! *Sixth Division*, A curious and beautiful ship in miniature, carried on eight men's shoulders, followed by Masters of Ships and Seamen, with poles and inscriptions, Trade! Navigation! *Seventh Division*, Six Tradesmen, with poles and inscriptions, the Honour of BRISTOL, – Defended by NUGENT! – Then followed Mr. Nugent and Alderman Elton, attended by the Gentlemen, Merchants etc., etc.

Thus tangible expression was given to the economic ideas of Tucker, the political goals of Nugent, and, above all, to the bread-and-butter interests of the inhabitants of Bristol. Broad national policies were taken note of, but their effect on the welfare of the locals was not of the first importance. Politicians who ignored this, as Burke was to do later in the century, did so at their peril.

By April Tucker was able to write to Birch,

> The Tories have given up this day. The Whiggs have therefore adjourned the count till tomorrow morning, in order to consider, whether Philipps or Beckford shall be second man, as they have it absolutely in their power to nominate either. The

general opinion is, and indeed the thing is as good as settled, that Beckford shall have the preference to Philipps; – Not that they are quite pleased with such a representative; but of the two evils, it is better to choose the least. And it would be quite inconsistent in us first to rouse the people against P as a J——te, and then choose him ourselves. I cannot say by what majority Mr. Nugent will be returned; but the real majority upon the canvass books, were they all to poll, is about 350.[22]

The final figures when the poll closed on 1 May were Nugent, 2590, Beckford, 2248, Philipps, 2163. The Bristol Tories, however, were so fond of Sir John, that they contributed £1200 towards obtaining him a seat at Petersfield, made available by William Beckford, who had been elected for the City of London, and he kept in close touch with his Bristol friends. An analysis of the poll book by occupation reveals that the electors were not always to be depended upon to follow what others at least thought were their economic interests. Although the Corporation was almost solidly Whig, a substantial number of glassmakers and those connected with shipping did not, as might have been expected, vote for Nugent, and Beckford, despite his West Indian sugar interests, failed to secure the support of the Bristol sugar trade. The Tory strength in an urban trading centre such as Bristol seems surprising, especially in the case of Sir John Philipps. He never reached much eminence, and to the extent that he was known it was as a leader of the country gentlemen, whose interests were generally not those of Bristol. Perhaps the electors who voted Tory did so out of dissatisfaction with government initiatives such as the naturalisation bills, as well as out of personal connections and loyalties which defy further analysis.

Once the smoke of battle had cleared, Nugent took time off to drop the Duke of Newcastle a line:

> Having read in this Day's newspaper that by the death of Mr. Dawnay a Prebend of Canterbury is become vacant, I can not refrain from putting your Grace in mind of poor Tucker. Thus much I must say in excuse for the liberty I take, that were I quite out of the question, and the man not my particular friend, I should still most earnestly wish that he who has so eminently distinguished himself, upon various occasions, in the Whigg-

Cause, and recommended himself beyond any other person whatever by his merits and his sufferings, to his majesty's best friends at Bristol, should receive a distinguished reward from your grace, and I wish this the more, as I sincerely desire to see your Grace rivetted in the hearts of my constituents.[23]

However, nothing came of this request, and Tucker had several years to wait for any recognition of his services.

In August, Tucker paid a visit to London. Although he missed Forster, he was able to see the Archbishop of Canterbury at Croydon, and Nugent at his seat in Essex. He also mentions having been in Cambridge and Hertfordshire. As both of these places contained estates belonging to the Yorke family, it seems to have been principally a fence-mending trip.[24]

The year 1755 was a quiet one, politically speaking. The *Elements of Commerce* was printed and distributed amongst Tucker's friends, and he fulfilled the requirements for his doctorate of divinity, which he received later in the year. In December Tucker told Forster about a rumour going the rounds that, owing to other promotions St James would become vacant and would be offered to him. 'And divers persons have strongly sollicited me, to give them the earliest *private* intelligence, when I am to quit St. Stephens, presuming upon my former declaration against pluralities of Livings.' However he was not at all convinced that this would take place, and, if it did, whether he should apply for it. 'The living itself could not be more than £60 a year above what I have at present: And if it was to be conferred as a *recompense*, I should not be willing to view it in that light.'[25]

Later that month the topic came up again. Referring to an enclosed letter, presumably from Nugent, which he asked Forster to burn, he said,

You see, by the enclosed, that my great man is as yet a very honest, sincere man in regard to me. . . . If you can contrive any scheme, wherein he can be of mutual service to us; I am of the present opinion, that his best endeavours will not be wanting. Some time ago, viz. just after our Bristol election, he mentioned me to the D. of N. as a candidate for a P. of C. [prebendary of Canterbury]: But he was put off according to custom; and I think, that stall has been since filled up. – One at Bristol would be as desirable to me as a better at a great distance.[26]

Early in 1756, he returned despondently to the same subject:

> In regard to ecclesiastical matters, and schemes of preferment I am in statu quo: Or rather I begin to grow weary of the thought and to give up all further expectations. The advancement of my friends will always give me pleasure; and in regard to you, I am willing to hope, that this pleasure is not a far off.[27]

Within a few days of this letter, however, events took an unforeseen turn. Richard Beckford fell ill while on a trip to France and died at Lyons on 24 January 1756. The resultant necessity for a by-election brought Tucker into the limelight again.

Because neither party in Bristol had recovered financially from the heavy expenses incurred during the election of 1754, it seemed only sensible to try to avoid a contested election. Two attempts were made at an accommodation, one after news of Beckford's illness had arrived and the other when it was learned that he had died. They were known respectively as the Bristol Compromise and the London Compromise. The background is given in a letter from Tucker to Forster.

> When I was last in London, Mr. Nugent spoke to me to use my best endeavours to bring about a compromise; and he spoke to several other persons of note among the Whiggs to help forward this good work. They all promised, tho some of them acted a very contrary part. The D. of Newcastle I found by the turn of his discourse, when I had the honour to be introduced to him, was in the same sentiments.... Thus armed and commissioned, as soon as I came down, I drew up the enclosed, which after having been approved of in the proper place was communicated to a few of both parties. The Tories nibbled at it very foolishly, saying, that it was done more to serve Nugent, and get him a re-election than to save them: And therefore they would stay till Mr. Beckford was actually dead. Had the Whiggs at that juncture insisted upon their compromising, else that they would contest the election at Mr. Beckford's death, the Tories must have submitted; and indeed many of them were inclinable. But

Political Activities

instead of acting with that spirit, the Whiggs could not be brought to joyn in a body. I was surprised at that conduct, and could not account for it: At last it appears: *That a certain person had, by himself and his agents been stirring up a club of low tradesmen among the Dissenters held at an Ale-House, whose sign is a Piece of Wood called a Leg in the Shambles, to insist upon a contested election.* These poor, silly mortals were taught to believe, that it redounded to the Honour of the Dissenting Cause, that they should make a member for the second city in the Kingdom. Thus all my peaceful schemes proved abortive.[28]

On the news of Beckford's death, the document was redrafted as the London Compromise:[29]

Proposed   London   10 February 1756

In order to preserve the Peace of the city of Bristol, that a person to be nominated by the friends of the late Mr. Beckford, be elected without any opposition to succeed him for the remainder of this Parliament: And in case Mr. Nugent's seat in the present Parliament shall be vacated by any means whatsoever, such person shall be elected by his friends; And that each seat shall be filled in like manner in case of any future vacancy during this present Parliament; And [in] case no such vacancy of Mr. Nugent's Seat shall happen during this Parliament, that then his friends shall have the like turn in case of such vacancy in the next. But this is not to extend to the choice of members at any general election.

    Unanimously agreed to by

Sir John Philipps Bart	Mr. Nugent
Mr. Berrow	Mr. Henry Swymmer
Mr. Brickdale	Mr. Love
Mr. Taylor	Mr. Elton Town Clerk

As Tucker explained to Hardwicke a few weeks later, one of the intended signatories turned out to be the villain of the piece:

But that is not all: – For when Mr. Nugent engaged me (when I was last in London) to promote a compromise, he likewise spoke to another gentleman, Mr. Henry Swymmer . . . to do the same: And we both then agreed upon the spot, that upon coming down, I was not to appear, lest my close connections with Mr. Nugent might give umbrage to some people, till he had prepared the way: And he was to have a week's time to do it. But upon my coming out, I found that he had been so far from preparing the way for peace, that he was actually laying a plan for a contest, and was working underhand with several sorts of engines.[30]

In his earlier letter to Forster, Tucker had explained the likely motivation:

And one man, whose only aim in this thing was to set up some member to eclipse Mr. Nugent, or to ruin the Whigg cause entirely, that he might have the nomination of places in the Custom House, which since Mr. Nugent's election have entirely become his province, – I say this man with these views, and a few instruments hath been able to throw the whole city into a greater uproar than ever I knew it.

Although the Tories had offered a compromise after Beckford's death, the Whigs had 'meanly chicaned' and chosen another candidate, with the result that the Tories did the same. Tucker blamed it on a club of seventy or eighty 'low tradesmen', who were also members of the Union Club. He concluded,

In regard to myself, I am resolved to be neuter; And so I believe will hundreds who were very active, the last election. Mr. Spencer [the Whig candidate] treats the silly people with a proper degree of contempt by refusing to come down. And indeed, as the case stands at present, I do not think it safe for him to attempt it, were he desirous; Our mobs becoming every hour more outrageous. But the Tory mob is by much the strongest at present: For the people in general were for peace, and are exasperated to a degree of fury against the disturbers of it. Just now I received a ticket from Mr. Castelman [a prebendary who had been involved in the negotiations] (For neither he, nor I stir out, but where we unavoidably must) that the Leg in the Shambles is almost demolished.[31]

Political Activities 151

We know from the Steadfast Society Minute Book that a joint committee was set up on 11 February to negotiate a compromise, and when that failed a local lawyer, Jarrit Smith, was approved by its members on 25 January 1756. The man chosen by the Whigs, John Spencer, was a great-grandson of the Duke of Marlborough and had a seat at Althorp in Northamptonshire.

On 27 February Tucker reported to Forster,

> The Tory party gains ground every day, scores of Whiggs within my own knowledge having joyned them on this occasion, who were strongly against them last time. And I am very certain, which side so ever shall get the election will get it by so small a majority as will bring on a long hearing before the H. of Commons. . . . If you come down, I would not advise you to think of taking any private lodging – For the College Green, and that part of town will be filled with roaring drunken mobs every night during the election. My house is retired, situated far back in a garden, and is as free from the noise of the busy town as its owner. Give me leave therefore to entreat you to accept a bed in it during your stay.[32]

Polling commenced on 2 March and continued for two weeks. In a letter written to Forster the day after polling started, Tucker enclosed an analysis of the factors likely to influence electors.[33]

> A Comparative View of the different Interests in the City of Bristol from the last Election to the present.
>
> ### Last Election
>
> The very great majority obtained by the Whiggs in the votes last election was owing to the following causes: 1st The unpopularity of Sir John Philipp's character on acct. of his attempt to prosecute the Associators during the height of the rebellion: 2dly The tyrannical proceedings of the Tories in refusing a compromise, when entreated to do it; which exasperated the town greatly against them as disturbers of the public peace. 3dly The peculiar talent of Mr. Nugent in accommodating himself to the humours and dispositions of all manner of people. These

reasons, joyned to those usually made use of on such occasions, created a majority on the poll of 432
The voters ready to poll had there been
occasion at least 120
                                                                                            552.

Present Election

	Votes
Deduct for a large number of absentees on board the fleet, or in the army: which circumstance must chiefly affect the Whigg interest because three fourths of the common people were Whigg voters, Upon a moderate computation about.........................	150
Deduct for a considerable number declaring at this juncture for the Tories, on account of the odiousness of the Whigg proceedings, who were themselves Whiggs before. They may be about 60 persons: But as they voted on the Whigg side before, all their votes are to be counted double...	120
Deduct for persons, who were neutral the last election, but now joyn the Tories, about..................................	40
Deduct for a great number that declare themselves neutral on this occasion, who voted before for the Whiggs, about...	150
Deduct for the want of Mr. Spencer's personal attendance; and for the popularity of Mr. Smith as a native of the city..	
Deduct for the want of unanimity and cordiality among the Whiggs at this juncture; – And for the most remarkable cordiality among the Tories, not to mention the largeness of the subscriptions on one side and the smallness on the other...	

Although Tucker did not complete his calculations, the total here is 460, which with the last two items, for which he gives no figures, would more than wipe out the 552 lead in the 1754 election.

As the election unfolded, Tucker continued his progress reports to Forster. On 7 March he noted, 'We have been very quiet for this and five nights past in regard to mobs; Jack Day, the Captain of Mr. Spencer's mob having exercised his valour a little malapropos on two women: and is now put into the Crown Office.' He was not going out of his house except to his church and spinning school.[34] On 13 March Tucker reported, 'Both sides are struggling very hard, and both pretend to be sure. But the poll will not be closed till Tuesday.' He gave the state of the poll as of that night as 1944 for Spencer and 2035 for Smith. Four days later, in a letter begun at noon, he wrote:

> I thought to have given you last night the concluding account of our poll: But the sheriffs adjourned the count till today, in order that some more of Mr. Spencer's friends may be brought to vote. The majority last night, according to Mr. Spencer's friends was 46 for Mr. Smith; But according the other party's count it is 71. This difference of 25 voices is what I cannot pretend to account for: – But very great outcries are raised by Mr. Smith's friends against the supposed partiality of one of the Sheriffs. And certainly Mr. Spencer's partisans do him and their cause no Honour by offering publickly to lay wagers, that tho Mr. Smith may have the majority upon the poll, he shall not be the sitting member. I have been hunted all day yesterday, and pressured prodigiously to break my neutrality: And as I expected the same, or stronger sollicitations this morning, I have absconded from my own house, and write this at a friend's house. You may remember that I told you, that the number of voters in this election would be about 300 short of the last: And there were all the reasons and probability in the world so to conclude: But the fact has proved the contrary: For there have voted above 100 more already: And where such numbers can be picked up, is a matter of surprise to everybody. I find one party talks of a scrutiny, and the other objects to the proceedings of the Senior Sheriff: So that we are likely to have fine work of it. I can tell you of one circumstance more, that will, if anything can, surprise you: His Majesty's own name, *by permission*, was made use of, to induce the Whigg committee to drop all thought of a contest at this critical juncture, and embrace a compromise: And yet even this had no effect. And they secreted this circumstance from the knowledge of their fellow-citizens as long as they could.
>
> Wednesday night –
> The books were closed at two a clock: And from that time till six, the Sheriffs were busied in settling the poll. Mr. Morris and

his friends demanded a scrutiny on behalf of Mr. Spencer; the others objected, saying, that the whole poll was a scrutiny: At last the Blue mob without became violent and outrageous, vowing that the Sheriffs should not come out alive, unless they made a fair return, – that is, returned Mr. Smith without a scrutiny. But I am told they were pacified by being assured that the Sheriffs would declare a majority tomorrow in favour of Mr. Smith of 52. This is all that I have been able to pick up. But as my information is all hearsay, I will not be answerable for the truth of particulars: I most sincerely wish to be removed from this place, where an honest man can do no good.[35]

All that remains is to note Tucker's concern that his reasons for neutrality would be understood by his patrons. He asks Forster in several letters to give his excuses, and then does so himself to Hardwicke in the letter of 13 March, which lays out his personal position in the affair. Referring to the previous election he says,

One principal reason, why Mr. Nugent got so great a majority was, that he was set up by those who declared themselves the friends of the peace of the city and the promoters of a compromise; and consequently that all their proceedings in the election were to be looked upon as acting on the *defensive* side. This was a topic which I made great and successful use of on that occasion both in conversation, and in print. And next to the personal objections to Sir J. Philipps on account of his attempts to prosecute the Associators there was no one thing which contributed to the success of our cause so much as our continued insisting upon the ill behaviour of the Tories in rejecting a compromise. It would be hard, extremely hard to expect from me, considered as the principal agent in the last election, to give the lye so soon to all that I had said before. And if I had been induced to do so, I must have sunk in your Lordship's opinion, and in that of all good men; But more especially I must have acted such a part, as would have given me the most uneasy reflections for every after. . . . It appears therefore to me, that in my peculiar situation, I had no other course to take but that of perfect neutrality; And I humbly hope, that my acting upon these motives will give no displeasure to your Lordship. . . . The Whigg cause may yet want assistance; And sure I am, that it hath lost ground prodigiously since the affair came on; If therefore I had voted at this conjecture I never could have served it more, but must have been the scorn and derision of both parties; whereas now, I shall be able for the future to give it more effectual assistance than ever I could before: – And, perhaps, what is as necessary a part as any at all, shall be able to restrain the furious, indiscreet people of my own side within proper bounds, and cause them to act upon the true Whigg principles of a moderate and judicious use of power.

He goes on to say that the Tories 'are so sensible of the advantages of having the opinion on their side, that they are not the disturbers of the peace of the city, that they publish it abroad already, that in case of a victory on their side, they themselves will be the first to propose a compromise for the future'.[36]

Such a compromise was reached and, even though it broke down in the 1770s, it was later revived, so that in 1816 Oldfield could write about Bristol, 'One of its representatives votes uniformly with administration, and the other commonly with opposition; so that six thousand persons, to whom the right of election is supposed to be confined, have virtually no representation at all.'[37] This is the reformer speaking, but he does raise a question which needs to be asked in any discussion of Tucker's position. Given the modern assumption, which was shared by Oldfield, that the whole point of the representative process is to give the electors a genuine choice, was not the kind of agreement that Tucker sought so assiduously an affront to the British system of government?

What we need to remember is the important underlying differences between then and now, despite the similarity of terminology. As Sir Lewis Namier has pointed out, 'There were no proper party organisations about 1760, though party names and cant were current. . . . Parliamentary politics not based on parties are to us a non-Euclidean system, and similarly require a fundamental readjustment of ideas and, what is more, of mental habits.'[38] Today we should expect Tucker to close ranks and support his party regardless of his personal feelings. However, at a time when the members had a free vote, the party label was not so significant. There was no need to elect an individual solely that he might be one more digit in the numerical total which decided whether his party would form the government or not. What was obviously of greater importance was to have a member who would represent local interests, whether he was called a Whig or a Tory. Smith was a more logical choice in this respect than Spencer, who did not even bother coming to Bristol.

However, although this may have been implicit in Tucker's position, what he really wanted above all was to preserve the peace in the city of Bristol by avoiding a contested election. First there was the question of cost. Tucker later estimated that the two contested elections had cost £60,000, and his figure has met with a general acceptance by later commentators. Given the electioneering practices then prevalent, furthermore, much of that money was spent in corrupting public morals, such as they were. A contested election in a large constituency was not an edifying spectacle before the advent of the secret ballot and stricter controls over voting lists and procedures. Rather than being a triumph for democracy, it may have had the opposite effect. Halevy thinks that these contests were worthwhile in providing ordinary people with a sense of participation in the political process, and that even the rioting could be seen as a useful reminder to the upper classes of popular power in a country without a significant standing army or adequate police forces. However, true as this may be, having to live through these picturesque episodes, as Tucker did, was a different matter. From that perspective, it was easy to see the faults rather than the virtues. Thus, if we accept the vast differences between political realities then and now, there is much to be said for the policy of compromise which Tucker pursued. Certainly there is no evidence that the interests of Bristol suffered. Whether both local representatives were selected by the Union Club or whether the Steadfast Society was allowed to choose one hardly seemed a matter of much moment.

One way of interpreting the election is open to those who are looking for early signs of the radicalism which emerged in the last few decades of the century. The fact that it was Dissenters and 'low tradesmen' who opposed the compromise and insisted on a contest may be seen as a revolt of the lower middle class against the 'establishment', both Whig and Tory. The fact that John Wesley urged his supporters to vote Whig might be seen as confirmation. However, it is hard to reconcile this with their choice of a descendant of the Duke of Marlborough as standard-bearer, and, if we give any credence to Tucker's suspicions, distribution of patronage may have been far more significant than class struggle as a determinant. Furthermore, the Whig organisation took part in the campaign. Tucker's behaviour was governed by his desire to retain personal credibility.

His predictions about the outcome being close and the result being protested turned out to be correct. A petition that itself was criticised by some Tories as containing forged signatures was presented to the House of Commons on 30 March 1756. The grounds for the protest were the inclusion of invalid votes for Smith and the exclusion of valid votes for Spencer, who should have won the election. The hearing of the petition was twice postponed, and then abandoned with the end of the session. Earlier on, the Tory *Bristol Journal* had aired a number of complaints about the election. It accused one of the sheriffs of partiality, the Low Churchmen of lack of moderation, and the Union Club and Corporation of influencing the votes of publicans by threatening to withhold licences. It also charged its opponents with arranging the impressment of Smith voters while 'ransacking the navy even at a critical time . . . and summoning the marines and soldiers who were freemen' to vote for Spencer, and with utilising the support of 'the whole crew of pensioners of the Excise and Customs'. One of the articles led to a libel suit against the printer, who was eventually acquitted.

The final outcome was the electoral compromise which had been Tucker's goal. Writing about it later he said,

> And a reconciliation ensued amongst the citizens, which led to a solemn agreement between the agents of both parties, that the candidate to be named by one, should be supported by the other during three successive parliaments; which compact was universally acquiesced in, and acknowledged by five unanimous elections and re-elections, of Mr. Nugent, named by the Whigs, and by two elections, one of Sir Jarett Smith, and the other of Mr. Brickdale, named by the Tories.[39]

Tucker's services went unrewarded as yet, but they were not unrecognised. During the summer the Duke of Newcastle wrote to Nugent,

> I beg you would make my particular compliments to my friend Mr. Tucker. I am truly sensible of his great merit, and what is

much more to the purpose, the King is so too. If I don't point out any particular preferment, it is, because I would not disappoint him. The Deanery of Bristol, or Gloucester, was what he seemed to wish for; that of Bristol is absolutely engaged to Dr. Warburton, at the recommendation of Sir John Legonier, and the Attorney Genl. – I don't love to make promises or engagements, but you may assure Mr. Tucker, that I will endeavour to serve him as soon as I can, consistently with my prior engagements.[40]

However, another offer appeared within a few weeks. On 23 August Tucker wrote to Birch,

My first duty is to express my gratitude in the sincerest manner for the great honour my Lord Royston did me in your last letter. And I hope I shall ever retain a proper and respectful sense of the obligation, and study any profitable means of shewing it. My present living which I hold from My Lord Chancellor's Bounty is worth £200 without any deductions. And, as I have now weathered the storms of party rage, and am enjoying the succeeding calm, attended with some degree of popular influence (a popularity got by an obstinate perseverance in right measures) the former inducements for quitting my present station lessen every day. Besides, it has pleased the D. of Newcastle to give very strong assurance that if the Deanery of Gloucester should become vacant during his ministry, he would use his best endeavours to serve me. Upon these considerations, after expressing the warmest gratitude and the liveliest sense of the obligation I humbly beg leave to decline the favour and to wait the event of the above engagement.

Our city is at present tolerably free from the epidemical madness of addressing, instructing, etc. And sure I am, that nothing of the kind will be attempted by the Whiggs; but I cannot answer for the Tories. Yet if such an attempt shall be made, the government might depend upon a counter address, instructions, etc. if that measure should be thought advisable.[41]

The latter was a reference to the turmoil caused by the fall of Minorca. The government was greatly embarrassed by this event and the opposition wasted little time in taking advantage of it. At ten o'clock the following evening Tucker heard that the Tories were advertising a meeting to be held the next morning to address the King. Shortly after eleven o'clock the same evening, his advertisement for a counter-address had appeared from the printer. The result was that the Tories were largely unsuccessful in obtaining signatures at the Exchange Coffee House and had to resort to going from house to house. Tucker was instructed by Nugent to draft a counter-address, which after some alterations was presented with hundreds of signatures in early September, to counter the effort of the Tory address. Nugent used the occasion again to remind Newcastle of Tucker's value: 'Is not Tucker a fine fellow? He deserves a Bishoprick.'[42] As it turned out, the petition was of little help to Newcastle, who fell from power shortly thereafter. Admiral Byng was eventually tried and executed, an unfortunate scapegoat for British reverses in the early part of the war.

Fortunately for Tucker, Newcastle was back in power by 1758, when a long-awaited event occurred. In a letter to Newcastle Nugent reported, 'The Dean of Gloucester is dead, and as your Grace told me there had been some solicitors for his preferment upon a vacancy, I thought it best to give your Grace early notice of it, that a speedy nomination of Doctor Tucker may save you from further importunity.'[43] The letter is endorsed, 'Dr. Tucker to be made Dean of Gloucester'.

Having finally received his reward, Tucker decided to resign the Bristol stall but remain Rector of St Stephen's. Although he had once taken a position against pluralism, he probably felt now that, given his long wait, he was justified in retaining his old post, especially since the new one was not immediately very lucrative. As he wrote to Birch, 'But in regard to money affairs my usual ill luck still attends me. For the present year will be one of the poorest that ever was known, the last having been an extraordinary good one. So that the Preb. of Bristol bids fair for the next ensuing twelve months, to be near double in value to the Deanery of Gloucester'.[44]

Tucker did not really leave Bristol when he moved to Gloucester. Although he had a curate at St Stephens, he took his duties as Rector seriously and was often in Bristol. However, as might be expected, he also took an interest in politics in his new home. He followed there much the same line that he had in Bristol, as is indicated by the following letter to Hardwicke, written in 1760:

> The considerable property which your Lordship has in this neighbourhood, – And the disputes which are going forward in this city (in regard to which I may suppose your Lordship to be no unconcerned spectator) induce me to believe, that your Lordship who has so just a right to enquire into my conduct and behaviour, would not be displeased with hearing an account of it.
>
> Before coming to this place, the people were made to believe, that I was a monster made up of the vilest parts of Whiggism and Judaism. This caricature did me no real disservice; For the little incidents in my behaviour among them, which otherwise would not have been taken notice of, served in this case to convince them, that they had been grossly imposed upon in regard to my character, and that I had as much of the human species in my composition as another man. In a little time I became popular; And this popularity still continues, and gains ground.
>
> When the talk of an election began to revive I declared myself to be no partisan, but the friend to peace: – And that I would strictly adhere to the same rules at Gloucester, which I had steadily pursued at Bristol; viz. To endeavour at the choice of one Whigg and to be equally ready to assist the other party in the choice of a Tory.[45]

Tucker did his best to avoid a disturbance of 'public tranquillity' and had the support of a substantial number of electors, but again he was foiled by a group of shop-keepers and tradesmen who wanted a contest. The result was everything that Tucker dreaded; in fact, the election was used by Namier to illustrate the corrupt practices of the time. George Selwyn, who represented Gloucester from 1754 to 1780, described one incident in a letter to Lord Holland:

> Two of my voters were murdered yesterday by an experiment we call shopping. That is locking them up and keeping them dead drunk to the day of the election. Mr. Snell's agents forced two single Selwyns into a post-chaise, where being suffocated

with brandy that was given them and a very fat man that had the custody of them, they were taken out stone dead. Here follows a hanging; in short, it is one roundeau of delights.[46]

So it may have been to Selwyn, who loved a good hanging, but for Tucker it can only have confirmed all his misgivings about elections.

8 Dean of Gloucester and 'Defender of the Faith'

The year 1758, when Tucker became Dean of Gloucester, marks something of a watershed in his life as an author. The first phase was over, and a decade and a half was to elapse before he took up his pen actively again. This hiatus was probably mainly owing to the demands of his new post. Since his predecessor had not been very diligent, there was much that required his immediate attention, particularly the fabric of the Cathedral. With plenty to do at Gloucester and frequent visits to Bristol, where he maintained a second home, it is not surprising that his output declined to a trickle over the next few years.

Gloucester owes its existence to the fact that its site commanded the principal passage over the lower Severn and therefore the main road to Wales. Its importance was recognised in the days of Edward the Confessor and the first two Williams, when it shared with Westminster and Winchester the honour of being a royal city, where once each year the King wore his crown and met with his advisers. Despite this it was not until 1541 that it became the centre of a bishopric, having previously formed part of the diocese of Worcester. The Cathedral, an early example of the Perpendicular style, had earlier been the church of the Abbey of St Peter, the origins of which went back to 681.

Economically, Gloucester was early associated with the cloth trade, which had its own guildhall there twenty-five years before one was established in London by the Cologne merchants. However, although this trade continued to grow for several centuries, and was briefly stimulated by the arrival of Flemish weavers fleeing from the Duke of Alva, it eventually went into decline, and the Guild of Weavers disappeared in 1692. Unfortunately for Gloucester, Bristol was a much better port and was thus enabled to seize a commanding position in the regional economy.

Although bell-founding had been carried on in Gloucester since the thirteenth century, the industry for which it was famous in the eighteenth century was pin-making. This was introduced there by John Tilsley of Bristol. Pins had, of course, existed from antiquity, but metal ones were too costly for the use of ordinary people. Tilsley's improvements in the method of manufacture were so impressive that he was credited with the invention of pins. He is so honoured in the following verse by Charles Dibdin:

> The ladies, Heaven bless them all!
> As sure as I've a nose on,
> In former times had only thorns
> And skewers to stick their clothes on.
> No damsel then was worth a pin
> Whate'er it might have cost her,
> Till gentle Johnny Tilsley
> Invented pins in Gloucester.[1]

There was a saying that it took nine tailors to make a man, but four men to make a pin. This refers to the four steps involved: heading, drawing, pointing and sticking. It is somewhat surprising that Adam Smith, writing at the dawn of the Industrial Revolution, should have chosen pin-making as his example of the benefits to be derived from the division of labour, but there is no doubt that the tremendous increase in output which could result from a limited amount of specialisation and the use of a few simple tools was striking enough. By 1802 there were nine pin factories in Gloucester, employing 1500 workers out of a population of almost 7600.

This industry foreshadowed many of the problems associated with the Industrial Revolution. Tilsley's original agreement with the city officials called for him to be supplied with at least thirty boys, and children remained the backbone of the labour force in the eighteenth century. The district in which pin-making was concentrated was noted for its dirt, and the workers for their unhealthy appearance. As one writer puts it, rather romantically, 'The children grew in Stroud and the Golden Valley as flowers grew, but soon lost their beauty and fragrance in dirt and bad habits.'[2] The latter were of great concern to the respectable people. Even quite young children could earn enough to give them a considerable degree of independence. 'Sunday was a Saturnalia – the day of sports and drinking. Bull baiting, bear baiting, badger baiting, cock fighting, dog fighting, running and wrestling were the principal pastimes.'[3]

It was this riotous behaviour and the foul language that went with it which finally drove Robert Raikes, the publisher of the *Gloucester Journal* as well as many of Tucker's works, to launch the Sunday-school movement. Its aim was to utilise the working children's one free day more constructively by making it possible for them to acquire the rudiments of learning as well as some knowledge of the Christian faith. After he had opened his first Sunday schools, in Gloucester in 1780, and publicised them in his paper, the idea caught on, and the number of schools increased rapidly. By the time he died, in 1811, 400,000 children were attending Sunday schools. The success of these schools in suppressing Sunday 'revels' was so noticeable that at the Easter Quarter Sessions of 1786 the Gloucestershire magistrates publicly thanked the gentlemen responsible.[4]

Raikes was not only Tucker's publisher but also one of his most conscientious parishioners. He attended the early service at the Cathedral practically every morning, usually accompanied by another local worthy, Jimmy Woods, the 'Miser', whose grandfather had, in 1716, opened the first private bank in the country, except for Child's. A glimpse of his operations in Tucker's time is given by a contemporary. 'His shop was in the main street, he had a sort of haberdashery shop and bank – one counter for each. On one side he'd sell you a farthing's worth of pins, and on the other shovel gold to any amount.'[5]

It was unfortunate that from 1760 until 1779 Tucker had as his bishop a man who bore him no love: William Warburton. However, Tucker was in good company; among the host of enemies the pugnacious Dr Warburton had attacked in his literary and theological writings were Bolingbroke, Wesley and Hume. Luckily for Tucker, Warburton did not take his duties as Bishop of Gloucester too seriously and spent most of his time in London or at Prior Park near Bath.

Prior Park was owned by Ralph Allen, who had made his fortune by contracting to improve the postal system. His benevolent character is indicated by the fact that he was Fielding's model for Squire Allworthy. He was so impressed by Warburton, who was introduced to him by Pope, that he eventually offered him the hand of his favourite niece and heiress. Warburton's good

Dean of Gloucester and 'Defender of the Faith' 165

fortune was compounded when Allen used his influence with William Pitt to obtain for his protégé the deanery of Bristol in 1757 and then the bishopric of Gloucester in 1760. Warburton's best work is considered to be his *Alliance between Church and State*, an attempt to justify the special position of the Church of England, published in 1736. Since it was one of the books Tucker recommended in his *Instructions for Travellers*, there is no evidence that Tucker was predisposed to anything but respect for his new bishop. However, his interest in economic affairs obviously irritated Warburton, whose own inclinations ran to commentaries of doubtful merit on various poets, and general scholarly quibbling. This annoyance was vented in a malicious *bon mot* concerning Tucker. The story went that, when Ralph Allen asked Warburton to comment on the relative merits of another man and Tucker as candidates to replace him as Dean of Bristol, Warburton replied that one made religion his trade and the other trade his religion. The chronology is obviously wrong, as Tucker was already Dean of Gloucester when Warburton was promoted from Bristol, but, regardless of the occasion on which it was said, it obviously hurt Tucker, who is quoted as having replied,

> The Bishop affects to consider me with contempt; to which I say nothing. He has sometimes spoken coarsely of me; to which I replied nothing. He has said that religion is my trade and trade my religion. Commerce and its connections have, it is true, been favourite aspects of my attention, and where is the crime? And as for religion I have attended carefully to the duties of my parish, nor have I neglected my cathedral. The world knows something of me as a writer on religious subjects, and I will add what the world does not know, that I have written over 300 sermons and preached them all again and again.[6]

Warburton's attitude towards his dean is further indicated in a letter he wrote concerning a visit made to Tucker with the Headmaster of Gloucester Grammar School. He calls Tucker's conversation a 'flow of transcendent nonsense', adding that the Headmaster 'would needs understand him; and here the Dean, who did not understand himself, must needs have the advantage'.[7] Since it was Warburton himself who said, 'Orthodoxy is my doxy; heterodoxy is the other man's doxy', one does not really need to quote the many critical comments made about him in order to question the quality of his judgement.

Eighteen months before his preferment to Gloucester, Tucker began a correspondence with Henry Home, Lord Kames, which was to continue until the latter's death in 1782. The printer in Glasgow who was responsible for a new edition of the *Essay on Trade* in 1756 suggested to Tucker that Kames would not object to any overture on his part. This he made in a letter written on 29 January 1757, and obviously well received, although we unfortunately do not have the letters of Kames to Tucker.

Through this friendship Tucker was brought into contact with the Scottish Enlightenment. In addition to being a well-known jurist and author, Kames was a friend and supporter of most of the Scottish intellectuals of his day, including David Hume and Adam Smith. As we have seen, Tucker came into contact with Hume through Kames. What is surprising is that his path and that of Adam Smith do not appear to have crossed. Smith was Professor of Moral Philosophy at Glasgow when this correspondence started, and he published *The Theory of Moral Sentiments* in 1759. Although his major work in economics was yet to come, Smith had already been covering economic topics in his lectures and he had a copy of the Glasgow edition of the *Essay on Trade* in his library. In addition to Kames and Hume, he shared several other friends with Tucker.

Some of the correspondence with Kames has been quoted already, but there are several other items of interest. Early in 1758 Tucker described the deplorable effects of war in Bristol:

> My parish, which is partly composed of the habitations of merchants, and partly the receptacles of common sailors, is become an Hell upon earth. And the wickedness is got to such an height, that the most respectable characters in the city, even such men as comprise the body of magistracy (if they are adventurers in privateers, – as there is scarce any person that is not) do not scruple, not only to countenance, but also to be in confederacy with the most notorious Bawdy-Houses, in order to retain them in their interest towards procuring crews for their respective privateers. When these ships return from their cruises, they bring home the gaol fever, and I am sometimes obliged to bury two, or three in a day. If the crews stay any time

ashore, they die of other fevers: And when any prizes are brought in, great are the rejoicings – because there is so much wealth added to the Nation! But, my Lord, the wealth is of such a nature; that I can assure your Lordship from the insurance books, that the adventurers in the gainful trade have already sunk near £100,000 and that it is expected that great numbers of them will soon break. The wary, rich men (who have not entered into privateering – or if they did at the beginning, immediately left it off) declare, they know whom not to trust and that the town is rotten, which is true in more senses than one – And I have known, a very considerable partnership, always accounted rich before the war, be refused money, though they offered 4½ per cent, when the same money was offered elsewhere at 3½. Such are the effects and credit of our increased riches! But this is not all. For when the prize goods are sold by auction, they are generally sold from 30 to 60 or 80 per cent under the prime cost in France; then the person who buys, gives a bond, and takes an oath, that he will export them. The goods are really shipped off, in order to save the bond; but it is contrived in some manner, or other, that great quantities are landed and sold daily in the town, to the great stagnation of British manufacturers. As to supplying the enemy with provisions, it is constant practice with those persons, who were *loudest for the war*, to freight ships from Cork to Eustatia: the beef usually sent for that market, is of an inferior sort and generally passes under the denomination of low priced beef; which is a term by which you may always know, that it is designed for the French market. These ships first touch at our English islands to sell their high-priced beef and to take part of their lading of English sugars: – Together with these they take many empty hogsheads, with English markings and an English clearance. These empty casks are filled with French sugars at Eustatia, and so brought to Europe and even to England. Nay, it is a certain fact, that the Joseph of Bristol sailed to Eustatia – there was new painted, took a Dutch name, master, and crew: and carried a cargo of French sugars to Amsterdam.[8]

This is the kind of personal experience with the ways of the world which lies behind Tucker's suggestions for reform and gives them their specificity and practicality.

There are further comments on the war in the next letter:

> My fate hitherto has been too similar to that of Cassandra, never to be believed till 'twas too late. In the years 53 and 54 I was incessant in my endeavours to stop the rage of the people in calling out for the present war; and did not fail to point out the miseries it might lead us into, and the impossibility, that even a series of victories and conquests in N. America could be attended with any real advantage to this nation. But all that I could say, both in conversation and in print had no other effect, than to induce the people to believe, that I had studied politics so long; till my head was turned.[9]

This is his first reference to the Cassandra analogy, which impressed him so much that he used it as a pen name for some of his writings during the American Revolution.

One of Tucker's few publications of this period was his 1760 pamphlet *The Manifold Causes of the Increase of the Poor*. The Advertisement contains an explanation of his relative inactivity.

> In the first place, the arts of peace are but little attended to, and less understood in times of war – To tell a nation, flushed with conquests, that trade does not depend upon victories, and that it can never be acquired by power, but will always find its way to the cheaper, even tho' it should be the vanquished country, is what they will never believe: – or if they do believe it, they will nevertheless prefer the shining and rapid acquisitions of the sword to the silent progress of industry, and to those slow returns of wealth, which arise only from greater goodness and cheapness of manufactures. To knock a man on the head is to take from him his all at once; and this is the short and compendious way; But to excite that man (who perhaps is called your enemy) to greater industry and sobriety, to consider him as a customer to you, and yourself as a customer to him, so that the richer both of you are the better it may be for each other; – This is the kind of reasoning which is as unintelligible at present, as the notion of the Antipodes at the time of Galileo.[10]

The title of the pamphlet is somewhat misleading, since it is devoted largely to a scheme to improve poor-law administration.

The Act of Settlement had created a situation in which 'every parish is, in fact, in a state of war both offensively, and defensively with every other parish throughout the kingdom concerning pauper-settlements and removals'.[11] Tucker's answer was to encourage parishes to unite into larger poor-relief districts. This would provide economies of scale, and reduce the inequities and animosities amongst the parishes concerned. As was his custom, Tucker provided detailed instructions concerning the day-to-day operation of the poor-houses and the means of raising money for their support. The Webbs called his scheme for the union of the parishes 'an interesting anticipation of the Poor Law Commissioners of 1834–47'.[12]

Tucker got a taste of his own medicine when he received from Lord Kames a copy of his best known work, *The Elements of Criticism*, with a request for his comments. He found the task too much for him.

> After repeated trials I am fully convinced that I have not a capacity for making proper remarks on your Lordship's book. How should a man, who understands not a note in music, be able to write a criticism on the finest of Handel's compositions? Now this is exactly my case: I know not one of the fine arts; And find moreover, that I have nothing within me, which can be called a genius for them or be made capable of cultivation . . . . In this situation, what can I do better than turn informer against myself, and confess my own ignorance? In one word, I know nothing of the matter. And if this be guilt, I dare believe that your Lordship will pardon it much more readily, than if I had added to it the provoking aggravation of a dull, impertinent criticism.[13]

In a letter of 1764, Tucker gives us a rare glimpse into his personal situation at Gloucester:

> I came into an house which wanted to be almost rebuilt, and into a chapter where many disorders required to be rectified. And I have a Cathedral and cloysters to examine and repair, which in some respects are the finest Gothic structures in the world; And which are now perhaps the best kept. Add to this, that I do not understand music, yet . . . I have, for the number

of voices, the best choir in the kingdom out of London. After this I need not mention family concerns, which are very perplexing: For tho I have no children of my own, I have no less than eight of an only sister, all thrown upon me, whom I must breed up to get their bread in some shape or other.[14]

This appears to be the only reference he ever made either to a sister or to family responsibilities.

In a postscript to this same letter he comments on one facet of Hume's work as an historian:

> In Mr. Hume's History of the Anglo-Saxons he follows the stream of historians in asserting that they exterminated all the natives; and consequently had no slaves, or villains. But I could never find any proof of this: and the appearance of things during the Heptarchy strongly indicate the contrary: the feudal system being as evidently the system among them, as among all the other nothern nations. And it is hard to say what could induce them to be so very singular in this respect. I am myself a Welshman: and we have no tradition in our country of any such massacre: On the contrary we suppose that all the slaves remained slaves to their new masters; and the gentlemen fled into Wales: Ergo the Welsh are all gentlemen . . . .

With the return of peace in 1763, it was again possible for the British to visit France. Many took advantage of the opportunity over the next couple years, including Tucker. An additional attraction in Paris was David Hume, who was secretary to Lord Hertford, the Ambassador. Tucker saw him in the summer of 1765 at Compiègne, where the philosopher had gone with the court. Lord Hertford, who had just been offered the lord lieutenancy of Ireland, wanted to take Hume with him, but there was too much opposition. It was jokingly suggested that, since the Lord Lieutenant had a number of bishoprics at his disposal, he should make Hume an Irish bishop. When Tucker wrote to Hume from Paris thanking him profusely for his hospitality, he followed up this idea, imagining himself being asked to preach Hume's consecration sermon. He even considered the miraculous possibility of the sceptical philosopher's being consecrated and converted at the same time. However, he concluded that Hume was 'not unbeliever enough for the episcopal mitre'. He suggested a more deserving candidate: the notorious John Wilkes, who was a fugitive in Paris at that time.[15]

Tucker must have met some of the leading literary figures of France during his stay, but, unfortunately, further confirmation is lacking. We know that he did not meet Turgot, who was Intendant of Limoges at that time. In 1768 the latter wrote to Hume asking a number of questions about Tucker's work, and Hume passed them on to Tucker.[16] Tucker replied by sending to Hume 'a parcel by the Gloucester coach (which stops at the Green Man and Still in Holbourne) containing six pamphlets, *viz*. The Elements of Commerce, Instructions for Travellers, three copies of the Case of going to War, and the Letter from a Merchant to his Nephew concerning the Colonies'.[17] Hume passed these on via a mutual friend at the French embassy, but they were lost by the Paris post office.

In his letter informing Turgot that the parcel had been sent, Hume passed on Tucker's compliments,

> When he was in France, he had frequently enquired concerning his translator; but cou'd meet with no-one, that cou'd give him information. He is very proud, that he has so much reason to value himself on that head. The thin quarto [*Elements of Commerce*], which he sends you, was never published; tho' the author printed off about a hundred copies near fifteen years ago: He sent copies to his friends and to persons for whom he had an esteem; and he desired them to return the copy with their remarks on the margin, which was left large on purpose. He desires the same favour of you, and does not limit you to any time. On my suggestions he permits you to communicate the work to M. de Montigny and to the Abbé Morellet, who, he hopes, will also be so good as [to] communicate their remarks. I think there are passages, which may be useful to the Abbé in his dictionary.
>
> I am sorry to find, that Dr. Tucker has little intention of finishing and giving to the public this valuable work. He was extremely discouraged with the bad reception given to this pamphlet against War, of which he sends you two copies. There were not fifty copies of it sold; tho' surely it merited a much better fate. But it was wrote, as I told him, when the public were

intoxicated with their foolish success; and a pamphlet, if it does not take during the first moment, falls soon into oblivion, and very often indeed, tho' it does take. But this is not the case with a greater work to which the public sooner or later does justice.[18]

The links between the members of a select group of like-minded persons is indicated by the list of people to whom Morellet asked Hume to present the prospectus of his *Dictionnaire du commerce*: General Conway the politician, William Robertson the historian, as well as Adam Smith, Dean Tucker and Benjamin Franklin.[19] Morellet had met Smith when the latter arrived in Paris with his pupil the Duke of Buccleuch, several months after Tucker's visit in 1765. Years later, the Abbé translated *The Wealth of Nations*, but his version was never published. When he paid a visit to England in 1772, Morellet spent several days with Tucker at Gloucester, but he does not mention seeing Smith, who was at Kirkcaldy.[20]

Turgot's *Réflexions sur la formation et distribution des richesses* was published initially in three successive issues of *Ephémérides du citoyen*, the house organ of the Physiocrats, during the winter of 1769–70. In 1770 Turgot had 100 to 150 copies of a corrected version of *Réflexions* printed, one of which he sent to Tucker. The accompanying letter was quite complimentary.

> A translator owes to his author every kind of homage, and I now request of you to accept as such a pamphlet which, while certainly conveying to yourself nothing new, may, I have been told, prove useful in spreading elementary ideas on subjects with which we desire to see the public better acquainted.

After regretting that he had not made Tucker's acquaintance on the latter's visit to France, he continues,

> I should have been all the more flattered by it, for I find in your works that our principles on liberty and on the main objects of political economy are much in accord. I confess I cannot help being astonished that, in a nation enjoying the liberty of the press, you should be almost the only author who has known and felt the advantages of a free commerce, and who has not been seduced by the puerile and suicidal illusion of a commerce fettered and exclusive.[21]

Dean of Gloucester and 'Defender of the Faith' 173

With the exception of works connected with America, to be examined in the next chapter, Tucker's publications in the latter half of the 1760s and the early 1770s were devoted to religious topics. The first of these was the 'Charity School sermon'. This school sermon of 1766 was preached in London at the annual meeting of Charity School children and published under the auspices of the Society for Promoting Christian Knowledge (SPCK).[22] In it he dealt with some of the criticisms which had been levelled at these schools. For example, there was the question of whether lower-class children should receive an education at all. Tucker's reply was that, since they were going to learn by imitating those around them anyway, was it not better to instruct them in virtuous behaviour instead? But, others might say, if they must have an education, at least confine it to the acquisition of a useful trade. Tucker agrees in principle, but he feels compelled to point out the many difficulties associated with organising a 'working school'. One had to choose a product that would remain in demand, find teachers willing to accept a percentage of the sales instead of a salary, and locate cheap raw materials while at the same time abiding by the corporation and apprenticeship laws.

One common fear was that education of the poor 'elevates them above their station, and destroys that balance of condition which ought ever to subsists between rich and poor' (p. 18). The fact that such an attitude was not uncommon explains why Tucker often adopts the tone he does; he is talking to the kind of people who think this way and he can often only appeal to them through prejudices such as these. But here he draws the line. If by balance of condition 'they mean to say, that the poor should not be permitted to enjoy the fruits of their own labour, or to rise gradually in the world by superior industry or skill, by greater frugality, or better economy: this is nothing else but saying in other words, that the poor ought to be kept in a state of slavery of the most abject kind, without a possibility of emerging from it' (p. 19). He cannot resist adding that slavery not only is morally repugnant but also, 'is known, *experimentally* known, to be incompatible with an extensive progress, much less any great perfection in manufactures, and the mechanic arts', not to mention agriculture.

As to preserving the 'balance of condition', Tucker continues that, if this means that the more genteel and lucrative occupations should be reserved for the higher ranks, he not only agrees but thinks that the purpose of the charity schools is to enable their children 'to get their bread in the meanest, the most labourious, and the least gainful imployments that belong to society'. Having reassured his listeners, however, he modifies this harsh judgement by adding,

> But after due care has been taken of that point; then surely, if any among this present set of poor objects should exert greater industry, or display superior skill, or practise better economy than others of their rank and station; surely, I say, in such a case, there can no sufficient reason be assigned why they should not be permitted to enjoy the benefit of these virtues.

He goes even further: 'They ought to be permitted, nay encouraged to grow rich, according to their rank or station, and in proportion to their diligence' (p. 20).

He concludes with a defence of the SPCK, which he imagines a critic accusing of accomplishing little at great cost, since 'practical religion was never at a lower ebb' – virtue is not more noticeable than it was before the founding of such societies. Tucker's answer is that, given the nature of the British constitution and the freedoms it guarantees, there is no way of encouraging better behaviour than through voluntary societies such as the SPCK. How would wrong-doers be prosecuted? 'And as to the ancient practice of decennaries or tithings, when every man was responsible for the good behaviour of his neighbour, and consequently had a right to inspect his actions, and in some degree to regulate his conduct; can this be revived in modern times?' Officially people were required by law to attend church and receive the sacraments at least three times a year, as well as send their children and servants to do the same, but they would not do so. Only by supporting such voluntary work can his listeners advance the cause not only of religion but also of patriotism and liberty.

A collected edition of Tucker's sermons was not published until 1772, when the *Six Sermons*[23] appeared, but the topics covered were ones which had obviously exercised him for many years. The first five of these (the sixth being a reprint of the Infirmary sermon of 1745) were concerned with texts which, in his eyes, could be seriously misleading. For example, sermon 1 dealt with Romans 11: 21: 'Hath not the potter power over the clay of the same lump,

Dean of Gloucester and 'Defender of the Faith'   175

to make one vessel to honour, and another to dishonour?' This text had been used to support the doctrine of predestination.

Tucker's attack on such an interpretation starts off by accepting the fact that God had created a world in which there is a great variety of individual endowments. 'Yet let the talents be few, or many, we shall only be called to an account in proportion to what we have received. . . . It can surely be no wrong to me, that I am not created an angel: Nor is it any injury to the brute that he is not a man' (pp. 18–19). We must learn to accept our station in the hierarchy of creation and improve the talents that we have been granted. Whatever inequality there may have been in the original dispensation, there will be no inequality in the final judgement. Thus, he concludes, 'Good and pious persons may be taught to banish all gloomy and melancholy apprehensions concerning the supposed degrees of absolute predestination', for the Lord had no intention 'of dooming persons unconditionally, and without allowing them a trial, to external misery and woe' (p. 36).

Similarly, in sermon II and III he defends good works against those who would overemphasise either grace or faith. Sermon IV is a restatement of his earlier argument against the Methodists' position that only an instantaneous conversion is efficacious, and sermon V is a caution against believing that a deathbed repentance is always sufficient to wipe away the effects of a life of sin. Tucker had obviously found that certain biblical texts were capable of causing confusion and dismay amongst members of his congregation, and he felt obliged to defend the moderate position of the Church of England by the application of commonsense to these passages.

One of the reasons why Tucker published the sermons when he did was to lay the ground-work for a defence of the Church of England itself: *An Apology for the Present Church of England*, which appeared the same year (1772). This was written in the knowledge that a petition to Parliament was being prepared, asking that subscriptions be abolished. The law required that ordinands as well as students matriculating at the universities subscribe to the Thirty-nine Articles. Opposition to subscription had been growing, and culminated in a meeting held at the Feathers Tavern. The result was a petition signed by about 200 clergy and fifty lawyers and physicians, which was presented to the House of Commons in 1772. After a debate in which Edmund Burke spoke eloquently against it, the petition was rejected by a substantial majority. In his *Apology*, Tucker argues on behalf of the idea of an established church:

> First therefore, I do assert, that as the establishing of religious societies is unavoidable in one degree, or other, it becomes the duty of the public magistrate to give the preference to that society, which upon comparison with others, shall appear to his own judgment and conscience to be the best, and the most deserving; – and consequently the fittest to assist him in the administration of a national, equal, and just plan of civil government. Similarly, it is both his duty and his interest to support and encourage the ministers of it. . . . And thirdly, as to all those other sects, or parties in religion which may happen to exist within the boundaries of his state, it is most certainly his duty, and evidently his interest to tolerate and protect them all, as far as a regard to good morals, and the safety of the state can possibly admit.[24]

This was not the sort of stuff which would convert the unbeliever, but the petitioners, to the extent that they were sincere, were not trying to do away with the Established Church but were trying to alter the rules which governed its adherents. Since they were free to leave any time and set up their own sects if they so desired, Tucker wondered if 'the circumstance becomes a temptation to several, who do not in their hearts approve of the terms of union, (and perhaps would rejoice at the destruction of it) to wish nevertheless to partake of its endowments' (p. 30). He had no objection to attempts to persuade the other members of the church that a change was necessary, but the petitioners were somewhat premature, since they represented a tiny minority of the total number of communicants.

Tucker was quite prepared to admit that there were flaws. The Thirty-nine Articles reflected the circumstances of the period in which they were formulated, and he himself suggested several changes. But he saw no necessity to pull down a venerable structure because two or three rooms were ill proportioned, especially when those who would do it appeared to have no plans of their own for a replacement. Furthermore, would they allow complete freedom to all to preach whatever they wanted? He doubted it. In fact, if the Established Church were destroyed, he foresaw a desperate struggle for dominance. In a passage that reflects his strong feelings about the type of people who favoured radical change, he says,

> [They would likely be] a set of bold and daring declaimers – a set of ecclesiastical fire-brands, – who being half enthusiasts, and half knaves themselves, could the more easily impose on the credulity, and work up the knavery of others; – who being possessed of the gifts of popular oratory – and by chiming in with passions, the prejudices and even vices of the giddy multitude, could enflame them into fury, and inspire them with an enthusiasm, bordering upon madness.   (pp. 46–7)

They would crush their enemies, and anarchy in the Church like anarchy in the State would be succeeded by despotism. Here was Burke's *Reflections on the Revolution in France* in embryo.

Although he felt that subscription to the Thirty-nine Articles was no great hardship for those who wanted to become clergy in the Church of England, Tucker was in favour of relieving the university students of this requirement. He was also prepared to support the Dissenting clergy in any move to rid themselves of their obligation to subscribe to all of the Thirty-nine Articles except those relating to church government.

This suggestion was taken up by the Rev. Andrew Kippis DD, who wrote, in his *Vindication of the Protestant Dissenting Ministers*, that he was happy that many of those who defended subscription for the Established clergy were opposed to requiring it for the Dissenters, who were now proceeding with their own petition. He went on, 'We saw, with still greater pleasure, that Dr. Tucker, the ablest apologist for the Church of England, had declared – "Let the ministers of Dissenting congregations, if they will choose to apply, be heartily wished a good deliverance from the burdens of our subscription."'[25]

However, when Kippis went on to criticise the Thirty-nine Articles on the grounds that only Christ can legislate for his church, Tucker felt obliged to reply, which he did in his *Letters to Dr. Kippis* of 1773. In the first of the two letters Tucker begins by admitting the 'unalienable right of private judgment, and the liberty of following the dictates of conscience in every case whatever if really consistent with good morals, and the just rights of other men'.[26] But individuals also had a right to associate with each other and make rules to regulate the behaviour of their members, always with the understanding that those who disapproved could leave peacefully to join another society or form a new one.

For example, in the case of a church, a day and hour of meeting has to be agreed upon, as well as the place where the faithful will assemble, the nature of the service to be conducted there, and even the dress of the clergyman. Christ may be the supreme legislator, but he expects his followers to use their own judgement on such matters. Furthermore, no sect, including that of Dr Kippis, can afford to have members who disagree about the day of worship or who insist upon the right to interrupt the service.

The second letter discusses another point raised by Dr Kippis, who was struck by the fact that the Calvinists were amongst the staunchest defenders of the Thirty-nine Articles, which they regarded as supporting their own beliefs. Tucker had admitted in the *Apology* that such an interpretation could be placed on at least one article, because of the influence of Bucer and Peter Martyr, who were in England when the Articles were being drafted. Here he looks at the broader issue of 'whether the English reformers in the reign of Edward VI intended to establish the doctrines of predestination, redemption, grace, purification, and perseverance, in the Calvinistical sense, as the Doctrine of the Church of England' (p. 5).

These five points collectively made up what was known as the Quinquarticular controversy, but essentially the quarrel was between the Augustinians and the semi-Pelagians. Tucker's studies had convinced him that 'nobody before St Augustine ever dreamed, that all unbaptized infants and the whole heathen world, were to be consigned to Hell, and the Devil' (p. 80), but since then 'the whole western church, before the Reformation, was Augustinian. . . . And if it was Augustinian, it could not avoid being Calvinistical; because in reality there is no difference', except for the insistence of the Catholics on the intrinsic merit of good works (pp. 84–5). Otherwise, the only difference was that the Papists did not put their position as bluntly as did the others.

The issue of predestination was an important factor in the break between Luther and Erasmus. In his *Diatribe on Free Will* of 1524,

Erasmus expressed his concern that a denial of free will might relieve man of moral responsibility for his actions. Luther stood firm on the omnipotence and omniscience of God, and Calvin, of course, made predestination the cornerstone of his theology. As far as the Church of England was concerned, when a settlement was reached under Edward VI, Tucker noted that it was a paraphrase of Erasmus that was ordered set up in the churches, rather than Luther's *Commentary on the Galations* or Calvin's *Institutes*. To clarify the whole question, he put in parallel columns the ideas of Calvin and those of the Arminians, with quotes from the liturgy, to see which were closer. Although he let the material speak for itself, it is clear that he found little evidence to support the charges of Calvinism.

As for the Dissenters' petition, their pleas were listened to with more sympathy than was received by their brethren in the Established Church. Although the House of Lords rejected Dissenters' Relief bills passed by the Commons in 1773 and 1774, such legislation was finally approved in 1779.

Despite the fact that Tucker felt obliged to defend the principle of an established church, as well as, within limits, the creed of his own church, he made it clear throughout the *Apology* and the *Letters to Dr. Kippis* that he was opposed to religious intolerance no matter from which quarter it came. Disturbed by the fact that the Bible itself was used to justify it, Tucker published a pamphlet devoted specifically to religious intolerance in 1774.[27] It was true that in the Old Testament the Jews were instructed to attack other nations with fire and sword, but Tucker believed the motivation to be political rather than religious. For example, although their other neighbours were equally idolatrous, it was only the Canaanites who were singled out for extermination. Furthermore, while strangers dwelling amongst the Israelites were forbidden certain practices, they were allowed to believe what they wished. As for the New Testament, it offered even less support for religious persecution than the Old. Tucker quoted many passages, the emphasis of which was on teaching, healing, cleansing and preaching. Christ's followers were instructed to be prepared to suffer persecution, not to inflict it on others.

Tucker has a number of eloquent things to say on the subject but nothing so characteristic as what he had already said to Dr Kippis:

You, Sir, suppose that the English independents were the first persons who founded the right of liberty of conscience. I am not disposed to detract from my countrymen the honour of this discovery: But I fear the fact is otherwise. I believe the Dutch were the first people who forebore to persecute, by discovering that those who could agree about buying and selling, need not cut one another's throats about religion. . . . The principle itself did not originate from divines and philosophers, but from tradesmen and mechanics. (p. 32)

Another question which exercised the Church during the eighteenth century was the dispute over the Trinity. In fact, differing views on this issue undoubtedly had something to do with the petition for relief from subscription, since, when it failed, a number of clergymen left the Church of England to become Unitarians. The controversy was sufficiently intense at this time for Tucker to make a modest contribution with *A Brief and Dispassionate View of the Difficulties Attending the Trinitarian, Arian, and Socinian Systems*. Again, common-sense is his guide.

Feeling that all the primary attributes of God are absolutely above the reach of our mental powers, and in their own nature incomprehensible; and seeing also that the doctrine of the Trinity is evidently, and according to the very state of the case, one of this incomprehensible sort, the Trinitarian judges it to be wiser and more prudent, as well as the more modest part, to accept the doctrine in the gross, without entering into any curious disquisitions about it, or pretending to fathom such bottomless depths by the short line of his scanty reason.[28]

In sum, although the Trinity attitude is hard to accept, he finds that it satisfies Scripture while the alternatives do not; and, since they create problems of their own, why not leave well alone?

This attitude is developed further in sermon XIV of the *Seventeen Sermons* published in 1776. Using as his text John 21: 22, 'What is that to thee? Follow thou me', he attacks excessive and profitless speculation. The nature of the Trinity, the incarnation, and redemption are beyond our limited understanding. The same is true of questions about why the wicked are allowed to flourish, when the day of judgement will come and what the precise boundaries

Dean of Gloucester and 'Defender of the Faith' 181

between good and evil are. People should try to live their religion instead of constantly quibbling about it.

For him religion was so much a part of daily life that its ends were inseparable from those of commerce and politics. Sermon VII is devoted to this theme.

> Now the greatest end of government is to promote the good and happiness of the governed: And if you ask, how is this to be done? I will answer, that this is best effected by causing each individual to conduct himself in such a manner, as shall contribute to the general good, and by protecting those that so behave from the fraud and violence of others. And what is this, but religion appearing under another shape. . . . And how are the ends both of religion and government to be answered, but by the system of universal commerce? – Commerce I mean, in the large and extensive signification of that word; commerce, as it implies a general system for the useful employment of our time; as it exercises the particular genius and abilities of mankind in some way or other, either of body or mind, in mental or corporeal labour, and so as to make self-interest and social coincide. And in pursuing this plan, it answers all the great ends both of religion and government; it creates social relations, it enables men to discharge their duty in these relations, and it serves as a cement to connect together the religious and civil interests of mankind. It is a friend to both, when rightly understood, and is befriended by them.[29]

This sermon together with no. VIII, an attack on excessive luxury and extravagance, was also published with the *Four Tracts* of 1774. In addition to the above-mentioned sermons and the six previously published, Tucker's *Seventeen Sermons* include several on the flaws of Catholicism, two on the religious value of Lent, one directed against narrow patriotism, one on the necessity for a general but not absolute obedience to earthly rulers, and a reprint of the Charity School sermon. Despite the fact that commerce and politics entered into his discourses quite often, as one might expect, Tucker was able to demonstrate that his religion consisted of a great deal more than trade and that he was able to hold his own in the area of theological controversy as well.

9 American Affairs

Tucker was best known in his own time for his writings on the American Revolution. This was a subject with which he became deeply involved, because it touched on practically all his major interests: his belief in free trade, his hatred of war and his suspicion of political radicalism. Although he was at times intemperate in his judgements, he saw more clearly than most of his contemporaries what was really at stake. Unfortunately his warnings went unheeded and he was forced to stand by helplessly as his most pessimistic prophecies came to pass. No wonder that he saw himself as a Cassandra and used that name to sign the occasional pieces he contributed to the press during the war.

The opening shot in his campaign was fired in 1766 with the publication of *A Letter from a Merchant in London to his Nephew in North America*. This was Tucker's reply to the protests of the American colonists over the Stamp Act. According to the Preface of the *Four Tracts* of 1774, in which it was reprinted, it was written at the suggestion of an elderly gentleman who had relatives over there and was familiar with the American smuggling trade with the enemy during the recent war. The arguments which he attacks were those commonly used in America against the imposition of stamp duties by the British in March 1765. The reorganisation of the Empire after the defeat of the French in the Seven Years' War required an expensive civil and military establishment. Grenville hoped to relieve British taxpayers of at least a portion of the cost by raising revenue in America. Unfortunately, the tax, though not a heavy one, was levied on newspapers, pamphlets, commercial transactions and legal documents. This meant that it had to be paid by the most articulate members of colonial society, who promptly organised a successful opposition, which included mob violence and non-importation agreements. The latter had an immediate effect on British trade, and it was largely pressure from merchants at home which caused the new Rockingham administration to repeal the Stamp Act in March 1766. The long-term significance of the affair was that it raised the question of exactly how much authority the mother country had over the colonists, and led the more radical Americans to look for acceptable reasons for resisting that authority. The one which dominated the Stamp Act crisis was the principle of no taxation without representation.

Although the colonists claimed that taxation without consent was contrary to the spirit of the British constitution, Tucker asks them to look at the *facts* of that constitution. 'Now the first emigrants, who settled in America, were certainly English subjects: – subject to the laws and jurisdiction of parliament, and consequently to parliamentary taxes, *before* their emigration: and therefore subject *afterwards*, unless some legal, constitutional exemptions can be produced.'[1] Is there any evidence of such exemptions? 'Nay, many of your colony charters assert quite the contrary, by containing express reservations of parliamentary rights, particularly that great one of levying taxes' (p. 9).

As far as the question of representation was concerned, Tucker noted that 6 million Englishmen as well as the 2 million Americans were not represented in Parliament. However, Tucker did not regard the question of whether any specific individual did or did not have the vote as significant. If one believed in the widely held theory of virtual representation, as he did, then all 358 MPs spoke for all the people under the British crown and 'every member of parliament represents you and me, and our interests in all essential points, just as much as if we had voted for him' (p. 19).

In practice, the lack of American representation in Parliament had not hurt the Americans. On the contrary, for tobacco-growing in Britain was forbidden and the British actually paid a bounty on certain colonial products. At this point the Americans usually shifted their ground from the legality of the tax to its excessiveness and unreasonableness. Tucker answered by showing that the internal debt of the colonies, which had grown exceedingly rich during the previous thirty years, was about eight shillings per capita, whereas that of Great Britain was £18 per capita. While the Stamp Duty was expected to raise one shilling per person, British taxes amounted to twenty shillings per person. Yet this modest request brought forth nothing but 'perverse and scandalous' behaviour which was especially shameful considering that the one shilling per head plus much larger sums from the mother country were to be spent in America.

Since it seems obvious to Tucker that the stamp duty was not the real cause for the outcry, he proceeds to discuss what he considered to be the real grievances, the first of which was the recent attempt at stricter enforcement of the acts of trade. This, Tucker felt, was a legitimate effort to carry out the law, particularly against smugglers. The second grievance was the constraint the colonists were under to pay their just debts. They had openly spoken of an association against the payment of debts.

The third grievance was by far the most significant: it was nothing less than the sovereignty of Great Britain.

> For you want to be independent: You wish to be an empire by itself, and to be no longer the province of another. This spirit is uppermost; and this principle is visible in all your speeches, and all your writings, even when you take some pains to disguise it. . . . 'What! an island! a spot such as this to command the great and mighty continent of North-America! Preposterous! A continent whose inhabitants double every five and twenty years! Who therefore, within a century and a half will be upwards of an hundred and twenty millions of souls! – Forbid it patriotism, forbid it politics, that such a great and mighty empire as this, should be held in subjection by the paltry kingdom of Great Britain! – Rather let the seat of empire be transferred: and let it be fixt, where it ought to be, viz. in Great America! (p. 42)

Tucker naturally thought these calculations somewhat premature, but the question still remained of what was to be done with a people who obviously intended to provoke Britain into extreme actions and who did not seem interested in reaching an accommodation. There were three alternatives: 'Shall we now compel you, by force of arms, to do your duty? – Shall we procrastinate your compulsion? – Or shall we entirely give you up; and have no other connections with you, than if you had been so many sovereign states, or independent kingdoms?' (p. 44). Although he had no doubt that Britain would triumph if she resorted to arms, he opposed military action because it would bring no benefit to her: 'For a shop-keeper will never get more custom by beating his customers: And what is true of a shop-keeper, is true of a shop-keeping nation' (p. 46). The second proposal, the one actually adopted at that time, was equally, if not more futile:

> For if recourse is to be had at last to the military power, we had better begin with it at first; – it being evident to the whole world, that all delays on our side will only strengthen the opposition on yours, and be interpreted by you as a mark of fear and not as an instance of lenity. . . . So that at last, when the time shall come of appealing to the sword, and of deciding our differences by dint of arms, the consequences of this procrastination will be, that the struggle will become so much the more obstinate, and the determination the more bloody.
>
> (pp. 47–8)

In a footnote to this forecast in the 1774 edition, Tucker noted that events had proved 'this conjecture to be but too justly founded'.

Thus the choice came down to continuing to subsidise the Americans without much in the way of return, or cutting them adrift to fend for themselves. Tucker obviously would have chosen the latter, but it was still a novel and rather startling idea which he did not pursue any further. As it was, he had laid out the alternatives in stark clarity and had already seen beyond the policy of drift, fuzzy thinking and futile expedients that was to prevail over the years that followed to the logical conclusion of the affair.

However, the crisis had to develop at its own pace. Charles Townshend, the son of Tucker's correspondent, and a man who had chosen Adam Smith as the tutor of his stepson, was responsible for the Townshend Duties of 1767. This attempt to tax the Americans eventually suffered the same fate as the Stamp Act and, with the exception of the duty on tea, was repealed in 1770. The quartering of troops in Boston and the attempts to deal with smugglers led to further violence, which culminated in the Boston Tea Party in December 1773. This in turn led to the so-called Intolerable Acts directed at Massachusetts, which resulted in enough support from the other colonies to pave the way for the meeting of the Continental Congress in September 1774. A brief survey such as this cannot, of course, do justice to the skill of radical leaders such as Samuel Adams in arousing popular support, in organising provocations such as the Boston Tea Party, and in taking advantage of the inevitable reaction so as further to polarise public opinion. Along with this went a propaganda campaign which succeeded in making the British government the villains of every confrontation and the colonial leaders the heroes in the eyes not only of Americans but also of many British sympathisers.

Tucker was not aware of everything that went on behind the scenes, but what he did see was enough to lead to a series of publications, the earliest of which was the *Four Tracts* of 1774. The first three tracts have already been discussed. Tract I, although never published before, was the comparison of the relative advantages of rich and poor countries. Its exact relevance here is not obvious, but Tucker offered it as a 'kind of introduction to those that follow'. Tract II, *The Case of Going to War*, was included because, as an attack on war in general, it could also be used against an American war in particular. Tract III, the merchant's letter to his nephew, gave 'the argument such a turn, as expressed rather a casual threat to separate, than a settled project of doing so'. This possibility was now to be made more explicit in tract IV, 'The True Interest of Great Britain Set Forth in Regard to the Colonies', since 'the more we familiarise ourselves to the idea of a separation, the less surprised, and the more prepared we shall be whenever that event shall happen'.[2]

First, Tucker places the recent events in their historical context:

> A very strange notion is now industriously spreading that 'till the late unhappy Stamp Act, there were no bickerings and discontents, no heartburnings and jealousies subsisting between the colonies, and the Mother Country. It seems, 'till that fatal period, all was harmony, peace, and love. Now it is scarcely possible even for the most superficial observer, if his knowledge extends beyond the limits of a newspaper, not to know, that this is entirely false. (p. 144)

The truth was that almost from the beginning there was discontent, as evidenced by a steady stream of complaints, instructions, memorials, petitions, remonstrances and resolutions. As early as 1670 violations of the Navigation Acts and the impossibility of enforcement through American courts and juries resulted in an act providing for prosecution in Admiralty courts in England. But, far from improving, the situation actually worsened, leading, in the reign of William III, to further legislation. This act declared that 'all laws, bye-laws, usages, or customs' of the colonies 'repugnant' to British laws were 'illegal, null, and void to all intents and purposes whatsoever' (quoted by Tucker on p. 149). The colonies, especially the chartered ones, which could elect their own councils and even governors, however, managed to evade this act, and the issuance of paper money in New England to pay debts, for example, had had to be disallowed as recently as 1751. If it were said that the Stamp Act made a bad situation worse, Tucker would agree, but only with the proviso that any legislation compelling the colonists to contribute a single shilling towards the general expense of the British Empire would have had the same effect.

The real cause of the increased wilfulness of the colonists, in Tucker's opinion, was the conquest of Canada. 'For an undoubted fact it is, that from the moment in which Canada came into possession of the English, an end was put to the sovereignty of the mother country over her colonies' (p. 153). The removal of the French threat at their borders meant that they no longer needed the protection that Britain had always provided.

But was there no provocation on the part of Britain also? Tucker is prepared to concede that there were faults on both sides.

> But what doth this serve to prove? If to exculpate the colonies in regard to their present refractory behaviour, it is needless. For I am far from charging our colonies in particular with being sinners above others; because I believe . . . that it is the nature of them all to aspire after independence, and to set up for themselves as soon as ever they find that they are able to subsist, without being beholden to the Mother Country. And if our Americans have expressed themselves sooner on this head than others have done, or in a more direct and daring manner, this ought not to be imputed to any greater malignity, or ingratitude in them, than in others, but to that bold free constitution, which is the prerogative and boast of us all.   (pp. 153–4)

Given the current situation, what were the possible courses of action open to Britain? Tucker this time saw five alternatives: to take no action in the hope that things would improve, to arrange for the colonists to send over representatives to sit in the British parliament, to defeat them in war and rule them by military force, to move the capital of the Empire to America, or to separate from the colonies entirely.

The first – the policy of hopeful drift – Tucker criticises as follows:

> This first proposal is very unhappy at first setting out; because it takes that for granted, which history and experience prove to be false. It supposes, that colonies may become the more obedient in proportion as they are suffered to grow the more headstrong, and to feel their own strength and independence; than which supposition there cannot be a more palpable absurdity.
>
> (pp. 158–9)

Furthermore, it ignores the fact that they have revolted and thus denied that the British parliament has any right to intervene in their affairs.

Tucker examines the second alternative by discussing a pamphlet entitled *Considerations on the Expediency of Admitting Representatives from the American Colonies into the British House of Commons*, published in London, in 1770. The author's plan was to admit about eighty colonial representatives, chosen not by the individual colonists but by the assemblies, which would issue written commissions empowering them to represent the colony and consent on its behalf to legislation concerning the colonies. The major problem with this arrangement was that, since these 'commissioners' would doubtless be subject to instructions from their governments, not only would they vote against any legislation contrary to these instructions, but in addition, such legislation, if enacted, would not be considered binding on their colony. Tucker's concept of a representative was quite different: each member of Parliament represents the whole nation, not just the constituency which elected him, and, as a result, any instruction from his electors must be subordinated to the interests of the country as a whole. Thus, it is not necessary for each deputy to consent personally to each act of the legislature, 'because a vote of the majority is in fact a vote of the nation to all intents and purposes' (p. 172)

There were other problems with the scheme. Who would decide

when intervention in American affairs was necessary? Would the commissioners have a voice in purely British affairs, accepting that the British would have little say in those of America? As for the author's suggestion that no legislation regarding a colony should pass into law until a year after its first reading, in order to give the colonists times to make representations against it, Tucker notes that it was precisely such a year's grace before the passing of the Stamp Act which allowed its opponents to mount such an effective campaign against it. The fact that the author himself had little hope that such a modest plan would be accepted by the colonists indicated how visionary it was, except, perhaps, to show how uninterested the Americans really were in obtaining representation, despite all their talk about it.

The third possibility – unfortunately, the one adopted – was war. If Britain acted decisively, she might well be victorious. 'But, alas! victory alone is but a poor compensation for all the blood and treaure which must be spilt on such an occasion' (p. 189). Furthermore, the occupying authorities would be faced with a dangerous dilemma. If they ruled despotically, how long would it be before 'the enslaved part of the constitution . . . [would] contaminate the free'? But, if the colonies were granted all the liberties of the British constitution, including the right to trial by jury, how long would it be before conditions were right back where they started before the war? Good examples of Tucker's logic at work were to occur in later years, as in the case of the Boer War and its aftermath. His conclusion is that, whichever choice were adopted, it would come to the same end: 'That England would be the greatest sufferer; and that America is not to be governed against its own inclination' (p. 193)

The suggestion that Britain should be governed from America is treated with scorn by Tucker, who then moves on to the last choice, which was his own solution: 'For if we neither can govern the Americans nor be governed by them; if we can neither unite with them, nor ought to subdue them; what remains, but to part with them on as friendly terms as we can? And if any man should think that he can reason better from the above premises, let him try.' Aware that the idea of separation was a shocking one to many people, Tucker examines 'the supposed disadvantages attending such a disjunction' (p. 195). The first and most important, the possible loss of trade, he dismisses as unlikely. The colonies have always been prepared to trade with anyone, even their bitterest enemies in a war undertaken on their behalf. Britain provided a better market for American goods than they could find elsewhere, and Britain produced a multiplicity of goods which the Americans could find no cheaper elsewhere. If it is assumed that there could be no loss of trade, then the second disadvantage, that the decline in shipping would reduce the number of seamen, was disposed of. The third source of concern was the danger that France might take over the colonies as soon as Britain had relinquished them. This Tucker considered a very extravagant notion. If the Americans objected to mild British rule, it was unlikely that they would accept the more authoritarian system of the French.

Turning to the advantages of his policy, Tucker sees it as first of all putting a stop to the massive emigration which had been taking place over the previous few years. Why he thought this should happen with a change of regime is not clear. A second benefit would be the saving of the £300,000 to £400,000 spent on the civil and military establishment in the colonies. A further sum of at least £200,000 would be saved in bounties. Furthermore, merchants would be better able to collect their debts. He also saw an important improvement in the image of the British, who would no longer be regarded as 'robbers and usurpers'.

But, Tucker imagines the reader asking, is the author 'still such a novice as not to know, that measures are rarely adopted merely because they are right, but because they can serve a present turn'? Tucker's reply is that right measures will prevail in the end. 'Therefore I make not the least doubt but that a separation from the northern colonies, and also another right measure, viz. a complete union and incorporation with Ireland (however unpopular either of them may now appear) will take place within half a century' (p. 212). In the event, it was nine years in the one case, and twenty-one years in the other.

The next of Tucker's American tracts to appear was *The Respective Pleas and Arguments of the Mother Country and the Colonies Distinctly Set Forth*, with an 'epistle dedicatory' dated 20 January 1775, and addressed to the plenipotentiaries of the various American 'republics' meeting in congress at Philadelphia. It was reprinted as tract v in the third edition (1776) of the *Four Tracts*.

Tucker begins by thanking the plenipotentiaries for the favour they had done him: 'Most people here in Britain thought that you would not so soon have thrown off the mask, and set up for independence. And very many there were, who either could not, or would not see, that you intended it at all.'[3] By coming out in the open they had 'acted a fair and consistent part', but how consistent had they been in their other behaviour? They claim the rights of life, liberty and property by the 'immutable' laws of nature, but 'Permit me therefore to ask, why are not the poor negroes, and the poor Indians entitled to the like rights and benefits? And how comes it to pass that these immutable laws of nature are become so very mutable, and so very insignificant in respect of them?' The negroes never ceded any right over their lives and liberties, and the Indians ['the only true and rightful proprietors of the land you inhabit'] over their property. 'These things, Gentlemen, ought not to be: For whilst you, and your constituents, are chargeable with so much *real* tyranny, injustice and oppression, you declaim with every ill grace against the *imaginary* tyranny, and the pretended oppression of the mother country' (p. v).

Every colony in its time seeks independence: only America wants to retain all the old benefits as well. And in order to strengthen themselves the Americans had shown a desire for 'the large and extensive province of Canada'. They might have spared themselves the trouble: 'Canada, when it has grown rich by our means, and our capitals, will assuredly set up for independence, as you have done' (p. vii). Another prophecy come true, albeit more slowly. But, as Canada for the moment remained faithful, the Americans, despite their attack on the Catholic religion in the *Address to the Inhabitants of Great-Britain* (a response to the Quebec Act of 1774) had now made an *Address to the Inhabitants of the Province of Quebec*, in which they gave the example of Switzerland as a union of Protestant and Roman Catholic cantons living peacefully together. Tucker does not feel that Switzerland was an ideal example, since the Protestant cantons inclined towards oligarchy, but, if the Americans wished to emulate the Swiss and become independent, by all means let them do so. When this happened, perhaps British merchants would be welcomed as they were in Switzerland, and not tarred and feathered, as was likely to be their fate in America.

Tucker begins the tract itself by noting that events since his last publication have confirmed that a policy of separation, at least from the northern colonies, was the only sensible way of terminating the dispute. The sooner this took place the 'less blood will be spilt: – And I add likewise, as no unworthy consideration the less *ill blood* will be occasioned' (p. 20). Many people still believed that concessions on either side could lead to a reconciliation, but, as Tucker points out, compromise was not really possible at this stage: 'For the claims of right on either side must be universal, or there is no claim at all: And neither party have it in their power to recede a tittle from their pretensions without subverting the very foundation of their claim to all the rest' (p. 21). The remainder of the work is an attempt to demonstrate the inescapable truth of this statement.

Tucker's first dictum is that in every society there must be a 'dernier resort' – a final authority. 'Here in Great Britain it is both the law, and the constitution of the realm, and the voice of reason, that we should stop at King, Lords, and Commons, when in Parliament assembled' (p. 22). Locke, perhaps, and certainly his disciple Dr Priestley, would go beyond Parliament to the people, and insist that laws are not really binding until they have reached the 'sanction of some political club, a popular assembly convened for that purpose: – Or that taxes shall not be levied, "till the people shall appear to be willing to pay them"' (p. 23). Tucker will admit only that a complete breakdown of the present system of government may necessitate such drastic action, but takes the view that no one in his right mind would go out of his way to upset it for some unforeseen contingency.

The next question is whether any part of the British Empire is outside the jurisdiction of this 'dernier resort'. The only exceptions he can see are those territories which the King rules by different titles, such as Hanover, of which King George was the Elector; Holland when King William was Stadtholder; and Scotland prior to the Act of Union. In each case the inhabitants of the other countries were aliens and foreigners with respect to England. The other possible exception was Ireland, which Tucker discussed at length. He concluded that any uncertainty had been laid to rest by a law of George I which explicitly defined the powers of Crown and Parliament over that island. The case of the colonies was far weaker, because a similar law had been passed 'in the patriotic days of our glorious defender King William' (p. 36). Thus, if the Stamp Act and the other acts of George III were usurpations, then the colonists' grievances were much older than they claim, for 'King William and his parliament were the prime usurpers' (p. 38).

Tucker devotes the second part of his tract to the resolutions passed by the Congress to justify its stand. What the Americans claimed, 'by the immutable laws of nature, and the principles of the English constitution and several charters or compacts', was all the rights, liberties and immunities of free-born Englishmen, especially the right to be taxed only with their own consent. Tucker then proceeded to compare the arguments of the two sides. The British position rested on 'facts and precedents', while the Americans depended on 'immutable' truths. 'Former laws and precedents carry little or no conviction to people who argue after this manner: And they are seldom or never mentioned by the Americans: For all these, they well know, would surely make against them' (p. 49). For instance, in the 1757 edition of Crouch's *Book of Rates*, there are 'no less than ninety clauses, or extracts from acts of parliament, for governing and controlling the subordinate legislatures of the colonies, for regulating their police, and restraining their trade; also for dispensing with the trials by jury in contraband causes . . . and lastly for laying on of duties and rates of various kinds' (p. 49n).

> And as to any claims to be derived from regal charters, they are not insisted upon as the main pillars of the American cause. (Indeed, if they were, such supports must fall of course; because every charter granted solely by the king, must, in the very nature of things, be subordinate to the supreme legislature both of king and parliament.) But these claims, pretended to be derived from charters, are quoted only by the bye, as a kind of super numerary proof, and as a sort of analogical reasoning, fit only for those, whose weak minds cannot digest arguments of a superior strength and quality.   (pp. 49–50)

Tucker therefore concludes that, as the two sides have no common meeting ground, they must either quarrel constantly or separate. There are those generous spirits who say, 'Let Great-Britain allow the colonies the sole right of taxing themselves: And on the other hand let the colonies allow to Great-Britain the exclusive right of regulating their external commerce' (p. 51). But the expectation that this would restore the former harmony was, in Tucker's eyes, naïve. The Americans would never renounce the right of regulating their own commerce; in fact, they could not renounce it, since it was founded on the indefeasible, inalienable laws of nature. In any case, Great Britain would be foolish to continue attempting to regulate their commerce. The laws of trade were unenforceable, because a jury of smugglers was not likely to convict a fellow smuggler. No, unless Britain wanted to continue a situation in which the Americans enjoyed all the benefits of being part of the Empire, while contributing nothing to the costs, the only way out was a peaceful separation.

Probably the most famous exponent of the policy mentioned above – that of letting the colonies go untaxed while retaining the right to regulate their external trade – was Edmund Burke. His party, the Rockingham Whigs, had been responsible for the repeal of the Stamp Act as well as the passage of the Declaratory Act of 1766. This asserted the right of King and Parliament to 'make laws and statutes of sufficient force and validity to bind the colonies in all cases whatsoever'. Burke stuck by the Act until events made it irrelevant, because he really did believe in the supremacy of King and Parliament over the whole Empire, but he was reluctant to exercise that power if the result was to antagonise the Americans. His position was made even more ambiguous by the fact that he was the colonial agent for New York from 1770 until the outbreak of hostilities.

Despite these contradictions, or perhaps because of them, two of his most famous speeches were made on American affairs. They did not alter the course of British policy, but they had a tremendous impact on later generations, both as models of oratory and as expressions of a generous and accommodating spirit towards the Americans which, if it had been adopted by the ministry, might well have kept the Empire together. That the latter was a serious oversimplification is widely recognised today and was certainly recognised at the time by Tucker, who published his reactions in *A Letter to Edmund Burke*. He had good cause to say something, because he had been personally attacked in the first speech, on American taxation. Burke, after referring to the 'vermin of court reporters' who had claimed that opposition to the Stamp Act in Parliament had encouraged the Americans in their resistance, went on to say, 'This has even formally appeared in print in a regular volume, from an advocate of that faction, a Dr. Tucker. This Dr. Tucker is already a dean, and his earnest labours in this vineyard will, I suppose, raise him to a bishopric.'[4]

Tucker began his *Letter* as follows,

> As you have been pleased to bestow much abuse and scurrility on me in your public speech of the 19th of April, 1774; – and also many commendations in private before, and since that publication; – I shall take no notice of either, than just to assure you, that I am neither elated by your praises, nor chagrined at your censures; and that I hold myself indifferent in respect to both. My business with you is solely of a public nature; and therefore, without farther preface, I beg leave to inform you that I propose to examine your last performance, entitled, *The Speech of Edmund Burke, Esq., March 22, 1775*, with as much freedom, as you do the writings and opinions of other men; but, I hope, with more decency and good manners.[5]

There is no need to examine in detail Tucker's discussion of Burke's conciliation speech. Burke said that the Americans were characterised by a love of freedom, which he ascribed to six different factors. The Dean agreed with all of Burke's arguments, although he naturally saw them in a less favourable light. An example is the sixth point, which says that this 'disobedient spirit' is encouraged by the 3000 miles of ocean between them and the mother country. Tucker exclaims, 'Pray, sir, on which side of the question were you retained? . . . It is a matter of astonishment that you should bring such arguments as these, to prove the necessity of continuing an union of empire between Great-Britain and the detached continental powers of North-America' (p. 39).

What then was Burke's solution? Tucker quotes the famous passage early in the speech:

> The proposition is peace. Not peace through the medium of war; not peace to be hunted through the labyrinths of intricate and endless negotiations; not peace to arise out of universal discord, fomented from principle, in all parts of the empire; not peace to depend on the juridical determination of perplexing questions: or the precise marking the shadowy boundaries of a complex government. It is simple peace, sought in its natural

course, and in its ordinary haunts. – It is peace sought in the spirit of peace, and laid in principles purely pacific.

These rolling periods left Tucker unmoved: 'What a pompous description is here!' The logic had a like effect. 'Why truly; if we grant the colonies all that they shall require, and stipulate for nothing in return; then they will be at peace with us. I believe it; and on these simple principles of simple peace-making, I will engage to terminate every difference throughout the world' (pp. 44–5). As for Burke's optimistic belief that the colonies would be willing to substitute voluntary payments for taxes, Tucker is scathing. The colonies had shown little interest in helping each other in the past, never mind Great Britain.

Tucker also dealt with Burke in his next tract, *An Humble Address and Earnest Appeal* . . . , usually known by the title given at the top of each page: *Address and Appeal to the Landed Interest*.[6] In his *Letter to Burke*, Tucker had not mentioned a brief reference in the conciliation speech to his own policy for dealing with the Americans. After listing three ways of proceeding, Burke adds,

> Another has indeed been started, that of giving up the colonies; but it met so slight a reception, that I do not think myself obliged to dwell a great while upon it. It is nothing but a little sally of anger, like the forwardness of peevish children, who, when they cannot get all they would have, are resolved to take nothing.[7]

However, it came up early in the *Address and Appeal* in another discussion of alternatives. Now that war had actually broken out, what was to be done? There were three possibilities, according to Tucker: the Parliamentary scheme of maintaining supremacy through the use of force; that of Burke for giving the colonies what they wanted subject only to an acknowledgement of the prerogatives of the Crown; and his own scheme of separation, 'which Mr. Burke, in his speech of March 22, 1775, is pleased to term a childish one' (p. 5).

Because the Parliamentary alternative was actually being tested, Tucker decided to confine himself to a comparison between his plan and that of Burke. Imagining himself as on trial before a jury, he desires first to exclude from passing judgement on him all those he considers 'under wrong bias'. He begins with 'courtiers and placemen', which leads him immediately to the charge that he himself was one. This he denies, 'For I thank God, I have no cause to complain of any disappointment; having since my advancement to the Deanery of Gloucester, in the year 1758, neither directly or indirectly made the least or the most distant application for any other or higher state.' He claims that Burke was fully aware of this through various people, including 'a noble lord, formerly high in office and a great favourite at court, but now his coadjutor and a flaming patriot' (p. 7). This was doubtless Lord Shelburne, whose relationship with Tucker will be considered in another chapter. Also he did not want his exclusion of courtiers construed as a criticism of the present ministry: 'For I think it may be fairly allowed, without paying them any compliment, that they are to the full as able, and as honest as the best of those endeavouring to supplant them' (p. 8). That this was not exactly high praise is made clear when one looks at his second group of those to be excluded from the jury, the 'mock patriots', who were always searching for excuses to oppose the ministry. America, of course, was a fertile source of such material. 'For example, had the ministry proposed at first the very scheme, which Mr. Burke himself has now thought proper to recommend, the heads of faction, and even Mr. Burke himself (if he had not been a pensioner to North-America) would most probably have proposed just the reverse' (p. 9).

Another group to be rejected for jury duty was all those 'from the roaring patriot in the Senate, to the miserable scribbler in the garret, who are the pensioners of France, or Spain, or of any rival power' (p. 11). He has no specific evidence but he thinks it highly probable that such people exist, given the nature of the times. He offers an interesting sidelight in a footnote:

> In the year of the Rebellion 1745, and for the many years afterwards, the *London Evening Post* (now a Republican) was then a flaming Jacobite paper: During which period the author of these tracts has frequently the honour of being abused by him, under the character of a low-church, fanatical, Oliverian Whig. Once in particular (above 20 years ago) he was complimented on the high-flown strain of Josiah ben Tucker ben Judas Iscariot. The times are now greatly altered; and so is the tone of

the abuse. But the author is perfectly resigned to these viscissitudes of human affairs: And he has no other favour to ask of this, and of all his brother scribblers, whether weekly or monthly, in sheets, or in pamphlets, than that they would *never praise him*; because that, and that only he should look upon to be a real disgrace. But it is not the *London Evening Post* alone, who from a violent Jacobite has commenced a fierce republican. Many like instances may be recollected. And indeed the transition is natural enough; for if a man can be so absurd as to think there is an indefeasible right in any one family, when that family becomes extinct, he turns a republican. (p. 16n).

Next he excepts all those with republican principles, 'for though they dignify themselves by the name of Whigs, yet as they are not the genuine, constitutional Whigs of this kingdom, but an unnatural superfoetation, and the avowed enemies of the British Constitution, they ought not to be allowed to sit in judgment in a British cause'. They only support the colonial republics because they think they are preparing the way for the introduction of similar institutions in Great Britain. 'Therefore *republicism* is the bond of union between these unnatural Englishmen and their fellow-labourers of America' (p. 17).

Having disposed of all these other groups Tucker asks that the case between Burke and himself be tried by the landed interest only.

> They are certainly the properest and most unexceptionable judges; for they have the most at stake; and their interest, and the interest of the public must coincide. They can gain nothing either by war, or peace, by a submission to, or a separation from, the revolters in North-America, but what must tend to the general, as well as to their own particular advantage. (p. 19)

Again this assumption, shared by Adam Smith, that the interests of the landowners and the public are identical.

Having chosen his jury, Tucker now presents his arguments. His plan is easy to execute. It requires a manifesto in the form of an act of Parliament to be published when the British armies and fleets have first been withdrawn. It would be to the effect that after a certain date all colonies in rebellion would be 'totally cut off,

American Affairs

severed and separated from the British empire', and that all the privileges of British subjects would be withdrawn, but that any province or individual wishing to return to its original allegiance would be pardoned and have its privileges restored.

If the question is asked which scheme is cheapest, Tucker, of course, can claim that his costs nothing more than what would have to be paid for ink, paper and printing. Burke's scheme, on the other hand, could be very expensive. The 'great honours and great emoluments' suggested in his speech would have to be offered to the Americans ('a pretty periphrasis this to describe the art of bribing', says Tucker) and the cost of guarding the American coasts would have to be paid.

> And when they chuse to amuse themselves by going on smuggling, trucking, huckstering, and buccaneering parties on the Spanish main, then you must more particularly stand up in their defence, and insist on their vessels not being searched by the Spanish Guarda Costas. And if the Spaniards should think this an hard measure, and appeal to the practice and example of Englishmen themselves ... you must positively and vehemently say, that the case is widely different: Then you have a sufficient plea for declaring war against them; – then, my lords and gentlemen, resolve (as your predecessors did before) never to make peace till the right of searching is given up; – then spend another sixty to ninety millions in this new quarrel; – and at last make peace (as they did) without even mentioning the right of not being searched; for which alone they pretended to go to war. (pp. 27–8)

So much for the War of Jenkin's Ear.

Another question was that of which alternative was more likely to prevent similar troubles in the future. Tucker regards Burke's plan as 'a mere truce'. Even if Great Britain repealed all obnoxious acts of Parliament, removed the right to levy taxes, etc., there would still be endless opportunities for further quarrels about the regulation of American trade, which control could easily be and had already been interpreted as a form of taxation. And what exactly would be the relation between the little parliaments of North America and the King of Great Britain?

This brings Tucker to his last question: which scheme will 'least endanger, or rather, which is best adapted to preserve our present happy constitution?' (p. 35). If the King were able to deal directly with a large number of separate legislatures, would this not strengthen his position in relation to all? The success of the House of Austria was an example of how well a policy of divide and rule could work. Such a fate might befall the British if Burke's plan were to operate in the way he intended. He noted in this connection that it was the 'modern patriots and American Republicans ... who propose to exalt the prerogatives of the crown to the subversion of the rights, privileges and liberties of the British Parliament, and the British nation' (p. 34). This attitude is to be found in many passages in the declarations of the Congress protesting that it has no desire to separate, and expressing the purest loyalty to the House of Hanover.

> In the meantime, because his Majesty is graciously disposed to join with Great Britain against America in this contest for empire, (for in fact *that* is the *real* dispute, whatever may be the pretense) not only among the Americans, but among Englishmen themselves [many] vent the bitterest reproaches against him for being the best friend and protector of the Mother Country. Surely posterity will stand amazed at such a procedure! (p. 41)

Tucker rests his case on the evidence before his readers and their capacity to understand the interests of the nation and of themselves. 'Your birth, your rank and education lift you much above the prejudices of the vulgar: whilst your patrimonial estates and ample fortunes screen you from a multitude of those temptations, to which other men are grievously exposed' (p. 45). If they did not exert themselves, they faced many dangers. If the republican party prevailed, the estates of the Church might be the first to fall.

> But nevertheless if you, my Lords and gentlemen, should be so weak as to imagine, that matters will stop there; and that your own large possessions, your hereditary honours, and ample privileges will escape unhurt, amidst the general wreck of private property, and subordination, which will necessarily ensure; you will be woefully mistaken. (p. 46)

Tucker could only look at America with its committee men and confiscations; the unpleasant fate of the French nobility still lay in the future.

The rest of the tract is devoted to commercial arguments springing from the fears of those who believed that the loss of the colonies meant the loss of trade. The notion that commerce between Great Britain and the colonies would cease if they were separated he has already disposed of by showing, in the fourth tract, that it is equivalent to saying that the Americans would no longer follow their own best interests. Now, in a series of 'Remarks', he questions whether the American trade is as important as many people think it is. Statistics for exports from 1764 to 1774, for example, show that those to Germany and Holland exceeded those to America by 50 per cent. Furthermore, imports from Russia would be cheaper if the bounties and duties which favoured America were removed. The truth was that, although 'we are gravely told, that as soon as ever the Americans shut their ports against us, famine to our manufacturers, bankruptcy to our merchants, destruction and desolation to our seaport towns, must inevitably ensue', the worst had happened and British trade, far from declining, had actually increased (p. 71).

Along the way, he admits the practical difficulties in dismantling an empire. In words very similar to those used by Adam Smith the following year, he says that he does not believe there is 'a single instance in all history, of any nation surrendering a distant province voluntarily, and of free choice, notwithstanding it was greatly in their interest to have done ' (p. 69).

Tucker's last American tract was the *Series of Answers* of 1776.[8] In the Preface he refers to a dispute concerning Benjamin Franklin's actions during the Stamp Act crisis, which had been mentioned briefly in his Postscript to the previous pamphlet. 'Now, in the first and second editions of my Fourth Tract, unhappily for me, I had charged him with procuring a place for himself in the American Stamp-Office; whereas, alas! it proved to be not for himself, but for a friend' (p. vi). Franklin's name had not been used, but apparently the reference was clear to all. Despite the fact that the offending paragraph had been removed from the third edition of the *Four Tracts*, Tucker had been under pressure from Franklin's friends to do more. As a result he quoted a letter he had received from Franklin in which the famous American gave his side of the story. While prepared to admit his mistake, Tucker still felt that Franklin's behaviour was inconsistent with his public opposition to the Act. Furthermore, since Franklin had been implicated in the theft of some letters which had been used against the colonial administration, his reputation was not so pure as to have suffered much damage in the affair.

Tucker then goes on to blame the present discord between Britain and America on the Regency Bill, which led to the fall of Grenville, who had passed the Stamp Act. The new administration were forced to repeal the Act, 'though I do not believe it was their inward choice'. Then they made the situation worse, 'hoping (vainly hoping) to patch up the breach they had made in the constitution, by the *soldering* of a declaratory law' (p. xi). This only convinced the Americans of British weakness, and gave them another grievance.

> To pretend to bind the colonies *in all cases whatsoever*, after having given such a recent proof, that we dared not bind them to pay even an halfpenny tax on a newspaper, was such an instance of gasconading folly, as is hardly to be paralleled. No wonder then, that the colonists should first treat it as a ridiculous bravado; and then make use of it as a weapon against ourselves, by putting it into their list of imaginary wrongs. (p. xii)

Thus it was the Rockingham administration which was, as Tucker put it, the 'exciting' cause of the war, and it was Burke himself who was one of the authors of the law under the oppression of which the Americans were groaning. Furthermore, as he had already pointed out, the Declaratory Act was nothing but a copy of a Declaratory Law of George I relating to Ireland, and a re-enactment of the colonial law of William III. 'All these Whig Princes! Whig Parliaments! and Whig Administrations!' (p. xv).

In the Introduction to the *Series of Answers* he complains that no serious attempt has been made to confute his previous pamphlets.

> Low, scurrilous epithets, such as childish, visionary, mercenary, mad, etc., etc. have been the only mode adopted for answering these treatises. But it . . . may appear unaccountable why so many of the Americans themselves, and why *all* their republican abettors here at home, should condemn this pro-

posal of an amicable separation with such asperity of language
... and such heavy execrations on its author; – a proposal,
which they cannot but confess, would put a total end to all their
present complaints, and redress every grievance pretended to
be imposed upon them by Great-Britain. (p. xi)

The reason, he thinks, is that the colonists want to continue to
enjoy the advantages of British protection as long as possible and
thus save themselves the cost of fleets, armies, and fortifications.
As for republicans in Great Britain,

[They] are most violently incensed against the author of this
proposal, because it would quash at once all their darling
projects of introducing similar liberty-meetings, similar congresses, and similar forms of government here in Britain; – and
because it would cut off all pretence for clamouring against
government on account of its tyrannizing over the natural rights
and liberties of their dear persecuted brethren, the poor,
innocent Americans. (p. xii)

Tucker's answers to various objections which had been raised to
a separation from the colonies were numerous, and many of them
had been touched on previously. The objections themselves are of
some interest, because they indicate the sorts of problems which
concerned Tucker's contemporaries. Some were strategic: the
danger that America might seize the West Indies, that it might
become a great maritime empire, or that Britain might suffer a loss
of seamen owing to the shrinkage of her possessions. Others were
commercial, such as the threat of American competition in manufacturing, or the possibility that it might raise tariff barriers.
Tucker considers the latter unlikely, because 'the Southern
independent republics will never consent to prohibit the introduction of the manufacturers of old England merely for the sake of
encouraging (to their own loss) the manufactures of New England
(a people whom they both hate and despise) nor will the New-
Englanders give a monopoly to the Southern provinces against
themselves' (p. 45). This turned out to be the case until the North
defeated the South in the Civil War and was able to impose tariffs
for protection instead of revenue only.

Along the way, Tucker refers to the influential pamphlet

Common Sense. He did not know that the author was Tom Paine (it was supposed, at that time, to have been written by Franklin and Samuel Adams) but he agreed completely with the author that 'it is time to part' (p. 27). His opinion of two of the leaders is given a little further on in reference to smuggling: 'Hancock himself, the nominal head of the Congress, and the tool of artful Adams, was one of the greatest smugglers on the whole continent' (p. 35). He again quotes *Common Sense* with approval when answering the objection that Britain and America could remain united as separate states under the same prince, as was already the case with Hanover. However, Hanover could never compete with Britain for supremacy in the way that America could. With the latter, it was possible to conceive of control being transferred across the Atlantic – 'as Dr. Franklin elegantly phrased it, from the cockboat to the Man of War'. He continues,

> Moreover the famous American pamphlet *Common Sense* declares it to be preposterous, absurd and against the course of nature, that 'a great continent should be governed by an Island. In no instance hath nature made the satellite larger than its primary planet. And as England and America, with respect to each other, reverses the common order of nature, it is evident they belong to different systems; England to Europe, and America to itself'. (p. 59)

The strange sense of weakness and foreboding that haunted Britain in the years after its notable success in the Seven Years' War is reflected in objection XI: 'Will not the severing America from England have the same effect in political constitutions, as that of cutting off, or striking away a main prop, a massy pillar, or a strong buttress from an antient, crazy building?' (p. 60). Tucker refuses to accept this metaphor, but, even if it were true, he feels that the separation would be more likely to preserve the constitution than otherwise. 'As long as ever North-America shall remain connected with Great-Britain, under any mode whatever; the republican party among us will ever find an asylum for sheltering themselves under that connection' (pp. 61–2). He does not deny that democratic governments may be good ones, but that alone is not a sufficient reason for pulling down governments which are equally good. These ideas are expressed even more forcefully a few pages later when he says,

> And from these [particulars] it must appear that as long as ever the continent of America shall remain connected with Great-Britain, under any mode or form whatever, so long will the champions for American republicanism be stirring up the people to rebel; and to establish a republican tyranny, the worst of all tyrannies, instead of the present government, which is certainly the least oppressive, the mildest, the best poised, and the most reasonable upon earth. (p. 72)

Objection XII raised the question: If separation from America is good, why not separation from Ireland also? This, of course, ran contrary to one of Tucker's favourite schemes. His answers were that Ireland was much closer; that, as it is too small to be a separate state, it must be under the influence of another power, if not Great Britain; and that it was a nursery of seamen, because the Irish trade between small ports was larger than commonly realised.

He refers to the Loyalists in objection XIII. 'If we should separate from North-America, what recompense shall we be able to make to those faithful Americans, who have suffered for their loyalty to the King and their allegiance to the British Government?' (p. 79). First of all, a continuation of the war was not the best method of assuring them a reasonable compensation. Even if the British won, the country would be devastated in the process. The rebels would retire across the Alleghenies and the poverty of the rest would prevent them from paying taxes for many years to come. He suggests compensating the Loyalists from a lottery or a million-pound sinking fund. Even a very large sum of money would be cheaper than a year's campaigning, not to mention the saving in life. The Loyalists could also be rewarded by offices in the public service. For those who wanted to return, perhaps the central provinces of New York, Pennsylvania, New Jersey and Maryland, which were the least disaffected and most open to British forces, would become independent republics where they could settle. 'And as to their neighbours to the north, or to the south, a greater, and a more deserved punishment could not be inflicted upon them, than to leave them to themselves. And then the fanatical hypocrites on the one side, and the tyrants over slaves on the other, would afford a useful lesson to mankind' (p. 83).

Tucker begins his Conclusion by noting again a similarity between the attacks on him by the republicans then and those by the Jacobites in former years. In fact, he had discovered to his amazement that many of those in Bristol who gave evidence of being Jacobites at that time now showed every sign of being republicans. 'Perverse infatuation! as if there were no medium between Scylla or Carybdis! And that the reverse of wrong is always right!' (p. 94n). Finally he attempts to defend himself from an accusation made by Dr Price in a popular pro-American pamphlet. In his *Letter to Edmund Burke*, Tucker had called the Americans disciples of Mr Locke. Price picked this up and at one point says, 'One of the most violent enemies of the colonies has pronounced them "all Mr. Locke's disciples": – Glorious title! – How shameful is it to make war on them for that reason?' (quoted by Tucker on p. 100). Tucker naturally took exception to the implication that he had recommended a war against the Americans, when he had been arguing for years to let them go their own way.

The *Series of Answers* ended with a Postscript in which Tucker noted that, as it was going to press, news had arrived of a British victory. Because he feared that this might have an effect on men's minds, he reminded his readers that the fortunes of war cannot change 'the necessary course of things'. His suggestion was to seize the opportunity thus afforded and 'terminate the war with more speed, and with greater reputation' (p. 107). Thus ended Tucker's American tracts. Together they come to 544 pages, and, even if we exclude the first two as not applying strictly to American affairs, they still make up a respectable contribution to the debate.

His advice, of course, was ignored and the war went on. Tucker continued to express his opinions on current affairs, but only in short pieces written for the newspapers. This was when he used the pen-name 'Cassandra'. Other comments are to be found in his letters to his friend Dr William Adams, Master of Pembroke College, Oxford. In one written in 1777 he notes wryly that, since Congress had decided to impose heavy penalties on those who refused to accept its paper money as legal tender, there existed the unusual situation in America of creditors being pursued by debtors, rather than *vice versa*. He thought that Dr Price and the like-minded Dr Priestley might be interested in applying the same techniques in England. 'For several of their own friends, the patriots, both Lords and commoners, would have no objection, I dare believe, against paying their tradesmen's bills in Congress paper currency instead of solid cash.'[9]

In another letter of the same year, he makes quite clear his primary motivation:

> For to tell the truth, my chief scheme was originally more to stop the growth of republicanism at home, than to attempt to make converts in the rebellious colonies: and I used the one rather as a pretext for executing my plan respecting the other. The present patriotic system, I am very certain, is, to represent both church and state as equally deserving to be laid level with the ground; – the church as being literally anti-Christian, which it seems all churches are, if by law established: – and the state, as being a most tyrannical usurpation on the rights and liberties of mankind, because it is not founded on the equal suffrages of a free people.[10]

With the entry of France into the war came threats of a French invasion of England. In order to calm the fears of the populace, Tucker published his *Reflections on the Terrors of Invasion* in 1779.[11] His arguments were mainly logistical: the difficulties of getting the substantial numbers of troops required together with their horses, artillery, wagons, supplies, and so on, embarked, protected across the Channel and landed. He estimated that fifteen days would be required from the first appearance of the invaders until they were ready to move inland. Perhaps two-thirds of their time would be spent waiting for the ebbing and flowing of the tides. He also suggested a different strategy from that used by Harold, who had given battle with all his forces directly William the Conqueror had landed. Instead, he recommended constant skirmishing by small forces, harassing the enemy by night and day until it was exhausted and demoralised – in other words to resort to what was later called guerrilla warfare. Tucker wrote to Adams that he had never received so many compliments as for his latest production. More important, it had been translated and printed in almost every European gazette. It had even been discussed at the table of

M. Necker, where a visitor, the radical Duke of Richmond, had called Tucker 'an ignorant, mercenary priest'.[12]

As the war continued to drag on, Tucker decided to make a direct appeal to Necker, which took the form of a series of letters to the French minister, entitled *Cui Bono?* Unfortunately, Necker was dismissed just prior to publication in 1781 and Tucker had to refer to him as the 'late' Controller General of Finances. He begins by identifying himself as a friend of Necker's predecessor, Turgot, and someone not entirely unknown to Necker himself, 'particularly at that juncture, when the idle project of invading England, became the general topic of conversation throughout all of Europe'; and he assures him that he enters upon the work 'not as an Englishman but as a citizen of the world'.[13]

He begins by complimenting Necker on publishing the accounts of the French administration in his *Compte rendu*, which he assumes had been made public 'to shew the world, that France had so many resources remaining, as would exhaust and ruin England in the progress of this war'. Tucker then supposes, for the sake of argument, that all the French hopes have been realised and England completely subdued. However, before proceeding, in letter II, to the likely outcome of the happy event, he pauses to tell a cautionary tale involving his own countrymen.

> Almost thirty years ago, when our colonists in America were at least fifty to one more in numbers than the handful of men who could have invaded them from Canada ... common sense might have taught us to have suspected the truth of [their] pretended fears: – common sense might have suggested the expediency of pausing a while, and of examining into facts, particularly relating to the fur-trade, before we rushed into hostilities on such weak and frivolous pretences. (p. 9)

There was a man at that time who exposed the absurdity of the American's fears, and who offered to prove from the Custom House entries 'that the quantity of furs brought into England from America was almost double what it had been in former times; instead of being monopolized (as was asserted) by the French' (p. 10). This same person also foretold that removing the French from America would be a signal for the colonies to revolt. 'But, alas! he

American Affairs

was preaching to the winds and waves.' He was accused of being base and scandalous and nothing but a spy and pensioner of France. Necker, who had complained of the enormous amount spent on pensions, could best say, 'whether you have met the name of Tucker among the long roll of English mock patriots, and French pensioners' (p. 5). Since Tucker refers to his writings as 'letters', and nothing similar to his references here appears in his pamphlets of the 1750s, these opinions must have been expressed in contributions to newspapers. He told Lord Kames in 1758 that he had written on the subject in 1753 and 1754.

Returning in letter II to his original supposition that England had been conquered by France, he asks how a tradesman could benefit by beggaring his customers. The English purchased large quantities of wine and brandy and there was a steady demand for French fashions, coats, laundresses, milliners, dancing masters, and so on. The English were responsible for one-half to two-thirds of the large sum mentioned by Necker as having been spent in France by foreigners. An impoverished England could never be a good customer for France.

But political dangers as well as economic ones would flow from a French victory in a war fought on behalf of the colonists and the principles they espoused. Their great complaint was really not a halfpenny tax on newspapers or threepence on tea, but 'that they were not governed à la Monsr. Locke' (p. 20). This meant that no taxes could be legal which had not been passed by a government based on the consent of the people.

> Now, Sir, as you know, that this is the language of Mr. Locke, and of all his disciples, more especially the Americans, who have made these very maxims the ground of the present war, and of all the miseries consequent thereupon; – I ask, in the name of common sense, what are you about? And do you really wish, that these levelling destructive principles should be made the standard of the politics of France? – If so, what becomes of the title of your reigning prince? And what right has Lewis XVI to any one province in his dominions? ... Moreover, you yourself have acknowledged, that the system of taxation, which you have been considering, is a very bad one, is amazingly absurd, and very impoverishing; and that hardly any one part thereof is what it ought to be, either in the manner of assessing, or of

collecting, or in the various ways of expending the same. Now, after this frank confession, with what face can Monsieur Necker, or can any of the ministers of France, who have countenanced Dr. Franklin, and supported his cause, object to the bitterest remonstrances of the French parliaments, or to the most violent outrages of the people, even were they to break forth into open rebellion? – Or will you pretend to say, that Frenchmen have not at least as just a right to throw off those loads of numerous and absurdly complicated taxes, under which they have so long groaned, as the Americans had for revolting from under the British government . . . .   (pp. 21–4)

It was true that the French had 200,000 bayonets ready to maintain order, but, says Tucker, 'first to teach one the principles of rebellion, and then to condemn them, if they should offer to rebel, is characteristical of the worst of beings, whose employment is said to be, first to tempt, and then to punish'. He reminds the French 'that there are critical junctures, even in the most despotic countries, when government must yield to popular clamour, and give up the supposed delinquents as victims to appease an enraged mob, or fall a sacrifice itself'. Why therefore do the French support the American cause? With so many combustibles already existing in France, 'are you really resolved to set fire to the pile, and to blow the flames, in order to show, how dextrously you can extinguish them?' (pp. 24–5). Thus Tucker predicted the impact of the American Revolution on France and anticipated what took place eight years later when the combustibles to which he referred were ignited. One wonders if Necker recalled this warning at the time of his second dismissal, two days before the fall of the Bastille. It is curious also that it was Tucker, not Burke, who should have foreseen the events against which Burke himself was to react so violently.

In letter III Tucker reverses the hypothesis and predicates an English victory over the French. The results would be just as unfortunate. The French would then be too poor to buy the goods that the English were so adept at making. That people would buy the goods they wanted regardless of national antipathies was indicated by the fact that English goods were still being sold to the Americans, despite the war, and at prices at least 40 per cent higher than before.

American Affairs

Jealousy of trade was the theme of letter IV. Tucker mentions having received from Turgot a copy of the proceedings at the Bed of Justice ceremony at Versailles in March 1776, at which he had succeeded in abolishing many of the trade restrictions which plagued France. 'But alas! his triumph was but short; – a fine dream (beau Rêve) as he expressed it in a subsequent letter, a phantom, and no reality. And the reward he received, for attempting to do his country such eminent service, was to be discarded' (p. 53). The English had been more fortunate in the ending of monopolies and often in a characteristically English way. 'For though in such a constitution as ours, it is dangerous to meddle with antient charters, even where their faults are very apparent, yet we frequently correct their bad affects, without seeming to touch the foundation' (p. 56). National jealousy of trade is even unnecessary and wrong, especially between two countries as different as England or France. The Frenchman excels in fashion and ornaments; the Englishman in more practical articles of general use. Let each country specialise in what it can do best and they will be good customers instead of rivals.

In the next letter, Tucker casts a sceptical eye on the benefits which were supposed to accrue if England were victorious over her colonies. He pours scorn on all of them, whether they related to trade or to national glory. The only explanation he can find for the behaviour of all parties in the war is Bishop Butler's theory of collective insanity. Tucker concludes that there is no convincing case to be made for English conduct. On the contrary, 'Were America this moment to lay herself at our feet and to submit to a *carte blanche*, provided we take her again into favour, – it is evidently our interest not to accept such a present' (p. 87). England had been involved in a similar situation when she claimed lands in France centuries before. 'Happily for our country, happily, I say, for Old England, your female commander, Joan d'Arc, rescued us at last from the danger of being victorious. . . . And cannot you find one Joan d'Arc in modern days to command his most Christian majesty's fleets and armies, in order to drive us back into our own island?' (p. 88). The English were now reconciled to the loss of French territory because they realised that such involvement was not to their best interests. Yet how much truer this was of America, which was thousands of miles away and not desirable in any respect.

In letter VIII Tucker supposes the Americans victorious over a decadent England, now without bishops, nobles or kings.

> This, Sir, you know is the language of that celebrated republican, Dr. Price. But perhaps you have never yet been told the name of the original author of that prophetic sentence: It was your own predecessor, the late Monsieur Turgot. (Now he is dead I am at liberty to declare it.) In a letter of his, dated Paris 18th of February 1777, and sent to Glocester, he says, *Je sais des voeux pour la liberté des Americains, parceque ce sera le premier exemple d'un grand peuple, que n'ait ni rois, ni noblesse.* (What infatuation! He himself being, as I am informed, of a noble family of antient extraction.) But however they may be, as Dr. Price, when he went to Paris, conversed with Monsieur Turgot, it is probable, that he learnt this famous aphorism from him. For in his famous pamphlet in favour of America, he adopted this very expression. (pp. 92–3).

Tucker sees the victorious Americas awakening from their 'golden dream' to find that their own leaders make far greater demands on them than the British ever did. He imagines a rueful American orator reflecting on their changed circumstances: the enforcement of severe punishments instead of British laxity; the limitation of the freedom of speech and press; the quarrels that would break out once British control, which had temporarily united them, was removed; the necessity to pay for their own defence, and the taxes – not just 3d. on a pound of tea but real taxes – on practically everything. As for their future, Tucker was not optimistic. He foresaw nothing but strife. At least they would be no threat to others, since they would be so busy prosecuting their own disputes. Thus the folly of fighting the war was clear: the winners would be the losers and *vice versa*.

Tucker's last letter included his plan for pacification, which had appeared separately in the *Gentleman's Magazine* the previous year signed 'Cassandra'. Its main provisions were for territory to be set aside for the Loyalists in New York, the Carolinas and Georgia, with the rest to be given independence. The previous system of government was to be restored in the Loyalist colonies, but after ten years each assembly would be free to decide its own form of government. It is clear he had no desire to retain control of any part of America, but wanted to make sure that the Loyalists were provided for. In the event, of course, most of them were settled in the Canadian provinces.

The date at the end of the *Letters* is 28 November 1781, but there is a postscript.

> This moment an account is arrived, that the brave Cornwallis with his little army has been obliged to submit to a force of superior numbers. I am at a loss what to say on this occasion – To congratulate my country on being defeated is contrary to that decency which is due to the public. And yet, if this defeat should terminate in a total separation from America, it would be one of the happiest events, that hath ever happened to Great Britain. (p. 140)

He was tempted to offer condolences to the French. 'Time will shew what you have got and what we have lost, by the progresses of the present war' (p. 141). What time did show was that the huge debt accumulated by France in pursuit of this war helped to speed the coming of the French Revolution. In the meantime, Admiral de Grasse, whose fleet was the chief factor in the surrender at Yorktown, had unwittingly provided Tucker with his Joan of Arc.

10 The *Treatise Concerning Civil Government*

Tucker was only one of a large number of pamphleteers expressing an opinion on the American Revolution, although his solution of the problem had few supporters at the beginning. His old opponent John Wesley was moved to write *A Calm Address to our American Colonies* in 1775. Wesley's arguments were somewhat similar to those of Tucker: he, too, blamed the anti-monarchists in England for stirring up the colonists in America for their own selfish ends. As for taxation, if Parliament had the right to make laws of any kind for the colonies, it also had the right to impose taxes on them. He urged the Americans to come to their senses, since they were as free under the present system as they could ever be. Republican governments, even that of Holland, tended to be more tyrannical than the mild regime under which they lived. He was not optimistic, however. In a letter to a friend dated 26 December 1775 he wrote,

> I see no possibility of accommodation. The one point is, has the supreme power a right to tax, or not? If they have, they cannot, they ought not to, give it up. But I say, as Dean Tucker, 'Let them drop.' Cut off all other connexion with them than we have with Holland or Germany. Four-and-thirty millions they have cost us to support them since Queen Anne died. Let them cost us no more. Let them have their desire, and support themselves.[1]

Not all those who expressed an opinion on America were so easily converted by Tucker. Dr Samuel Johnson had something to say on the matter in his *Taxation no Tyranny*, also of 1775:

> The Dean of Gloucester has proposed, and seems to propose it seriously, that we should at once release our claims, declare

The Treatise Concerning Civil Government 215

them masters of themselves, and whistle them down the wind. His opinion is, that our gain from them will be the same, and our expense less. What they can have most cheaply from Britain, they will still buy, what they can sell to us at the highest price they will sell.

It is however a little hard, that having so lately fought and conquered for their safety, we should govern them no longer. By letting them loose before the war, how many millions might have been saved. One wild proposal is best answered by another. Let us restore to the French what we have taken from them. We shall see our colonists at our feet, when they have an enemy so near them.[2]

He, too, believed that the fault lay with Englishmen who had encouraged American resistance to the Stamp Act.

We have on record several other comments by Dr Johnson on Tucker, thanks to the letters of Hannah More. She and her sisters operated a well-regarded girls' school in Bristol, although she did not teach there herself after 1767. In the 1770s she started her annual visits to London, where she met most of the famous people of the day. Among them were Joshua Reynolds, Dr Johnson, and her special friend, David Garrick. This was the period when she established her reputation as an author with several volumes of verse and a play, *Percy, a Tragedy in Five Acts*, which was a great success when performed at Covent Garden in 1777. After Garrick's death in 1779, she gradually withdrew from the fashionable world of the capital, and turned to the Sunday schools and improving tracts which were responsible for her later renown. At this time, however, she basked in the admiration of a group of literary and artistic friends which included Tucker.

Since he was present, along with Johnson and Garrick, at a *petite assemblée* Hannah held in London in the first half of 1776, we know that he and the famous Doctor had met. Hannah once asked Johnson for his opinion of Tucker, which he gave as follows:

> I look upon the Dean of Gloucester to be one of the few excellent writers of this period. I differ from him in opinion, and have expressed that difference in my writings; but I hope what I wrote did not indicate what I did not feel, for I felt no acrimony. No person, however learned, can read his writings without

improvement. He is sure to find something he did not know before.

After quoting this, Hannah went on in her letter,

> I told him the Dean did not value himself on elegance of style. He said he knew nobody whose style was more perspicuous, manly, and vigorous, or better suited to his subject. I was not a little pleased with this tribute to the worthy Dean's merit, from such a judge of merit; that man, too, professedly differing from him in opinion.[3]

Tucker's own comments on his style are also available, since Hannah on one occasion asked him if it would not be desirable for him to polish it more. He replied, 'Oh, no, they don't expect a fine style from me. All that I care for are the authenticity of my facts, and the truth of my principles.' When she told him that the subjects on which he wrote were beyond her power of comprehension, he replied, 'Pish! No such thing! Common sense will ever appeal to common sense.'[4]

Hannah had also valiantly defended Tucker from the slings and arrows of Edmund Burke.

> I have told the Reynolds's how angry I am with Burke for an unhandsome paragraph on the Dean of Gloucester. They are warm friends, but I would not give up my point. They seem to think that the man and the politician are different things: but I do not see why a person should not be bound to speak truth in the House of Commons as much as in his own house.[5]

One of her biographers refers to an anecdote frequently told by Hannah of the time when, by coincidence, 'Edmund Burke, Dean Tucker and Mrs Macaulay called upon her in Park-Street, Bristol, on the same morning, fortunately in succession, as they were all at that time writing against each other.'[6] Mrs Macaulay was a well-known republican historian who had recently attacked Burke in print.

David Garrick, in a letter in 1777 from Lord Palmerston's estate in Hampshire, where he had been convalescing from an illness, wrote to Hannah,

The Treatise Concerning Civil Government

> Your friend, the Dean of Gloucester, has most kindly sent me his book against Locke and his followers. I have read it with care, and like it, some few trifling matters excepted, but I cannot be conceited enough to make my objections in the margin of his book. What shall I do? You are, I suppose, in the same predicament.[7]

This is a reference to the early version of what was to be published in 1781 as Tucker's *Treatise Concerning Civil Government*. He had been promising such a work for years. In the fifth tract on American affairs he promised that 'Mr. Locke's theory of Government will be examined at large ... in a tract especially for that purpose'. In both the *Letter to Edmund Burke* and the *Series of Answers* he excused himself for the delay in the appearance of his 'animadversions', on the subject, giving as his reasons that the times were too turbulent for the public to be interested in 'metaphysical speculations', although he was still working on it. The fruit of his labours was first made available in a privately printed form to about fifty of his friends, under the title of *The Notions of Mr. Locke and his Followers*. Unlike Garrick, some of the recipients had no qualms about making comments in the margins, so that he was able to take these criticisms into account in the final version of the *Treatise*. He also left out, on the advice of his friends, a preliminary discourse enumerating Locke's errors in great detail, since they thought it was unnecessarily provocative. Even then Tucker published the book with some reluctance.

> When I first undertook the task of answering Mr. Locke, I thought it necessary to proceed with the greater caution, as I had so many popular prejudices to encounter with. Mr. Locke's writings on government had obtained a reputation and character little short of political infallibility; therefore any man who dared to depart from this standard of orthodoxy was deemed a state-heretic, or condemned of course, as an enemy to the just and unalienable rights of society.[8]

That this should still be the case this late in the century is striking, since Locke's version of the contract theory had been subjected to sporadic criticism starting with that of his own pupil, the third Earl of Shaftesbury, in his *Characteristicks*, and continuing with such thinkers as Hutcheson, Hume, and, more recently, Blackstone and Bentham. But, because of its links with the Glorious Revolution and its flattering conclusion that the authority of the government depended on the consent of the people, the doctrine retained its popularity – and a respectability that it might not have had if it had not been attached to the revered name of Locke. In fact, its critics generally avoided the kind of direct attack on Locke and his 'Second Treatise of Civil Government' in the *Two Treatises of Civil Government* (1690), which was undertaken by Tucker.

The notion of popular sovereignty had actually taken a new lease on life since the publication of Rousseau's *Du contrat social* in 1762. The British and American radicals seized on these revolutionary ideas, which could be propagated as part of a British tradition legitimised by the sacred name of Locke. This is why, when he wanted to attack Dr Priestley and Dr Price, the two most influential radicals of his day, Tucker was forced to do something about Locke. If he could have disarmed his opponents by showing that Locke was really a conservative, he doubtless would have done so. But this was impossible, since Locke's words were there for all to see, and many of them supported a revolutionary interpretation. Thus there was no way of avoiding a confrontation with Locke as well as his contemporary disciples.

In the Preface, therefore, Tucker defends himself against an obvious criticism: that Locke himself would never have supported the 'dangerous consequences' drawn by his followers from his principles. No one, of course, could know what position Locke would have taken in the last quarter of the eighteenth century. However, during Locke's own lifetime a friend of his, the Irish philosopher William Molyneux, inspired by the 'Second Treatise', published a book calling for the legislative independence of Ireland. In this work, *The Case of Ireland's Being Bound by Acts of Parliament in England Stated*, he used such intemperate language as 'I have no other notion of slavery; but being bound by a law, to which I do not consent' and 'To tax me without consent is little better, if at all, than down-right robbing me.'[9] When asked for his opinion of the book by the author, Locke, with his usual caution, did not commit himself (he never did acknowledge that he was the author of the *Two Treatises of Civil Government*, except in his will), but he did not disown Molyneux, even though the book was condemned by the British House of Commons. Here was an

The Treatise Concerning Civil Government 219

example of revolutionary use being made of Locke's ideas while he was still alive.

In order to save time, Tucker began by delineating those issues on which he was not prepared to dispute with Locke. He accepted that there is a sense in which 'no man is born the *political* subject of another', that government is a matter of 'public trust, not of private property', and above all, that there is a right of revolution if all other recourses had failed when dealing with a ruler who had betrayed this trust. 'All these points being previously settled, there can be no controversy between Mr. Locke's disciples and me about the patriarchal scheme in any of its branches, or indeed about any sort of an indefeasible hereditary right whatever: – Much less about unlimited passive obedience, and non-resistance' (pp. 3–4).

In the hope that he had thus allayed any suspicion that he was trying to revive the Jacobite cause, Tucker went on to make clear exactly where the difference between the Lockians and himself lay. The sole question to be decided was, 'Whether that government is to be justly deemed an usurpation, which is not founded on the *express* mutual compact of all the parties interested therein, or belonging thereunto' (p. 4). Tucker lets them speak for themselves in sixteen pages of quotations from their works. In addition to Locke's 'Second Treatise' and Molyneux's *Case of Ireland*, he uses the 1771 edition of Dr Joseph Priestley's *Essay on the First Principles of Government* and Dr Richard Price's *Observations on the Nature of Civil Liberty*, an influential tract of 1776.

Both Price and Priestley were Dissenting clergymen with a wide range of interests, as witnessed by important discoveries in chemistry in the case of Priestley. They were both associated with Lord Shelburne, Price as a friend and adviser of many years' standing and Priestley as his librarian from 1772 to 1780. Their radical sympathies led them to welcome the French Revolution when it broke out. It was Price's sermon before the Revolution Society in 1789, published as *A Discourse on the Love of Our Country*, to which Burke replied with his *Reflections on the Revolution in France*. Priestley's defence of the Revolution in his *Letters to Burke* of 1791 was one of the reasons for his unpopularity with the mob, which destroyed his house near Birmingham the same year.

The burden of these selections is that society did not evolve naturally but is the result of a compact. Tucker chooses as most representative the words of Dr Priestley, 'the fairest, the most open, and ingenuous of all Mr. Locke's disciples, excepting honest, undissembling Rousseau'.

> To begin with first principles, we must, for the sake of gaining clear ideas on the subject, do what almost all political writers have done before us, that is, we must suppose a number of people existing, who experience the inconvenience of living independent and unconnected; who are exposed without redress, to insults and wrongs of every kind, and are too weak to procure to themselves many of the advantages, which they are sensible might easily be compassed by united strength. These people, if they would engage the protection of the whole body, and join their forces in enterprises and undertakings calculated for their common good, must voluntarily resign some part of their natural liberty, and submit their conduct to the direction of the community: for without these concessions, an alliance cannot be formed. (Priestley, *Letters to Burke*, p. 6; quoted in Tucker's *Treatise*, p. 23)

Tucker's reaction is one of surprise that the author would assume not that men had a natural propensity to live in groups but that they had to be brought together by artificial means, 'driven by necessity, and not drawn by inclination to seek for any sort of civil government', which became 'rather as a necessary evil, than a positive good'. He notes, ironically, that although the Lockians were not prepared to allow human nature any innate need to live in society, they made up for this by insisting that each individual had an innate right to choose whether or not he wished to join such a society. But that was not all:

> For Mr. Locke and his followers have extended the privilege of voting, or of giving *actual* consent, in all the affairs of government and legislation, beyond what was ever dreamt of before in this, or any other civilized country; – Nay, according to their leading principles, it ought to be extended still much farther than even they themselves have done.... Now, according to the principles of Mr. Locke and his followers, ... the right of voting is not annexed to land, or franchises, to condition, age, or sex; but to human nature itself, and to moral agency.... For whosoever

is a moral agent is a person; and personality is the only foundation of the right of voting. To suppose the contrary, we have been lately told by a Right Reverend Editor of Mr. Locke, is gross ignorance, or something worse. (pp. 25–7)

Tucker believed that this idea was derived from the great principle of freedom of conscience in religion, with which he heartily agreed. But to apply it to civil society created a number of problems. For example, how can you deny women, and even children, the right to vote except by proving to everyone's satisfaction, including theirs, that they are not moral agents. Tucker touched on a sore spot here, because his opponents had no satisfactory answer, at least as far as women were concerned, yet they had no intention of giving women the vote. Tucker was not just trying to make a debating point here: although he believed the franchise was a privilege, not to be handed out indiscriminately, he honestly did not believe that there was any good reason for excluding women. As he wrote near the end of the *Treatise*,

During an experience of upwards of fifty years, I have observed, that in every contested election, the females of all ranks, ages, and conditions both in high and in low life, married or unmarried, those of rigid, and those of easy virtue, – so far from not concerning themselves at all in such matters, – have entered into the spirit of electioneering with much greater zeal, and keener appetites than the males. (p. 365)

Another question raised by the practical application of the doctrine of consent was this: Why should a dissident have to accept the will of the majority? 'For as a plurality of votes is no evidence of infallibility, a man's inward conviction may not be altered by his being overpowered by numbers' (p. 34). Locke himself admitted that government would be impossible without majority rule, but he failed to justify it except on pragmatic grounds. Priestley attempted to face the dilemma by having his original contractors agree unanimously to be bound by a majority. But for Tucker this is no more satisfactory. In addition to the lack of actual evidence that unanimous agreement was ever obtained, there is the much more serious objection that inalienable rights cannot really be surrendered, and, even if they could, only those who made the agreement would be bound by such a surrender. Tucker concludes that, 'according to the Lockian system, nothing less than *unanimity* in every measure can keep such a society as this from the danger of breaking to pieces every moment; for a single *dissentient voice*, like the veto's [sic] of the republican tyrants of Poland, is sufficient to throw the whole constitution of the state into chaos and confusion' (p. 36).

The same argument applies to the surrender of these rights to representatives. It cannot be done if we accept Locke's principle. For support, Tucker calls upon his opponent Dr Price, who had said,

> As no people can lawfully surrender their religious liberty, by giving up their right of judging for themselves in religion, ... so neither can any civil societies lawfully surrender their civil liberty, by giving up to any extraneous jurisdiction their power of legislating for themselves, and disposing of their property. Such a cession being inconsistent with the unalienable rights of human nature would either bind not at all, or bind only the individuals who made it.
> (*Observations on the Nature of Civil Liberty*, p. 15, quoted in Tucker's *Treatise*, p. 37)

Price was here defending the Americans from English usurpations, but, as Tucker points out, the same argument could be used against any representative assembly in England or America.

Only 'honest, undissembling' Rousseau, a man who never 'boggled at consequences', faced the issue: 'The English imagine, they are a free people: they are however mistaken: they are only free during the election of members of parliament. When these are chosen, they become slaves again' (*Du contrat social*, ch. 15, as quoted in Tucker's *Treatise*, p. 39). There was one further problem, which Tucker mentions later on: 'What express covenant or stipulation have Mess. Priestley, or Price made with the rest of the members of parliament, – perhaps not so few as 550 in number, whom they do *not* elect – and for whom they have no votes to give?' (p. 144). How far we have come from the right of the individual not to be bound by laws to which he has not given his consent. He not only has to be bound by majority decisions, but also must transfer his inalienable rights to a representative and, worse still, to

The Treatise Concerning Civil Government

hundreds of others, over whom he does not even have the measure of control contained in his single vote.

What all this means is that, if the doctrine of individual consent is to be taken literally, it can only apply, even partially, as its supporters in their candid moments admitted, to a state small enough for everyone to be able to assemble to decide in person all the issues – 'some paultry village, consisting of a few thatched cottages', as Tucker puts it (p. 40).

The one way out of these entanglements, Tucker concludes later, is to admit that there are only two kinds of genuinely inalienable rights: 'the functions of nature and the duties of religion'. The reason is that they are not transferable: no one else can eat or drink for us, nor can anyone perform our religious duties in our stead. But it is possible for political affairs to be carried out by proxy, as they are transferable and therefore not inalienable. This is admitted in their franker moments by Locke and most of the others, except, of course, Rousseau, 'who is generally consistent whether in truth, or error' (p. 236). Nevertheless, Tucker readily admits that, despite the difficulties, inalienable rights have become formidable weapons in the hands of radicals.

He next turns to another weakness of the social contract. If we take it seriously, 'no man ought to be deemed a member of the state politic, 'till he had enrolled himself among the number of its members by some express and positive engagement' (p. 43). This is no more than a paraphrase of several very explicit passages in Locke. One of the most obvious criticisms of the contract as an actual historical occurrence is that we have no evidence that it ever took place. But, even if it did, how does it bind later generations? Tucker uses as an example a father with seven sons. For the sake of argument let us allow that the father has personally contracted to become a British subject; but what of his sons? Do they not owe any obligations to the country of their birth? Suppose that the eldest son inherits the land and the other six are left the movable property. Locke attempts to provide for the case of the first son, at least, by introducing the concept of *tacit* consent. By accepting the land he has accepted the conditions that go with owning it. The father, says Locke, 'may oblige his son to be of that community, if he will enjoy those possessions, which were his father's; because the estate being the father's property, he may dispose, or settle it as he pleases' (*Two Treatises*, § 116, quoted in Tucker's *Treatise*, p. 45).

Tucker quickly points out the flaw here. Where did the father acquire the right to attach conditions to the possession of his property after his death? Presumably no such rights exist in the state of nature, where the property would revert to the public domain.

> But if it should be said, that he derived the right of bequeathing land, and of annexing various conditions to the bequest, from the positive laws of civil society (which is the truth of the case, and which Mr. Locke himself is obliged to allow, by stiling this father, a subject of some commonwealth) then I ask, why could not the commonwealth, if it so pleased, exercise the same right itself, which it had empowered the father to exercise? Why could not the state oblige the other six sons, as well as the eldest, to perform the several offices, and discharge the duties civil and military, of loyal subjects, if the exigencies of the state should so require? (p. 47)

And what essential difference is there, in this case, between the landowning son and his brothers? The only possible way out, in Tucker's eyes, is to accept 'that protection and allegiance, between prince and people, are reciprocal ties, and that the one necessarily infers the other, without the formality of an express personal covenant, or positive stipulation; so that if the duty of protection be performed on the one side, that of allegiance ought to be observed on the other, and vice versa' (p. 48).

One of the claims made by the Lockians, in line with their general presuppositions, is that taxes are free gifts rather than debts due for services rendered. After taking a detailed look at the various types of taxes and their historical origins, Tucker concludes that compulsory public taxation is a necessity for the existence of government, and remarks that after their declaration of independence the Americans resorted to it after the pattern of other states. However, this dispute is really superfluous to his major argument, since it is merely another aspect of the whole question of contract and will depend on how narrowly that term is defined. To assume, as Locke and his followers do in some of their statements, that personal consent is required before each and every tax is to be paid (witness Molyneux's 'To tax me without my own consent is little better, if at all, than down-right robbing me'),

The Treatise Concerning Civil Government

is so far removed from the real world as to be hardly worthy of comment, much less an extended rebuttal. But people were taking such ideas seriously in Tucker's day and he obviously felt that some solid facts would dispel much of the haze obscuring the issue.

He now tackles another 'capital error' of the Lockians. This is 'that dreadful notion, propagated by them with a kind of enthusiastic ardor, that *their system* of government is the only true one, in the nature of things: – And that all others, not built on this foundation, are, in deed and truth, so many detestable robberies, and barefaced usurpations of the unalienable rights of mankind.' In his mind this was 'in fact proclaiming war against all the governments upon earth, and exciting their subjects to rebel' (p. 81). Tucker notices here a similarity between the position adopted by the republicans and that of Sir Robert Filmer, against whom Locke wrote. For Filmer the heirs of a monarch retained the divine right to rule no matter how much time had elapsed since he had been deposed, and they remained a constant threat to successor governments, which were considered as nothing more than usurpers. Likewise, the Lockians called into question the legitimacy of any government that was not founded upon the consent of its people. The divine right of kings was replaced by the divine right of the people.

This represents another and disturbing side of the social-contract notion, because, if its opponents can say that there is no historical evidence that such a contract was made, its supporters can turn the tables by agreeing, and thus threatening the title of every government in the world. Dr Priestley himself says that 'all governments whatever have been, in some measure, compulsory, tyrannical, and oppressive in their origin'. Such a doctrine obviously undermined all political authority and contained the seed of continuous unrest and revolution, and all the misery that results from anarchy. It used to be a maxim, Tucker observes, 'not to be very inquisitive concerning the original title of the reigning powers' so long as they provided protection from outside enemies and a reasonable degree of justice and prosperity. How much better a basis this provided for peace and order than the constant question 'What is your title?' (pp. 85–6).

Although it is now acepted that Locke wrote his *Two Treatises* before the Glorious Revolution, they were generally regarded, after their publication in 1690, as a justification for the change in rulers at that time. 'We have therefore a right to expect, that his fundamental, political maxims tend immediately and directly to vindicate this necessary measure. How great therefore will be our disappointment, if the quite contrary should appear!' (p. 89). Tucker, of course, regarded the deposition of James II as completely justified. Locke's principles serve well for 'demolition', as he puts it, but what about rebuilding? Once James had gone, the people of Britain, according to the contract theory, had returned to a state of nature. Even if we did not demand that Locke's principles be observed to the letter, we should at least expect that all the adult males of the realm would have been consulted at a time when the whole legal basis of the state had been swept away. This, of course, did not happen.

> A few scores of noblemen, and a few hundreds of gentlemen, together with some of the aldermen and Common Council of London, met at Westminster, (but without any commission from the body of the people authorising them to meet) and requested (thereby empowering) the Prince and Princess of Orange to assume the royal prerogative, and to summon a new Parliament. (p. 95)

This Parliament proceeded to grant them sovereignty over Ireland and the colonies, as well as Britain, not only without the consent of the former but also without even informing them. Furthermore, in the Convention Parliament there was actually a majority against giving William the crown; the dissenters only acceded when he threatened to abandon them to James. In Ireland a minority of Protestants asked William to free them from James, who was the choice of the Catholics, an overwhelming majority in the land. How could this be explained on Lockian principles? Yet Molyneux, one of the ruling minority, demands independence and dedicates his book to King William!

There was also the current situation in America. Tucker directs his questions here especially at Dr Price, that tireless champion of American liberties. Are the Americans being governed according to the principles put forward by Dr Price? If we leave aside the tarring and feathering, and the plundering of Loyalists' property, and ask whether 'any of their Congresses, general or provincial, admit of that fundamental maxim of Mr. Locke, that every man

The Treatise Concerning Civil Government 227

has an unalienable right to obey no other laws, but those of his own making?', the answer must be a very definite 'No.' 'So far from it, that there are dreadful fines and confiscations, imprisonments, and even death made use of, as the only effectual means for obtaining that unanimity of sentiment so much boasted of by these new-fangled republicans, and so little practiced' (p. 105).

At this point Tucker inserts a brief defence of discretionary power, as embodied in, for example, the Declaratory Act, against critics such as Dr Price, who saw tyranny in such power. For Tucker, government must always be left with a residual and necessarily undefined power, because no constitutional arrangement can provide for every situation which might occur in the future. There must be an element of trust in the relationship between government and people. 'Yet can any man in his senses pretend to say, that the king and the parliament would be justifiable, or even excusable were they to abuse this discretionary power . . . so as to enslave the people by cruel, unjust and tyrannical laws?' (p. 110). He points out that even Filmer and the Jacobites do not defend such rulers, but, whereas they would defer punishment to the next world, he prefers it to take place here on earth, where it can act as a deterrent to others.

We now come to the conclusion of part I of the *Treatise*, the critique of Locke and his followers. Tucker admits that 'probably the original author, and several of his disciples never meant to draw conclusions so horrid in their nature, and so full of wanton treason and rebellion, as the Congresses have actually drawn from it in America, and as the republican factions are daily endeavouring to draw from it in England, had they power equal to their will' (p. 112). It is doubly unfortunate because, in his opinion, such excessive measures are not necessary to dispose of the patriarchal system of Filmer or the passive obedience doctrines of the Jacobites. These can be refuted without recourse to Locke. However, Tucker expresses satisfaction that he lives in a country where people are allowed freely to express such treasonable thoughts, rather than in America, where their lives and property would be in danger. This only demonstrates again that English 'slavery' is preferable to American 'liberty'!

In part II, 'The True Basis of Civil Government', Tucker offers, with some humility, his alternative to Locke's theory of the origins of the state. As might have been expected, it emphasises the social propensities of man. Unlike the contract theorists, he believes that mankind not only has 'a capacity for becoming members of a civil society', but also an inclination for doing so, and 'that the natural instinct precedes the capacity, much in the same manner, tho' not with the same strength, or in the same degree, as the innate instincts of individuals towards food, or of the species towards each other, precede the arts of cookery, and brewery, of marriage-ceremonies, and marriage-settlements' (p. 124).

Of what instincts is this general inclination composed? Tucker lists four: man is naturally gregarious; he needs the help of others, because of the unequal distribution of talents; he can make known his wants through language; and he enjoys helping others. In order to see how these instincts operate in practice, the obvious place to start is with the family, but, since Locke's most important objective was to refute the derivation of political authority from that of the father over his children, Tucker refrains from using that analogy, confident that it is not necessary for his argument. Instead, he tries to show how some form of civil government would arise spontaneously if 100 otherwise unconnected couples were brought together in isolation. As these couples went about seeking food and shelter, natural differences in the ability to perform various tasks would soon become apparent, and each individual would tend to devote his time to what he could do best, thus leading to a division of labour.

Human beings have another trait which results in a natural subordination in society: the inherent differences in dominance and submissiveness between various individuals. Whatever the explanation, there is no doubt that in any group of people we find what would today be called a 'pecking order'. Tucker mentions with approval the French term 'Le coq de village', used to describe an individual who dominates all the others in the vicinity. Affected therefore by differences in ability and temperament, as well as by their needs and their feelings of benevolence and gratitude, the 100 couples would soon become a society or economy founded on division of labour, and a political structure reflecting the differences in status accorded to individuals by the group. In Tucker's words, each 'would fall into that rank in society and that station in life, to which his talents and his genius spontaneously led him, – as naturally, I had almost said, a water finds its level' (p. 137).

The Treatise Concerning Civil Government

At this point, Tucker raises a question which is vital to any discussion of the social-contract theorists. Is the difference between them and critics such as Tucker only a matter of phraseology? Suppose that a Lockian were to say he meant only that 'no part of the human species, has a right to enslave the other'. Tucker would reply that, 'if you mean to say, that every man is a slave, who has not the power of electing his own law-giver, his own magistrate, his colonel, captain, or judge, I deny the position and call on you to prove it by better arguments, than your own bare assertion' (p. 138). However, if, when he talks about inalienable rights and social compacts, he means only that governors who abuse their power should be called to account, Tucker would heartily agree.

> But, surely, this is a very odd, and intricate way of expressing the plainest, and most obvious truths imaginable. Moreover, if you intended to say, that tho' government in general did not derive its existence from any personal contract between prince and people, between the governors and the governed; – yet, that it hath so much of what a civilian would term a *quasi-contract* in the nature of it, that the duties and obligations on both sides of the relation are altogether to the same effect, as if a particular contract, and a positive engagement had been entered into, – If this be your meaning, we are ready to join issue with you once more; – and this the rather, because of the ideas of a quasi-contract contain our own on this head, and those of every Constitutional Whig throughout the kingdom.   (p. 139)

Thus Tucker introduces his own substitute for the contract idea. It may seem odd that after his vigorous polemic against the whole concept he should decide to use a modified form of it himself. This is a measure of the immense popularity of the term as an analogy of the moral relationship between governor and governed. Despite its obvious weaknesses, it has been abandoned over the years only with reluctance, because it expresses, admittedly too sharply and legalistically, what is felt by most people to be a broad truth about political society. For Tucker this can be defined as follows:

> In all human trusts whatever, from the highest to the lowest, where there is a duty to be performed, which is not actually

expressed, specified or contracted for, – but nevertheless is strongly implied in the nature of the trust; – the obligation to perform the implied duty, is of the nature of a *quasi-contract*; – a contract as binding in the reason of things, and in the court of conscience, as the most solemn covenant that was ever made.

(p. 141)

The courts of equity, in his opinion, were concerned with little more than enforcing quasi-contracts.

But this does not appear to be what the Lockians really mean. If it were, why should they 'cavil at the phrases, implicit consent, tacit agreement, implied covenant, virtual representation, and the like?' (p. 139). Why is it that they believe that a 'man is a slave, who is obliged to submit to the best laws that ever were made, and to the mildest government, that ever existed, if he did not give his consent towards establishing the one, and enacting the other'? (p. 140). Tucker concludes that the key to the whole dispute is to be found in the word 'consent', and that, if his opponents are to be held to what they have actually said, they mean a degree of personal consent which goes far beyond the notion of quasi-contract.

Tucker is aware that all kinds of objections may be raised to his own theory, and he attempts to answer some of them. One of the first is especially interesting, because it exposes a problem which his analysis has hitherto ignored: the distinction made in political theory between the social contract and the contract of government. He imagines his objector accusing him of not distinguishing between *natural* society and *political* society. Even if we admit that man's herding instinct leads to some form of group life, this does not imply a political organisation.

> For no mere meeting together, or assemblage of the people, no contiguity of habitation, or vicinage of inhabitants ought to be allowed to constitute a state politic, till *legislation* hath been actually introduced, and *jurisdiction* exercised among them: – which it is apprehended, could not be done without common consent, or at least the consent of the major part. (p. 152)

This agreement would be based on fear rather than gregariousness, because only the apprehension of great danger would

The Treatise Concerning Civil Government 231

lead men to surrender as much of their natural liberty as they would be obliged to do.

Tucker replies first by challenging his objector to show when such a contract was entered into – when did a particular individual become a subject of Great Britain, if he were not born into that status. Secondly, if fear and insecurity drive a man into a political society, these motives would operate even more strongly in connection with natural society.

> Therefore, according to this system, neither the society which is called natural, nor that which is political can exist at all, till there has been a previous contract entered into for the safety and preservation of all parties. And yet methinks, it is rather difficult to conceive, how a connection could be formed, how terms could be settled, and a solemn contract entered into, for binding all parties, before men had once met together, or indeed before they could prudently, or safely trust themselves in the company of each other for this, or any other purpose.
> (pp. 155–6)

J. W. Gough accuses Tucker of misunderstanding Locke on the subject of contracts.

> He attacks Locke for supposing that there was a contract between king and subjects, and repeats the usual objections about the occasion when the contract was made in England.... But Locke never said that there was a contract between king and people; on the contrary his position was really the same as what Tucker suggests as an alternative, but without the additional and unnecessary complication of the quasi-contract.[10]

There are several answers that Tucker could have made to this type of criticism. First, he was criticising not just Locke but also his followers, who were often more explicit than Locke on this point. Secondly, his work is an attack on the whole concept of the contract, including the social contract, and he uses most of the arguments advanced against it by Gough himself. Thirdly, there is some question as to the validity of the distinction itself, which Gouch takes for granted. The complexity of the problem is indicated by the fact that Priestley and Pufendorf had felt it necessary to introduce a third contract between the two already mentioned. This was a compact whereby the newly constituted society unanimously consented to be bound in future by a majority. Tucker himself had suggested, in the passage quoted above, the need for yet another contract, to be entered into before the social contract: an agreement providing safe conduct for the participants. The more closely one looks at the original idea, the more it seems to come apart in one's hands.

No time is specified for the interval between the social and political contracts, but it seems likely that, if they actually occurred, it would need to be very short: for all practical purposes, they would have to be simultaneous. The assembled individuals would probably have to include the political arrangements – how the first ruler was to be chosen and the terms of office – in their original discussion before finalising the contract. Although the contract of government was the more tangible of the various subdivisions, since there were historical examples of actual covenants of this type, it was the one that was gradually dispensed with. As Gough points out, Locke replaced it with the notion of a 'trust' or 'fiduciary power'. The reason, of course, was that any contract with a ruler could be interpreted as a Hobbesian contract of submission in which the people surrendered all. What was attenuated in Locke disappeared completely in Rousseau, who insisted that sovereignty remained with the people.

There is another point at which two or more contracts would appear to be superfluous. That is when someone who is born after the original contract was made gives his tacit personal consent to the arrangement by deciding not to leave the country. When this happens, he is dealing with both the society and the political system, so that he is simultaneously entering into a social contract and a contract of government. Thus it can be seen that Tucker had several good arguments in his favour for not splitting the contract. That he did not go into this possibility in further detail is probably owing to the fact that the idea had so little credibility for him in the first place.

He does recognise the existence of one type of contract: that which occurs when a private society is incorporated. A person joining such an organisation surrenders certain liberties and takes on certain responsibilities. But, in addition to the fact that the day and year of such an agreement can be named, and the circumstances of its foundation known, it has nothing to do with civil government. Tucker observes 'that in the infancy of states and empires, political societies were not formed at once, as guilds of trades, or companies of mercantile adventurers, or bodies politic are formed at present, by means of paper, parchment, and wax, signing and sealing but . . . grew up by degrees from small, and in a manner, imperceptible beginnings' (p. 159). Put more rhetorically, this could be the later Burke speaking. He continues,

> That which the Lockians ought to have said, is probably to this effect, that tho' it be absurd to suppose, that civil government in general took its rise from previous conventions, and mutual stipulations actually entered into between party and party; – and tho', whenever such a contract as here supposed did take place, at some very extraordinary conjuncture, – (a contract, by the by, which could only bind the contracting parties:) – Yet as civil government in general is in reality a public trust, be the origin, and the form of it whatever they may; – there must be some covenant or other supposed or implied as a condition necessarily annexed to every degree of discretionary power, whether expressed or not. – Had they said only this, they would have said the truth; and their doctrine would have actually coincided with the ideas of a 'quasi-contract' before mentioned. Nay more, they would have avoided all those paradoxes, which attend their present system, and render it one of the most mischievous, as well as ridiculous schemes that ever disgraced the reasoning faculties of human nature. (pp. 160–1)

But, it could be objected, there were actual historical contracts which limited the powers of kings, the best-known example being the Magna Carta. Tucker replies that these contracts were negotiated from strength by aristocratic heads of clans or chieftains of armed retainers. There was no evidence that the power of these men was obtained by delegation from the people. The barons who dealt with King John were no more interested in the rights of those below them than George Washington was in the liberty of his slaves.

If we accept the quasi-contract as an adequate way of describing the relationship between rulers and ruled, what is the best means of enforcing it? In order to answer this question, Tucker undertakes a comparison of monarchy, aristocracy and democracy. He concludes that none is perfect, and that democracy in its pure form is not even feasible except at the village level. If the example of Athenian democracy is advanced, Tucker retorts that the citizens of Athens were very much a minority, something like the Liverymen of London, and that had it survived it would have become an hereditary aristocracy like Venice. A 'mixt' constitution, which combined the best features of monarchy, aristocracy and democracy, seems to him the most desirable. This was, of course, a belief shared with the vast majority of his countrymen.

Since Britain already enjoyed such a constitution, the only question that remained was whether there was a proper balance between the parts. Tucker disagreed strongly with those who suggested, as did the Whig opposition, that the influence of the Crown had increased. There was no evidence that bribery was any worse; the cost of disputed elections was far more than the income received by a placeman; and, most convincingly, when the 'outs' obtained office they never laid any charges against those they had accused. In any case, elections were rarely fought on national issues but over which family or faction should have the seat. Opportunities there were for corruption, but these were produced by the possession of colonies and the fighting of wars, both of which demanded heavy expenditure and provided opportunities for peculation. Yet the opposition ignored these, while raising a hue and cry over the cost of the King's kitchen.

There seemed to be little controversy about the power of the aristocrats, which was, if anything, diminishing. The same was not true of the popular part of the constitution. The programme of the Lockians called for more equal representation of the people as regards both numbers and property, as well as for annual or at least triennial elections. Tucker is against having each member represent an equal number of people, for practical reasons. Since London already exerted enough influence with eight members to secure, in his eyes, more than its share of public money and influence, what would it not be able to do with its representation increased in proportion to its population? To him London, with its disease and vice, was already too large and should not be given further encouragement. The Gordon riots of the preceding year only confirmed his opinion. As for annual elections, which were advocated on the grounds that they would eliminate bribery, Tucker felt that, whether this was true or not, the practically

The Treatise Concerning Civil Government

continuous electioneering with its attendant evils would bring trade to a standstill.

In his discussion of representation, Tucker points out the ambiguity of the Lockian position on property.

> Mr. Locke himself strongly leans towards the doctrine of representing property – and many of his followers directly maintain it. – Though the notion itself is little less than a contradiction to their favourite grand principle of unalienable rights belonging to each individual, whether poor or rich. For if such rights do belong to any beings whatever, they must belong to person, not to property. Moreover, according to this doctrine, every man, who has no property, ought to have no vote, notwithstanding the supposed unalienable rights of his nature. And a rich man, with large and extensive property, ought to have many votes in proportion to his riches. Consequently the Grand Turk, and every other despot, who is the only rich man, being the proprietor and lord of all, is justly entitled to every vote within his dominions: – Or rather, he is the only rightful voter and therefore represents all property in his own person. What a Revolution is this! (pp. 261–2)

Tucker's own criterion for the franchise is essentially as follows:

> Though it would be highly absurd to admit indiscriminately every individual moral-agent to be a voter, yet true policy requires that the voters shold be so numerous and their qualifications respecting property be so circumstanced, that the actual voters could not combine against the non-voters, without combining against themselves, against their nearest friends, acquaintances, and relations. . . . [The qualification for voting] ought to be placed in such a mediocrity of condition, between the two extremes of great riches, and of wretched poverty, that no sober, diligent, and frugal man could well fail of raising himself by his industry, in a course of years to the honourable distinction of a voter; – and that almost every idle, vicious, and abandoned spendthrift would be in danger of sinking beneath, and of being degraded from the privilege of voting.
> (pp. 275–6)

The current voting qualifications were acceptable, but they had to be vigorously enforced in order to eliminate abuses. For example, a requirement that all taxes should be paid a full year before the entitlement to vote would put an end to the practice of splitting freeholds for election purposes. Tucker also proposed qualifications for the candidate, including the ownership of substantial property in the constituency he sought to represent, so that he would have a genuine interest in its welfare. All this was gone into in considerable detail, with the hope that at some point a regulating bill could be put before Parliament.

At one point in his discussion of the constitution, Tucker offered a convenient summation of the reasons for his strong anti-democratic bias:

During an attentive observation, and the experience of 50 years, sorry I am to say, but truth obliges me to do it, that I hardly ever knew an unpopular measure to be in itself a bad one, or a popular one to be truly salutary. *Internally* the people violently opposed the best of all schemes for a commercial nation, – That of warehousing goods on importation, and paying the duties by degrees. They were also as bitterly averse to the making of turnpike roads, to the use of broadwheel waggons, to the enclosing and improving of lands, to the freedom of trade in cities and towns corporate, to the introduction of machines for abridging labour, and also to the admission of industrious foreigners to settle among them. Nay, they very lately were so absurd as to raise loud clamours against the execution of the act for preserving the public coin, and their own property from debasement and adulteration. *Externally*, they are perpetually calling out for new wars (though against their best customers) on the most frivolous or unjustifiable pretences. Moreover, if there was any convention or treaty to be broken through or disregarded, (the observance of which would have restored peace or prevented bloodshed) or if there was any new colony to be planted in a desart country, or conquest to be undertaken in a populous one, even in the most distant part of the globe. – All these measures, though totally opposite to a spirit of industry at home, and though the bane of a commercial nation, were sure to receive the applauses and huzzas of the

The Treatise Concerning Civil Government 237

unthinking multitude. Such was the *Vox Populi* for 50 years last past, which some persons blasphemously stile vox DEI.
(p. 212n.)

Part III is a collection of odds and ends related to the topic. Tucker's long discussion of the 'Gothic constitution' need not detain us, but his response to the 'cavils' of Major John Cartwright is worth glancing at. Cartwright, another 'Lockian', had recently written two pamphlets putting forth his views: *The Legislative Rights of the Commonalty Vindicated or, Take your Choice!* (second edition, 1777) and *The People's Barrier against Undue Influence and Corruption* ... (1780). Although he believed that the right of choosing representatives rested on personality alone, he referred Tucker to the Scriptures for reasons as to why women should not have the vote. He added, 'Were the Rev. Dean to receive no greater thanks from the Ministry than he is likely to obtain from the fair sex for such attempts, poor indeed would be his reward! Women know too well what God and Nature require of them, to put so absurd a claim for a share in the rights of election.'[11] Tucker says he would be happy to refute Cartwright from Scripture, but feels it is unnecessary, since Cartwright refutes himself on the following page, where he says that the sexes 'are equal in dignity with regard to God, and Salvation'. Cartwright's rather whimsical interpretation of Scripture is illustrated by another quotation, in which he claims that God himself only rules with the consent of the people.[12] As for Cartwright's reference to the possibility of ministerial rewards, Tucker says 'The Dean is a man, who, with a very moderate income, (which many people would think rather scanty) can truly say, that he has all he wishes to have, and more than sufficient to supply his wants' (p. 364).

Looking to the work of his predecessors for confirmation of his views, Tucker quotes from the writings of Aristotle, Cicero, Grotius and Hooker on the inherently social nature of man. His reading of the latter he found especially interesting, since Locke often buttresses his case by reference to the 'judicious Hooker'. Tucker was pleasantly surprised to find that Hooker's position was closer to his own than it was to that of Locke, who had been very selective in his quotations from the respected author of *The Laws of Ecclesiastical Polity*.

The final chapter of the book begins with a reference to the biblical injunction concerning rendering unto Caesar what is Caesar's. The Lockians can find little comfort here, since all the Roman rulers from Caesar to Nero were usurpers, yet the Bible approved. Tucker concludes that government is a trust regardless of how the ruler acquired his title. However, if the power, wisdom and goodness, which are the characteristics of good government, are lacking, then the ruler no longer has a right to his office. Thus Tucker admits that revolution can be justified under certain circumstances and in this he does not differ from Locke or most other political theorists. In any case, if one ruler were replaced by another one as a result of a revolution, he would be prepared to accept the inevitable peacefully and give his allegiance to the new ruler. What he could not accept was the alternative shared, in his opinion, by republican and Jacobite alike: that of agitating continually against any type of government but their own, on the grounds that its title was faulty. His own position, as summarised at the end of the book, is 'that every individual . . . ought to be subject in Christian sincerity, without guile or fraud, to the higher powers, the powers for the time being; notwithstanding any defect of title imputed to them' (p. 428).

Although Locke's ideas had been attacked earlier in the century, the man himself had been treated quite circumspectly. Hume even chided Hutcheson in 1743 for not being 'more express' in his condemnation of the theory of consent associated with Locke.[13] Hume did criticise Locke by name several times in his essay 'Of the Original Contract', first published in 1748, but his few words in the midst of a volume of essays obviously did not have the impact of a work specifically devoted to the subject. Furthermore, Tucker undertook his attack at a time when these ideas were being propagated by reformers with a substantial popular following. It is no wonder then that he took so long to get it out and that Hannah More, for example, reacted as she did.

The Dean of Gloucester has sent me his book against Locke, splendidly bound. I have not yet had the manners to write and thank him for it. I am afraid it will draw upon him a number of enemies and answers, which at his time of life cannot be very agreeable. I believe where the spirit of controversy has once possessed the mind, no time can weaken it.[14]

Several replies did appear, the most notable of which was probably that of Joseph Towers (1737–99) a London bookseller and editor, who was also a Dissenting minister associated with Dr Price at Newington Green.[15] Towers makes some common-sense criticisms of Tucker's juggling with property qualifications, but otherwise he refuses to come to grips with the hard core of Tucker's case. He produces moderate quotations from Locke to support his charge that Tucker misrepresented Locke and was 'combatting monsters of his own imagination', but he seems totally unaware of the legitimate questions which arise when the highly appealing notion of personal consent is diluted by reliance on majorities, representation and the concept of tacit consent.

One is left with the general impression that the *Treatise* was either received unfavourably or ignored. However, it may ultimately have had the effect that Tucker intended. The American Loyalist Jonathan Boucher, when writing about the American Revolution in 1797, had this to say:

> Mr. Locke had the good fortune to enjoy a pre-eminent reputation for political wisdom longer than most men who have degraded great abilities by employing them to promote the temporary purposes of party. Till the American war, he was looked up to as an oracle: and the whole nation implicitly pinned their faith in politics on his dogmas. But when the great controversy between the parent state and her colonies came to be agitated, men were under necessity of examining, thinking or judging for themselves. One consequence of their doing so was, that the high degree of infallibility, which, till then, had been ascribed to the name and the work of Locke was greatly lessened. At length, in 1781, Dr. Tucker, the celebrated Dean of Gloucester, wrote a Treatise (and one of the best he ever did write) on purpose to consider, examine and confute the notions of Mr. Locke and his followers, concerning the origin, extent, and end of civil government. Since that time writers in general venture to read Mr. Locke, as they do other authors, without being overawed by the unmerited popularity attached to his name.[16]

11 'A Well-Wisher to All Mankind'

In the years that followed the death of his first wife, Tucker made do with a housekeeper, but early in 1780 he ran into difficulties. After the death of his current housekeeper in February, he lost two replacements in two months. As he told Dr Adams, all he wanted was an old woman to look after an old man.[1] Then in a postscript to a letter of 4 April 1780, he wrote, 'I am at last fixt in an housekeeper, Mrs. Crow, a daughter of Mr. Crow the schoolmaster. If goodness consists in bulk, she must be at least twice as good as [I am]. Notwithstanding her size, she is the least eater and drinker that ever I knew.'[2]

But there was obviously more to her than size and it was not many months before she and the Dean were married. In a letter to Hannah More replying to her congratulations he says,

> I have very literally taken a help meet for me. She has all the useful qualifications but none of the brilliant... our tempers and dispositions, our pleasures, or pursuits, can hardly ever be brought to clash with each other. I reign sole monarch, or fancy I reign throughout the boundless regions of politics and metaphysics; whilst my queen acts the majestic part very well in the lesser domains of common sense, and common life. Whether these two empires may be so far extended as to approach each other, whereby we may hereafter complain of mutual encroachments, and quarrel about the limits, is more than I am able to foretell. But I think the probability is on the other side; because I do not feel a spark of ambition to invade her province, and she has too much sang froid on her part, to be capable of being worked up either into a metaphysical or political ferment.[3]

His new wife obviously was right for Tucker, if his frequent affectionate references to her in his letters are any indication. In 1782 he writes again to Hannah More, 'My good-natured, jolly

'A Well-Wisher to All Mankind' 241

Blowsabelle has made herself so necessary to me by the assiduity of her attendance, that I cannot dispense with her absence for a day.'[4] He often refers to her as 'Queen Joan'. His new domestic arrangements were of sufficient interest to be noted by an unknown versifier.

> When Israel's sons immersed in sin
> Brought turtle doves and pigeons in
> In hopes to be forgiven,
>
> Our Dean his penitence to shew
> In humblest form he chose a Crow
> To pave his way to heaven.[5]

In 1780 Tucker met a person who was to play a rather perplexing role in his life over the next few years. This was a young prodigy named John Henderson. Tucker first encountered him in a stage coach when he was about twenty-two. Henderson was born in Ireland but was brought to England at an early age by his father, who after serving as one of Wesley's itinerant preachers became a schoolmaster near Bristol and finally kept a lunatic asylum there. The son received some education at Wesley's school at Kingswood but was mostly self-educated. He taught Latin and Greek when he was twelve and, in addition to the principal European languages, knew Hebrew, Persian and Arabic. Tucker was so impressed by him that he immediately sent £200 to his father to get him started at Oxford. Henderson was matriculated at Pembroke College, where Dr Adams was Master, and was given Dr Johnson's old quarters. He soon became quite well-known. Dr Johnson and Burke, as well as Hannah More, took an interest in him. Even Boswell thought he was worth a visit. He was the subject of a number of anxious and exasperated letters between Tucker and several of his friends. One letter to Hannah More is unusual in that it contains a rare biographical detail. Tucker had sent £50 to Dr Adams at Oxford for the support of Henderson once he was settled in.

> But after he is entered what shall we do with him? This is a difficulty which neither Dr. Adams nor I can well resolve. He knows a great deal too much to want the instructions of a tutor.

And yet there is a knowledge, perhaps the most useful of any, in which he is deficient; – the knowledge of the world, and an experience in the ways of men. But this is a science which books and colleges are not calculated to teach. He talks well on all subjects; but he is dilatory, and seems unwilling to commit his thoughts to writing. I fear that he is a kind of voluptuary in learning, and regards books in the same view in which an alderman regards turtle. However, such parts and such talents as his, ought to have every advantage for displaying themselves. I felt the want of such assistance in my little way when I was somewhat in this situation; and therefore resolved with myself at an early period in life, that if ever Providence should enable me to call uncommon or useful talents out of obscurity I would do it. That opportunity has now been put into my hands.[6]

Unfortunately, Henderson did not live up to his promise. He began to drink heavily and his behaviour became more and more eccentric. Although he graduated in 1786, he never did settle on an occupation before his early death two years later.

Because of his publications during the American Revolution, Tucker attracted sufficient attention to be worthy of notice by Horace Walpole, who referred to him in several letters to one of his correspondents, the Rev. William Mason, Rector of Aston in Yorkshire. Mason enjoyed quite a respectable reputation in his own day as a serious poet, but he also published a number of satirical verses under the pseudonym of 'Malcolm M'Greggor'. In the 1770s and early 1780s he and Walpole shared a violent prejudice against the administration of Lord North and anyone who appeared to support it in print. Dr Shebbeare, a well-known writer on behalf of the ministry, and Dr Johnson, among others, were abused by Walpole as 'assassins pensioned to appease the champions and martyrs of freedom, and to recommend the chains and massacres prepared for America'.[7] Despite his objections to the war, Tucker did not escape censure, either. In 1775 Walpole, writing to Mason in despair at the current state of politics, said pettishly, 'Naturally I fly to books: there is a finis too, for I cannot read Dean Tucker, nor newspapers.'[8] In much the same mood he complained in 1781, 'Tucker has published his attack on Locke. In short we shall not stop till all virtue and all sense, as well as all Europe are our enemies.'[9]

Tucker received a brief mention in Mason's *Ode to Mr. Pinchbeck* of 1776, along with Dr Johnson, and a slightly longer one in his *Epistle to Dr. Shebbeare* of 1777. In the latter the poet imagines seeing a vanquished Congress

> Toast peace and plenty to their mother nation,
> Give three huzzas to George and to taxation,
> And beg, to make their loyal hearts the lighter
> He'd send them o'er Dean T .. k . r, with a mitre.

He also could not resist a reference to Tucker's oath that he would not accept a bishopric if one were offered:

> Hear me, like T. . k . r, swear, 'so help me muse!
> I write not for preferment's golden views'.[10]

When Tucker's *Treatise* finally appeared, Mason wrote to Walpole that he was 'somewhat of a blackguard' for reading it.

As I have in my time kept worse company than you ever did, and am more used to vulgarity, I have been able to read a great part of the Dean of Gloucester's long expected attack on Locke, but I am sure you will not be able to read a page of it; you could as soon drink gin with a Wapping landlady. I wish I could prevail on you to read the last paragraph which sums up his whole doctrine and which is neither more nor less than that of his worthy brother in the old song of the Vicar of Bray.

> That this is law I will maintain
> Unto my dying day, Sir,
> That whatsoever King shall reign
> I'll be the Vicar of Bray, Sir.[11]

Walpole's reply was a promise only to read the last sentence, if he came across the book, 'but I certainly will not buy it'.[12]

Mason, however, could not let the matter rest, and in 1782 another satirical poem issued from the pen of 'Malcolm M'Greggor', *The Dean and the Squire*. The Squire was Soame Jenyns, to whom this 'political eclogue' was dedicated. Jenyns was himself a writer of light verse, as well as of prose pieces on religion and politics. He was a country gentleman, justice of the peace, and member of Parliament from 1742 to 1780. About a year after Tucker's *Humble Address and Earnest Appeal* had appeared, Jenyns wrote a poem called *The American Coachman* in which he likened the American colonies to runaway horses who eventually return 'with bellies full of liberty but void of oats and hay'. In the last verse he wrote,

> Let all who view the instructive scene
> And patronize the plan,
> Give thanks to Glouceter's honest Dean,
> For, Tucker, – Thou'rt the man.[13]

It was no. VII of his *Disquisitions on Several Subjects*, entitled 'On Government and Civil Liberty', which caught Mason's attention. In this essay Jenyns examines a number of 'absurd principles' which were being propagated with great energy at the time. These were:

> 1stly That all men are born equal. 2dly That all men are born free. 3dly That all government is devised from the people. 4thly That all government is a compact between the governors and the governed. 5thly That no government ought to last any longer than it continues to be of equal advantage to the two contracting parties; that is, to the governed, as to the governors.[14]

Mason, in his Dedication, says that he had decided to read Tucker's *Treatise* since its principles were similar to those of Jenyns.

> Although I must own, that this exercitation of my patience cost me many a yawn, yet I found to my great satisfaction, that this writer allowed for true, what you held to be false, those two first principles of Mr. Locke, that men are equal, and that men are free. I concluded, therefore that he was a perfect person to dispute points with you. . . .
> If on your part, Sir, I have ever done more than elucidated any of those assertions, which you call arguments, I humbly ask your pardon: and on the Dean's, if *I have made him a little too lively*

and spiritual, I as humbly ask his. I know nothing does so much harm to an ecclesiastic, in the road of preferment, as the mere suspicion of being witty. But, as the Divine in question has long been a dean, and has sworn that he will never be a bishop, I hope no great harm is done.[15]

Not only is the dialogue quite amusing, but also, to support the opinions expressed by his proponents, the poet goes to the trouble of supplying footnotes giving quotations from their works. He also, rather quaintly, uses footnotes to explain his witty metaphors, in case his reader should have missed them. However, considering the vigour with which he had expressed his viewpoint, it is ironic that Mason switched sides when the younger Pitt took over. After thoroughly castigating him for his betrayal, Walpole ended the correspondence, and they were only reconciled by the outbreak of the French Revolution.

The proponents of radical reform remained unconvinced by the arguments that Tucker had put forward in the *Treatise*. The fact that the movement had aristocratic backers only confirmed him in his belief that the magic of Locke's name had combined with much loose thinking to mislead them as to the dangerous consequences which could emerge if the radicals were successful. His concern was expressed in his *Four Letters to Lord Shelburne*, who headed the government from the summer of 1782 until February 1783. The *Letters* were published in the latter year, but were obviously written before Shelburne's fall, since they are addressed to him as First Lord of the Treasury.

Tucker begins letter 1, 'The Occasion of the Work', with an autobiographical note:

> Some years ago, when your Lordship first began your political career, you honoured the Dean of Gloucester, with a visit at Bristol; and you were pleased to repeat it. The purpose of these visits was, to desire my opinion in writing concerning the best regulations for those four islands, which the French had ceded to us by treaty. I waited on your Lordship at Bowood, and brought my papers with me; . . . though I ventured to say at the same time, that I hardly thought these islands, or any other acquisitions, at so great a distance from the Mother Country, worth the costs both of men and money, which had been, and

would be, bestowed on them. Your Lordship then took me into your pleasure grounds, and there read one or two letters from a Nobleman of the first consequence; to which you added a comment . . . 'You see, Sir, how much it may be in my power to serve my friends, and promote deserving men. I shall be exquisitely happy in considering you among the number.' . . . To which I made answer, My Lord, I shall execute the task you have been pleased to set me, to the best of my abilities. As to any views of preferment, though I humbly thank your Lordship for your kind intentions, I have none at all, being quite contented with my station. It was very visible, that this answer rather chagrined than pleased you; and that the Peer did not expect such a speech from the Priest.

Soon after this your Lordship changed sides, and became as violently antiministerial, as you had been ministerial before. This, of course, made no alteration in my hopes or fears; though I own, it caused some variation in my opinion concerning the political merit of a certain great man. . . . To confirm me, that I was not mistaken, a pamphlet appeared some time afterwards (said to be written by a young smart dissenting Minister, who had frequent access to your Lordship) wherein, besides the usual strain of scurrility and abuse, I was also reproached with being a ministerial scribbler, hired to write against the colonies. This, I own, rather surprised me, because I thought it hard to be thus stigmatized, after the conversation which had passed between us. But now I am taught, by long experience, to be surprized at nothing.[16]

Tucker's personal experience with Shelburne throws further light on why that talented and reform-minded politician was regarded with such suspicion and distrust by his contemporaries. However, that Tucker had been prepared at least to play his previous role of provincial correspondent is indicated by a letter in the Public Record Office written in 1767, when Shelburne had last held power, in which he informs Shelburne of local troubles occasioned by a dearth and encloses a threatening letter from a firebrand.[17]

Tucker feels that events had only confirmed the correctness of his advice to let the American colonies go. Everyone would have been better off. 'Unless indeed the raising of a few American upstarts to be American princes, . . . the enriching of a few cormorants, and contractors here in Britain, . . . and the placing of the aforementioned patriotic fraternity on ministerial thrones, can be thought to have been objects sufficient to compensate such portentous losses' (pp. 8–9). The rest of this letter was taken up with the folly of those who had been agitating for the independence of Ireland, and the general dangers of the revolutionary principles expressed by the radicals.

Letter II is headed 'The Evil Consequences of Debasing the Regal Influence, and Exalting the Aristocratical or the Popular, beyond Their Due Proportion'. Tucker assumes that influence of one sort or another will always play a part in politics. Shelburne and his friends seem to take for granted that it is only the influence of the Crown that is always bad. Perhaps Shelburne is of a somewhat different opinion now that he has finally become the 'Pilot of the State' and would agree that 'either therefore all influence ought to be condemned alike; or that of the Crown ought not to be branded more than the rest, as being peculiarly criminal' (p. 28). There are, after all, other forms of influence.

> Your Lordship has the command of two boroughs already; And the public shrewdly suspect, that you have no qualms of conscience against commanding two more, . . . or even twenty-two. Mr. Fox and Lord Holland's family command one. The late Marquis of Rockingham had at least two, which he might, and did call his own: And were I to proceed after the same manner throughout the peerage, and the great landed interest of the realm, perhaps I might enumerate not less than two hundred, viz. boroughs and cities, and even counties, whose voters choose representatives, and return members to Parliament, more according to the good will and pleasure of who have the ascendancy over them, than according to their own private judgments, or personal determinations. (p. 29)

Tucker then goes on to ask the very pertinent question of whether Shelburne is prepared to bring in a bill to eliminate this sort of influence, and to provide penalties for the intimidation of tenants, tradesmen and dependants.

> But Oh! my Lord, lay your hand on your heart and tell me plainly, – or rather tell your country, which hath the right to ask

the question, – was this ever part of the plan either of yourself, or of your quondam, or present associates? Did either you, or they, when such tragical exclamations were raised against the influence of the Crown, ever intend to lessen your own? Did you ever propose to set the first example by enacting a self-denying ordinance against yourselves? – No, my Lord, so far from it, that many, if not most of your illustrious band grounded all their hopes, and all their schemes, for their own exaltation, on the depression, and humiliation of the Monarchy. In short, while the general liberty of the people was the pretence and cry, the particular emolument and grandeur of about a score of lords, and twice as many commoners, was the real end and aim of these patriotic endeavours. (p. 31)

The current situation in England could be compared, in Tucker's eyes, to that in Sweden after the death of Charles XII, when the popular leaders 'under the masque of procuring the liberty and independency of the subject' at the same time invaded their civil liberties, which were at the mercy of 'the Secret Committee, that state engine of a State Inquisition' (p. 33). The Americans had more recently been exposed to a similar experience. The truth was that, when a revolution was unleashed, it was likely to go further than its instigators bargained for. Referring to the radical Duke of Richmond, Tucker says,

It is confidently reported, that even this good, but mistaken man hath said, If we must have a K—, I should prefer the present to any other; but I do not see what need there is to have any K— at all. Little, surely, did he think, that with a very small change in the expression, and none at all in the sentiment, the same euphemism is applicable to himself, and to the very best and greatest landed men throughout the kingdom. 'If we must have landlords, saith the tenant, I should prefer the present to another. But I do not see what need there is to have any landlord at all. We are all his equals by nature, as free and independent as himself; and the Earth was given to us all. Therefore we ought to claim our rights, and no longer submit to such usurpations.' – Shall I add, that the modern doctrine, of the perfect equality of all mankind, – of their original, natural, and inherent rights, never to be transferred, or alienated, and of the necessity of contending for them even to the death, tend to confirm all these wild and extravagant conceits? – Yes, my Lord, they do tend to confirm them all; for they necessarily demolish not only *Crowns*, but *Coronets* too, levelling all distinctions with the ground. All ye great ones hear this, and tremble!

(pp. 40–2)

He notes a further inconsistency in the recent behaviour of the Whig reformers, related to legislation which had been passed disenfranchising revenue officers of the Crown. To strip the servants of the Crown of their rights as free citizens whilst at the same time defending the inalienable rights of all mankind was, in his mind, the height of hypocrisy.

Letter III, 'The Manifold Bad Consequences of Disturbing the Public Peace and Tranquility under a Pretense of Procuring a More Equal Representation of the People in Parliament', can quickly be disposed of, since it deals with the technical difficulties of substantially enlarging the electorate and Tucker had discussed of these before. Since the publication of the *Treatise*, Dr Towers had come up with another feeble reason why women should not have the vote, i.e. 'that we males, on account of the delicacy of the sex . . . have excused them from the trouble of voting' (p. 57). Tucker also for the first time raised the question of how the reformers intended to accommodate Scotland under the grand new scheme of things. On the assumption that it was home to one-quarter of the population of Great Britain, it should have 140 members instead of forty-five and, given that it contained one-third of the land in Great Britain, it would only be fair if Parliament assembled in that kingdom one-third of the time.

The title of letter IV, 'The Evil Consequence Arising from the Propagation of Mr. Locke's Democratical Principles', does not fully describe its contents. Tucker starts with a brief history of recent political theory. 'The destructive Civil Wars of 1641, to 1648, which ended in the tyranny of a single despot, set many persons on considering the nature and ends of government' (p. 87). They all agreed that Aristotle's 'political animal', in this case the people, was a capricious beast which required some form of control. Hobbes 'maintained with some degree of plausibility, that any man, or set of men, who could get into the saddle, and seize the bridle, had a right to ride this fiery, high-spirited, skittish horse, and to break ar manage him as he could' (pp. 87–8). Sir Robert Filmer, on the other hand, felt that only someone with an hereditary claim could have a Divine Right to hold the reins'. Algernon Sidney insisted that only those of noble blood, like himself, were 'fit persons to be the stateriders; and he bewailed the degeneracy of the times, which had abolished the honourable distinction of Baron and Vassal' (p. 88). Harrington, who was a gentleman, was of the opinion that 'gentlemen by birth (such as the rulers of the state of Venice, which government was his model) were the fittest of all to be riders'. He was pleased to find that Oliver Cromwell was a gentleman of ancient lineage. Tucker digressed here to note:

> This very man, Mr. Harrington, whose authority jointly with that of the great Sidney and Locke, has been urged in both prose and verse against the poor Dean of Gloucester, modestly wished, that your [Shelburne's] own country Panopea [as Ireland was called in Harrington's book, *Oceana*] had been leased out to the Jews in perpetuity . . . 'because Panopea (Ireland) is the soft mother of a slothful and pusillanimous race'.
>
> (pp. 89–90)

Richard Baxter opposed both Hobbes and Harrington, quite effectively in Tucker's eyes, but made the mistake of wanting to introduce an intolerant theocracry into the English system. And then came Locke, who made his first appearance as a political writer with his *Laws of Carolina*:

> In this system he was so far from supposing, that the people was the only fountain of power, that he goes on to an opposite extreme; . . . not indeed of absolute Monarchy, but of that which is rather worse, a tyrannical aristocracy; such as Mr. Sidney had been recommending. . . . A complete system of baronage and vassalage never yet appeared in the world, than is comprised in this little code of laws. Nay, Mr. Locke carries the matter of slavery so far, and grants such powers to masters to put their slaves to death, whenever they please, as exceeds even the tyranny of Poland. (pp. 92–3)

But after the Revolution, Mr. Locke veered about, and ran into an extreme quite opposite to his Laws of Carolina; – yet without publicly renouncing his former opinions. The people then, and not the barons, or the men of landed property became his sole fountain of power. In his Tract on Government, (the 2d part of which is nothing more than the resolves of the Cromwellian Levellers, worked up into a system) he maintains such principles, as must seemingly destroy every government upon earth, without erecting, or establishing any. (pp. 96–7)

Tucker believed that both Filmer and Locke made a similar error: they were too optimistic about human nature. Filmer's faith in one arbitrary ruler was as excessive as that of Locke in the people. Experience had shown that, 'when the multitude was invested with the power of governing, they prove the very worst of governors', because they are rash and capricious, and easily become 'the dupes of designing men'.

Besides, a democratic government is despotic in its very nature; because it supposes itself to be the only fountainhead of power, from which there can be no appeal. Hence, therefore, it comes to pass, that this many headed monster, an absolute Democracy, has all the vices and imperfections of its brother tyrant, an absolute Monarchy, without any of the shining qualities of the latter to hide its deformity. And what is still worse, it feels no remorse of conscience, and it never blushes. (pp. 98–9)

Tucker seems to have in mind here an extreme form of popular sovereignty, similar to what Rousseau was talking about in at least some parts of his *Du contrat social*, except that what were virtues for Rousseau were vices for Tucker. He thus recognised that propensity, discussed in J. L. Talmon's study *The Origins of Totalitarian Democracy* (1955), for 'total' democracy to slide over into totalitarianism.

Tucker's solution to the perennial problem of reconciling liberty and order was, as we know, the mixed form of government, which interposed between the regal and the popular a third power which served 'to maintain a balance between the opposite and contending parties, and to prevent either of them getting such an ascendancy as would render the other useless and unnecessary' (p. 100). Such a power, in Tucker's eyes, could only be an hereditary nobility possessing privileges sufficient to maintain its independence. In the British constitution this order was represented by the House of Lords. He notes, as an example, the useful role played in the Glorious Revolution by the nobility, who had taken the lead against James II.

Tucker also reminds Shelburne that the nobility could not look to Locke for any justification of their place in society.

> [Locke] sinks the nobility into a total insignificance, – never ascribing to them any right or privilege, or even so much as an existence in the state, any otherwise than as they make a part, and a very small one too, of the mass of the people. Nay in his 19th chapter, *Of the Dissolution of Government*, he lays down such a position, as annihilates the House of Lords at once, absolutely forbidding us to acknowledge them as a branch of the legislature, distinct from the people. His words are these: 'When any one, or more, shall take upon them to make laws whom the people have not appointed so to do, they make laws without authority, which the people are not therefore bound to obey, – and may constitute a new Legislature, as they think best.' The necessary consequence of which is, that a House of Lords, unless they will acknowledge that they are appointed by, and the creatures of the people, are a pack of usurpers, who ought at least to be set aside, if not punished for daring to infringe the perogatives of their emperors. A fine lesson this for your Lordship, and the whole body of the peerage! (pp. 103–4)

Tucker goes on to note some of the contradictions in Locke's theory, which he had already discussed in his *Treatise*, including the problem posed by the right of a majority over a minority.

> Now this I called a palpable contradiction. . . . But what say his advocate and defenders? Do they assert that these points are not contradictions? No; – at least not as yet. And they blame the Dean of Gloucester for having suppressed those passages which are explanatory of Mr. Locke's meaning. (p. 107)

But he had quoted the relevant passages at length at the beginning of the *Treatise* and elsewhere in it.

> Either, therefore, these boasted rights are alienable, or *unalienable*. – Let Mr. Locke's defenders choose, which side of the

question they will please to maintain; – provided they will adhere to it, and not shift about, and be guilty of those tergiversations which have hitherto appeared in all their writings. A searcher after the truth, and a practitioner of legerdemain, are very different characters. (p. 108)

Tucker insists that he had no personal animosity to Locke. As a young man he had considered him 'a kind of oracle', but as he grew older he became more aware of the error mixed in with the truth. He now felt that Locke's works had done more harm than good, not only in England but also in France, where, whether it was his intention or not, he had helped father the fashionable philosophy of atheistical materialism. Tucker therefore concludes that Locke's ideas did not 'promote either genuine liberty, real safety, or social happiness' and that Shelburne would be well advised not to support those who were agitating for change in Locke's name.

Although this was to be Tucker's last major publication, he was responsible for two more pamphlets, both on contemporary problems. The first of these, *Reflections on the Present Low Price of Coarse Wools*, had been published the previous year. The price of coarse wools had been falling for some time, and, although the stoppage of exports to America had played its part, Tucker believed that the principal reason was changing tastes.

> Females of all ages and conditions hardly use any woollens at present, except those of the finest texture, and made of the finest wools. Silks, cottons, and linens, combined in a thousand forms and diversified by names without number, are now almost the universal wear, from Her Grace in the drawing-room down to the lowest scullion in the kitchen. . . . And as to males, even they wear ten times the quantities of cottons and silks, under one denomination or another, more than was usual for them to do.[18]

Nothing much could be done about these early effects of the Industrial Revolution, but Tucker was not prepared to stand by helplessly. As was his wont, he put forward a plan which he hoped would at least alleviate the situation. One factor at work was the decline in numbers of the chief customers for coarse wools, the cottagers, whose lives were being made difficult by the parish-settlement policy. His remedy was to build cottages near the turnpike roads and offer them to men who could serve in the militia, raise produce on their plot of land, and be available for turnpike maintenance and day labour. The State should pay the poor rate and the money for the cottages could be raised by a lottery. In addition to thus creating a market for coarse wool, Tucker advocated a bounty on exports, especially to the Baltic states and Russia, that could use this type of cloth.

The reaction of a classical economist to this pamphlet is given by J. R. McCulloch in his catalogue of economic works, published in 1845: 'This pamphlet exhibits, though in an extreme degree, that singular medley of sense and nonsense that is found in some of Tucker's other tracts.'[19] The proposal to build cottages was such self-evident nonsense that McCulloch's only comment was to conclude his summary with an exclamation mark.

The other pamphlet, Tucker's last, appeared in 1785, and was entitled *Reflections on the Present Matters in Dispute between Great Britain and Ireland*. Tucker's attitude towards Ireland had been expressed in his *Essay on Trade* in 1749, and had not changed over the years. He believed that a union between the two kingdoms was desirable for a number of reasons, the most important of which was the elimination of economic discrimination against the Irish. British policy had actually moved in the opposite direction, with the granting of legislative independence to Ireland in 1782. The logical next step, taken by Pitt in 1785, was to move for free trade between the two countries, but intense opposition by British manufacturers and merchants, afraid of Irish competition, forced Pitt to make concessions which were unacceptable to the Irish, and nothing came of the project.

This only confirmed the doubts about the granting of independence which Tucker had expressed in his *Four Letters to Lord Shelburne*. He was convinced that union was the only answer and that it would eventually come about, but in his 1785 pamphlet, which was published, at the request of some friends, during the Parliamentary debates about free trade, he tried to look on the bright side of Irish independence, especially the possibility that ships sailing under the Irish flag would compete with the East India Company and the other trading monopolies. He also hoped that by purchasing their sugar at the cheapest market they would undermine the slave trade. The most expensive sugar came from the British islands, where slaves were treated the most harshly, while the cheapest came from the East Indies, where there was no slavery. He hoped that this would expose the 'momentous truth, not yet thoroughly understood, that of all monopolies, slavery is the most prejudicial to the true interests of a trading nation',[20] a truth which might affect those otherwise untouched by the inhumanity of the slave trade.

Tucker's attack on slavery did not go unnoticed. When Thomas Clarkson, the abolitionist, arrived in Bristol in 1787, he sought out Tucker, who, he reported, became 'a warm supporter of both me and my cause'. Tucker also introduced him to Raikes, who provided free space in his paper for Clarkson's ideas.[21]

The Dean's views on Ireland were given additional exposure at the end of the century, just before union was finally effected. A pamphlet of 1798[22] contained as a preface several pages of his arguments concerning the likely effect on English trade, and *Union or Separation*, published in 1799 by Dr Clarke, chaplain to the Prince of Wales, contained extensive quotations from Tucker, who had been questioned by Clarke on the subject in 1785.[23]

That Tucker still had fifteen years to live after his last publication was probably as much of a surprise to him as it may have been to others. Already in 1780 he referred to himself as an 'old man'. Three years later, writing to Mrs Jones, the wife of a minor canon at Gloucester, he mentioned that he liked to visit Bath each time duty called him to Bristol, in order to drink the waters. 'I have some indication of a flying gout, which I suppose at my time of life would not be malpractice if it turned into a regular one.' Characteristically, he noted that the ladies there were now ogling the gentlemen, which confirmed his opinion that 'revolutionary principles are continually gaining ground'.[24]

Writing to William Seward in 1790, he said that his faculties, 'which were never very good ones, are now so blunted by old age, that I hardly know what I ought to do, until I put pen to paper'. But he still followed current affairs with great interest. In the same letter he wrote, concerning Britain's dispute with Spain over the west coast of North America,

> For indeed I am a well-wisher to all mankind; and am sorry to find that the Spaniards and the English are so blind to their own interests, as not to perceive, that the cultivation of their own

countries in Europe is of much more consequence to each of them than the most splendid victories in order to obtain waste lands in foreign regions. . . . You have long known of my sentiments concerning the dispute which subsisted between England and North America, and the event has shown that I judged rightly in that affair. Were I at present a younger man, I think I could have wrote another 'Cui Bono?' as to the quarrel between England and Spain. But at my time of life, now almost completely 77 years old, I cheerfully resign that task to younger hands and abler heads.[25]

At about this time Tucker decided to give up St Stephen's in Bristol, because of his age. However, he wanted his curate, a man named Grenville with a large family to support, to receive the living. Since it was in the gift of the Lord Chancellor, who naturally wanted to choose his own man, this took some doing. But Tucker was stubborn, and made Grenville's appointment a condition of his resignation. He also organised a petition among the parishioners, who unanimously attested to Grenville's fitness for the job. The Lord Chancellor yielded, and in November 1793 Tucker severed his long connection with his Bristol church.[26]

Although we have no record of Tucker's reaction to the French Revolution, it can easily be imagined. Nevertheless, that contradictory opinions about both the Revolution and Tucker were possible is indicated by an exchange that occurred in the House of Lords in 1793, when it was debating an enlargement of the armed forces. The Marquis of Lansdowne, formerly Lord Shelburne, is quoted as saying,

> With respect to French principles, as they had been denominated, those principles had been exported from us to France, and could not be said to have originated among the people of the latter country. The new principles of government, founded on the abolition of the old feudal system, were originally propagated among us by the dean of Gloucester, Mr. Tucker, and had since been more generally inculcated by Dr. Adam Smith, in his work on the *Wealth of Nations*, which has been recommended as a book necessary for the information of youth, by Mr. Dugald Stewart, in his *Elements of the Philosophy of the Human Mind*. But

whatever these principles were, a metaphysical war was not the means of extinguishing them.

The Lord Chancellor (Lord Loughborough) was not prepared to accept this interpretation of events:

> And the new-fangled doctrines of that people [the French] could hardly deceive the penetration of the lowest graduate in the schools, yet the practical effect of these miserable lessons ought to be resisted to the utmost of our powers. In the works of dean Tucker, Adam Smith, and Mr. Stewart, to which allusions had been made, no doctrines inimical to the principles of civil government, the morals or religion of mankind were contained. And therefore to trace the errors of the French to these causes was manifestly fallacious.[27]

Although it was true that the dismantling of the ramshackle structure of internal trade restrictions accomplished by the Revolution would have met with Tucker's approval, the political ideas it embodied had been under attack by him for years. On the other hand, since he had also expatiated at length on the folly of war, it was likely that any commentary he might have produced at this time would have been as unpopular with both sides as his views on the American War had been. Indeed, if he had lived long enough to see the final outcome of the Revolution and the Napoleonic Wars, it would only have confirmed him again in the correctness of his beliefs.

However, being right in such circumstances would have given him no cause for rejoicing, and it was fortunate for him that he was spared the years of bloodshed which lay ahead. A paralytic stroke brought his life to an end on 4 November 1799, at the Deanery in Gloucester, when he was aged eighty-six.

In his *Anecdotes of Distinguished Persons*, first published in five volumes over the years 1795–7, William Seward wrote, 'One deviation only from the general plan of the work occurs – the introduction of a living character. In this the wishes of the reader, who may think a man like Dr. Tucker *omni major eulogio* should be also *omni exceptione major*.'

After awarding him this signal honour, Seward goes on to group him with Chatham, Mansfield, Dr Johnson, Garrick, Goldsmith and Reynolds.[28] The fact that all these other names have retained their lustre while Tucker's has sunk into relative obscurity shows that Seward was excessively generous, at least in the judgement of posterity. But the fact that such an assessment seemed reasonable at the time can also be taken as an indication that posterity has perhaps been excessively ungenerous in its appraisal of Tucker.

One area in which a difference of opinion has occurred is the history of economic theory. In his unsympathetic review of Schuyler's Introduction to his 1931 collection of some of Tucker's writings, the economist Jacob Viner gives short shrift to any claims made on the Dean's behalf: 'Only fairly comprehensive ignorance of what preceded and what followed Tucker in the evolution of economic ideas can explain the assignment to him of the role of an economic innovator.'[29] This crushing rebuke is mitigated somewhat by the fact that Viner believed Schuyler to have been unduly influenced by W. E. Clark's 'mediocre and naive monograph' *Josiah Tucker, Economist*. Viner unhesitatingly rejects any influence of Tucker upon Adam Smith, either directly or via the Physiocrats. Such influence could only be demonstrated '*if* it were shown that Smith and Tucker had many important ideas in common, *if* it were shown that their ideas were not widely prevalent at the time, and *if* it were not true that their ideas could readily be found in writers prior to both, some of them prior by a century'.[30] These are conditions which are difficult to fulfil in their entirety for any thinker. Even recalling the shade of Adam Smith and subjecting it to a vigorous cross-examination might not elicit the truth, since Smith could always justifiably claim that his ideas came to him independently of any books he happened to possess. Schuyler merely claimed that it was 'reasonable' to assume some influence, because Smith had in his library a substantial number of Tucker's books, published many years before. That it is not so completely far-fetched as Viner would have us believe is indicated in a work by James Bonar, who was responsible for the *Catalogue of the Library of Adam Smith*. His book is a series of dialogues with dead economists, the second of which is called *Adam Smith among his Books*. In it the interviewer says,

> You personally directed the binding of your Tracts, making

'A Well-Wisher to All Mankind'   259

your own list of contents in your own large handwriting. Dean Tucker's *Tracts* are here, for example, with others in one large volume. . . . You do not quote Tucker nor did he agree with you at all points; but there he is in your library and we feel sure that you had read him.[31]

Bonar's Smith is unable to offer a satisfactory answer to the implied question. But then there are many omissions in the list of acknowledgements that Smith might have made, as Bonar, in effect, points out.

In order to defend Schuyler and, even more, Clark, against charges of unwarranted enthusiasm concerning Tucker's contribution to economic theory, one must put the whole affair into historical perspective. The situation which existed in 1903, when Clark's work appeared, is explained by Edwin R. A. Seligman, of Columbia University, in his Introduction to the book.

> It is unfortunate that we have as yet no history of political economy worthy of the name. . . . For the period before Adam Smith, so rich that a contemporary writer collected no less than fifteen hundred works on economic topics, we have virtually nothing but a few short essays. . . . The absence of an historical school of economics in England and the glamour of a few great names which have thrown everything else into the shade explain, but do not excuse this neglect. Careful students of Adam Smith who are at the same time acquainted with the earlier literature, are well aware of how much he owes to his predecessors; but the ordinary manuals of the history of economics lay but little emphasis on this debt.[32]

Clark's monograph was meant to be one of a series which would help to fill this gap. Since then, of course, a substantial literature on the subject has accumulated and the contributions of Smith's predecessors have been acknowledged. As a result, there is not the excitement today that there was at the turn of the century in discovering that someone such as Tucker had, many years before the publication of Smith's masterpiece, held views similar to his on a number of topics.

Even then, Clark does not make excessive claims on behalf of his subject. Since Tucker had been largely ignored by economists from Adam Smith on, his direct influence on British economic thought has been 'nearly negligible'.

> On the other hand ... Through his advocacy of economic freedom in relatively ephemeral, but, at the time, highly influential tracts, published intermittently during fifty years, through his sermons and conversations, and through his correspondences, Tucker undoubtedly helped to create and to extend the demand for larger commercial and industrial freedom. He helped to prepare the British mind for a readier reception of the teachings of a *Wealth of Nations*.[33]

Clark was prepared to go further in connection with the Physiocrats, because, unlike in the case of Adam Smith, there are acknowledgements and other references in the records. He notes that, a minimum of two years before any of the Physiocratic writings were published, seven of Tucker's works were available to those who could read English. In French, the substance of Tucker's *Essay on Trade* was known through Plumart d'Angeul's *Remarques*, which Henry Higgs says 'was constantly present to Quesnay's mind in writing this article ["Grains" in the *Encylopédie*] and was quoted in the course of it'.[34] As we have seen, Turgot had already translated one of Tucker's works into French, and, when he sent his *Réflexions* to Tucker, he modestly said they would have nothing new to offer the British writer. It would be hard to deny on this evidence that the French economists felt that Tucker had helped clear the way for their struggle against the old order.

One other point needs to be classified before we move on. Viner sees Tucker's economic writings as of interest only because they are 'illustrations of the struggle of mercantilism to survive in the face of what should have proved crushing criticism by means of a superficial change in form while adhering to an outmoded substance'.[35] This is a good example of the kind of criticism mentioned earlier when these writings were being examined in detail. In the conventional history of economic thought, a new age of enlightenment began in 1776 when the *laissez-faire* doctrine was revealed to the world by Adam Smith. Those who had stumbled in darkness during the preceding period were known as mercantilists. Some of these mercantilists had been granted glimpses of the new dispensation and were thus not as perverse as the others. According to this schema Tucker was sometimes regarded as one who had almost escaped the bondage of mercantilism but at the crucial moment had fallen back into the bad old ways. Viner is unique in seeing him as a kind of mercantilist wolf trying to pass as a *laissez-faire* sheep.

It is ironic that Viner should have sought to eliminate Tucker from serious consideration by pinning the mercantilist label to him just four years before the publication in 1936 of Keynes's *General Theory of Employment Interest and Money*, which provided a new and more favourable assessment of the mercantilists, stemming from the apparent inability of *laissez-faire* policy to end the depression. But the problem is really with the word 'mercantilism' itself. Not only has it acquired pejorative connotations which allow it to be used for condemnation rather than description, but, in addition, exactly what it is supposed to denote is open to question. In the words of Charles W. Cole,

> As a matter of fact, mercantilism was never an entity, never a system, never a coordinated or coherent body of policy or practice.... Those who practiced and preached it never thought of themselves as a school. The very name 'mercantilism' was invented by its opponents when the old ideas were already on the wane.[36]

Thus 'mercantilism' as a concept was flawed from the start, and its usefulness is further impaired by the diversity of ideas and policies which it is intended to encompass. When an intellectual construct is likely to lead to confusion rather than clarity, it should be used with great caution if it is to be used at all. In the case of Tucker any attempt to divide his thought into what is 'mercantilism' and what is not merely obscures whatever internal consistency it possesses.

Tucker believed that, although self-interest is the vital force which drives the economy, it does not automatically act in a way that is beneficial for the community as a whole. If this assumption is accepted, then his desire to redirect self-interest, where necessary, into socially useful paths, makes perfectly good sense. In fact it made such good sense that even Adam Smith violated his own *laissez-faire* doctrine in a surprisingly large number of instances, as listed by Viner himself, in another article. From this evidence he concluded that, 'even in his own day when it was not easy to see, Smith saw that self-interest and competition were sometimes treacherous to the public interest they were supposed to serve, and he was prepared to have government exercise some means of control over them'.[37]

A more recent reference to Tucker by an economist can be found in Ronald L. Meek's *Precursors of Adam Smith*. In his introduction to a selection from tract 1 of the *Four Tracts*, Meek notes that 'the implied distinction between "productive" and "unproductive" labour in Tucker's consideration of his "Case 1" has a distinctly Smithian flavour and the Edinburgh illustration reappears, in very similar language, in the *Wealth of Nations*'. He continues,

> And in the latter part of the tract a whole number of 'Smithian' ideas are to be found in embryo. Conspicuous among these are the division of labour, duly limited by the extent of the market; the idea that 'Heaps of Gold and Silver are not the true riches of a Nation'; the notion of the crucial importance of capital, both fixed and circulating, and the advantages accruing from the possession of 'superior Capitals', the idea that in a rich country monopoly is ousted by competition, which lowers prices, and even, in one place, a concept of profit on capital which, with the exercise of a little charity, may be regarded as not essentially dissimilar to Smith's.[38]

If we move from Tucker's possible influence on economic theory to that he may have had on economic policy, the situation seems clearer. In 1945 R. L. Schuyler, whose book on Tucker has been mentioned above, published *The Fall of the Old Colonial System*. In it he sees Tucker as an early anti-imperialist whose arguments for American independence helped pave the way for the later emergence of free trade.

However, the whole question of whether free trade and imperialism were necessarily incompatible has been subjected to considerable discussion in recent years. The cross-currents at work in the nineteenth century have been analysed by Bernard Semmel,[39] who assigns Tucker an important place in the evolution of 'free trade imperialism'. The essence of this concept is that a policy of

'A Well-Wisher to All Mankind' 263

encouraging international free trade can work to the advantage of a country which has established such a commanding lead in manufacturing that it needs no protection from possible rivals. Britain enjoyed such a position in the first half of the century, when it could quite justifiably claim to be the 'workshop of the world'. Semmel traces the idea back to the Hume–Tucker debate, about which he had written earlier. Tucker's argument that a rich nation had little to fear from a poor one was sufficiently convincing to encourage Pitt in his moves towards freer trade in the 1780s. 'Indeed, the principal arguments in favour of Pitt's Irish proposals of 1785, for example, were drawn almost phrase for phrase from Tucker's rebuttal to Hume. Parts of the Tucker argument reappeared, though much less prominently, in the parliamentary support for Pitt's French treaty of 1787, and parliamentary opponents of the treaty borrowed from Hume.'[40] The reason why this is not more widely known is that Tucker was given no credit by those who used his reasoning. As Semmel says,

> It might be useful to ask why it was that – although the opposition made some allusion to the Dean of Gloucester in the debates – neither Pitt nor Shelburne, the leading proponents of these liberal trade proposals, made any acknowledgement to Tucker. Pitt was to say kind words about Smith, and Shelburne spoke of the influence upon his views of both Smith, and the physiocrat Morellet. Why was not a similar generosity displayed towards Tucker?[41]

The answer seems to be that, not only did Tucker, as we have seen, refuse to be patronised by Shelburne, but also his highly individual approach to the American war contradicted either the economic beliefs or the political views of both major parties. This made it embarrassing for anyone to admit being his disciple, although, as in the case of Shelburne and Pitt, they were willing to employ his arguments.

Referring to later developments Semmel adds,

> In the nineteenth century the English classical economists managed to identify free trade with cosmopolitanism, despite the efforts of List and Carey, and other material economists, to depict it as the necessary policy of an English nationalism. In

Tucker's views, and in the manner in which his arguments were employed in Parliament by Pitt and his supporters, the 'national' economists would have found some confirmation of their position. That Tucker's analysis was in essence similar to theirs is, of course, further indicated by Tucker's anticipation of the remedy which List and Carey were to offer the agricultural nations – tariff protection for industry. Tucker's analysis . . . also anticipates the general terms of the debate concerning the international economy which has been underway now for over a decade.[42]

The latter refers to a claim by Gunnar Myrdal, among others, that in the relative free-trade conditions prevailing since the Second World War, the gap between the developed and underdeveloped countries has been increasing. This seems to support Tucker's position against the classical international trade economics advocated in recent years by Jacob Viner.[43]

Turning to Tucker's political ideas, it might be useful first of all to see how they compare with those of his well-known contemporary Edmund Burke. The problem with Burke is to separate out what he genuinely believed from what was dictated by the imperatives of party politics. For example, although Burke's sympathy for the Irish is well documented, we find him opposing Pitt's moves towards free trade with Ireland. And, despite his defence of the old colonial system, even when sympathising with the Americans, we find him advocating economic liberalism in his *Thoughts on Scarcity* of 1795. Burke's shifting principles easily led to the kind of harsh judgement made by Karl Marx:

> This sycophant who, in the pay of the English oligarchy, played the romantic *laudator temporis acti* against the French Revolution, just as, in the pay of the North American colonies, at the beginning of the America troubles, he had played the liberal against the English oligarchy, was on an out and out vulgar bourgeois. 'The laws of Commerce are the laws of Nature, and therefore the laws of God.' (E. Burke, 1. c. pp. 31, 32). No wonder that, true to the laws of God and Nature, he always sold himself in the best market.[44]

Marx, incidentally, recommended Tucker's *Letter to Edmund Burke* as a reliable source on Burke's earlier period. 'Tucker', said Marx, 'was a parson and a Tory, but, for the rest, an honourable man and a competent political economist.'[45]

Burke could have responded, with respect to the French Revolution, that the very intemperance of his comments was proof of a passion that no money could buy. Whatever the reason, Burke provided in the course of his later speeches and pamphlets a philosophical foundation for modern conservatism. What interests us is that he did it largely in response to ideas which Tucker had subjected to a steady assault starting two decades earlier, when Burke seemed oblivious to them. The continuity is shown by the fact that Richard Price was the target, among others, of both men, and no one could suggest that his ideas had changed. Burke's insistence that the American Revolution was nothing more than a North American version of the Glorious Revolution has always made him popular with those who preferred to avert their eyes from its radical side. However, it was in the Declaration of Independence that, as D. W. Brogan puts it, 'the new revolutionary doctrine gets its first, clearest and most decisive expression, far more coherent and revolutionary than in the later French Declarations of the Rights of Man that were its children'.[46] Why was this not more evident to Burke and the others? One reason may have been that the outcome of the American Revolution did little to disturb their equanimity. To quote Brogan again,

> It was necessary, indeed, to put the American claims on the widest philosophical basis, to raise questions that put the very foundations of political society in question, but the social and economic realities of American society did not force the application of those principles or even seriously tempt any important body of Americans to apply them unconditionally and imprudently. It was possible to declare that 'life, liberty and the pursuit of happiness' were inalienable rights of all men and provide legal protection for slavery, to declare that governments derive their just powers from the consent of the governed and accept a constitution that limited, very seriously, the rights of the majority to rule themselves.[47]

For Tucker, on the other hand, the situation did not have to deteriorate as far as it did in the French Revolution for him to realise that the radicals were putting 'the very foundations of political society in question', nor that the very people who ranted on about 'liberty' were capable of the most breathtaking hypocrisy in flouting the very ideals for which they were supposed to be fighting. Furthermore, he foresaw the likely effects in France of the American example and warned Shelburne of the disaster which could befall landowning aristocrats who played the fashionable radical game.

However, Tucker did not formulate a philosophy of 'romantic' conservatism, as Burke did in response to this threat to the *status quo*. Above all, he did not take the potentially perilous step of attaching religious reverence to the State, in the tradition of Rousseau and Burke. Tucker's religious feelings were channelled through the body ecclesiastic rather than the body politic. Burke's concept of prescriptive rights, hallowed by time, also was alien to his cast of mind. He had faith in the value of an aristocracy as a mediating force between Crown and people and he shared the belief of most of his contemporaries that the landowners were somehow more disinterested than the mercantile and other politically active classes. However, it was because they played a useful part in the 'mixed' constitution, not because they enjoyed ancestral rights, that Tucker respected them. Finally, although he never swallowed the Rockingham Whig myth of the malign influence of the Crown, Tucker would certainly never have gone to the other extreme, as Burke did when he sprang to the defence of Marie Antoinette and the absolute monarchy of France. For Tucker the Crown occupied an important place in the mixed constitution, but that was all.

Tucker's defence of the *status quo* was essentially pragmatic. The British system of government worked. It offered a degree of personal liberty practically unknown elsewhere; it gave a share in decision-making to the various interest groups which made up the political nation; and it provided a balance between the monarchical, aristocratic and democratic principles sufficient to prevent one from overwhelming the others. Like Burke (and many others), Tucker accepted the hierarchical nature of British society and believed the subordination of one order to another was a positive good. Like Burke, and Rousseau, he rejected the extreme individualism of the Lockian contract and looked for man's roots in his family and community. But he was not prepared to deify the community, as was Rousseau, in the name of popular sovereignty, or Burke, on behalf of the *ancien régime*. For Tucker, society provided the setting in which the individual could improve himself, and the structure of honours and other rewards which provided him with the incentive to do so. Tucker's approach could be called utilitarian, although he would not have followed Bentham along the path which led to hedonism and the felicific calculus. The moderate conservatism of David Hume was probably the closest in spirit to Tucker's position.

Since Hume was widely regarded as a Tory, this may be a suitable point to determine whether Tucker also deserved this label, which was often applied to him in the latter part of his life. Tucker certainly regarded himself as a Whig – his active participation in politics was under that banner. He also was not a member of that group, largely composed of country gentlemen, who thought of themselves as Tories. However, during the period of the American Revolution 'Tory' tended to be used as a term of abuse against those who supported the ministry by those who did not. This usage was most clear-cut in America, where the revolutionaries called themselves Whigs, as well as patriots, and referred to the Loyalists (whom they considered to be traitors) as Tories. Although Tucker sided with the Loyalists, he was completely opposed to the policy of coercion adopted by the government and therefore it is unfair, even in this sense, to call him a Tory. If Burke in the 1790s could still think of himself as a Whig (albeit an Old Whig), there is no good reason why Tucker could not do the same. However, it did not really matter what he thought himself to be: posterity labelled him a Tory. The reason why this was unfortunate is that in the ideological smog which descended on the second half of the eighteenth century such tags made it easier to separate out the villains from the heroes without having to look too closely at them.

This tendency to oversimplify has itself received a name: the 'Whig interpretation of history', and Tucker can certainly be numbered among its victims. In British history, as Macaulay viewed it, 'there have been, under some name or other, two sets of men, those who were before their age, and those who were behind it'.[48] During the period with which we are concerned, the Tories were the reactionaries and the Whigs the agents of progress or 'democracy'. Historical research over the past fifty years has substantially altered once commonly held beliefs, particularly about the role played by George III. However, the lineaments of the age were sketched by the Whig historians in a way which has retained such a powerful appeal that it often has to be freshly challenged each time one deals with a specific individual. This is particularly true for someone such as Tucker, who openly advocated a position which is easily condemned as reactionary when viewed with the presuppositions of today.

For one thing, the meaning of such a word as 'democracy' has changed, and even today is defined differently in East and West. Certainly the complex mechanisms whereby people are governed in the Western liberal democracies are responsive to public opinion, but they are a far cry from the small-scale models of direct democracy familiar to the eighteenth century, and even further away from the ideal of the reformers, which required individual consent to legitimise the actions of the government. In actuality, someone like Tucker would not feel too much a stranger in modern America, still faithful as it is to its eighteenth-century constitution. The fact that, 200 years after a revolution fought at least partly over the question of representation, the inhabitants of the capital city of the United States are still unrepresented in Congress would not have surprised him.

In his attack on the Lockians Tucker was making essentially two significant points: first, that a system of government under which no one is bound to do anything without his own consent is impracticable and unrealisable; and, therefore, second, that anyone who puts forward such a programme, especially when he immediately excludes women and slaves, is either very simple-minded or has an ulterior motive. Most often the rhetoric of liberty is used to justify a change in rulers, and, once that change has occurred, the ideals which helped to bring it about are honoured in word more than in deed.

The American Revolution was the laboratory experiment which tested Tucker's hypothesis. As it unfolded, it confirmed all his suspicions. The liberties for which the American leaders claimed to be fighting were almost immediately suspended. Those who were slow about switching their loyalties soon discovered that guarantees concerning the protection of life, liberty and property did not apply to them. Even more striking was the reconstruction of governments which took place, with only the most cursory attention paid to securing the consent of all the inhabitants. These actions were excused by the revolutionaries, and by later historians, as occurring within the context of a war for survival. This is true enough if we are referring to the survival of the leaders themselves, but it begs the question of whether or not it is right, under any circumstances, for one party in a dispute to use intimidation and coercion against those who have not been converted to their cause by force of argument. War affords altogether too tempting a means of turning one's political opponents overnight into traitors.

However, although civil rights were restored at the end of the war, Tucker's assessment of the situation soon received further confirmation. The victorious leaders reacted with increasing dismay to the anarchic tendencies which prevailed in the 1780s and decided to restore order by means of the Constitution, which was pushed through at the end of the decade without obtaining the individual consent of all or even a majority of the inhabitants. The speed with which radicals became conservatives, or, perhaps, with which conservatives dropped their radical guise, once they had achieved power, must have been somewhat confusing to their followers. When in 1786 the pleas of the debt-ridden farmers in Massachusetts for relief were ignored by the legislature and they finally took up arms under Daniel Shays, Samuel Adams, who had master-minded the Boston Tea Party, referred to these new revolutionaries as 'wicked and unprincipled men' and George Washington was shocked. Regarding this and other disorders, he exclaimed, 'Good God! Who besides a Tory could have foreseen, or a Briton have predicted them?'[49] An even more ironic situation occurred after Washington had become President. Attempts to enforce the Excise Act of 1791 against the whisky-making mountaineers of western Pennsylvania were met by violence. These people had no more given their consent to this law than their predecessors had to the Stamp Act. There was even talk of another declaration of independence. Washington's answer was to call out 15,000 militiamen and crush the Whisky Rebellion, as it was called, without delay.

Thus the history of this period probably provided as much support for Tucker's position as any reasonable person could have expected. Although the narrow doctrine of consent could be used to undermine an established government, it could not itself provide a foundation on which a new one could be firmly erected. The only reason people believed this to be possible was that the concept of consent could be expanded or contracted according to the needs of the interested parties. The Americans were lucky in that, if they did not find the version known as tacit consent either convincing or convenient, they could always go west into the wilderness and enjoy a period of happy anarchy before the forces of law and order, and tacit consent, caught up with them again.

Events on the other side of the Atlantic have been treated in some detail because a discussion of them makes a suitable conclusion to any study of Tucker's life and thought. The American Revolution, which began when Tucker had already reached the age of sixty, was the occasion for his best-known writings and the period in which he received the most public recognition. It was significant also because it brought together practically all the strands of his thought. Even his religion was involved, in the sense that it never permitted him to take seriously the belief, popular with so many revolutionaries, that there are political solutions to all mankind's problems and therefore that some kind of heaven is possible on earth. But the Revolution was a testing ground chiefly for his political and economic ideas. Not only did it appear to justify the stand he had taken against the more simplistic assertions of the Lockians, but in addition, the fact that after the war was over trade prospered as never before between the former combatants, just as he had said it would, seemed to prove once again the folly of both war and commercial imperialism, against which he had inveighed for so many years.

In politics, also, Tucker would have had some grounds for satisfaction. As we have noted, it was not America and its fate which concerned him: it was the growth of republicanism at home. True, he was unduly pessimistic about the effect of enlarging the electorate; but, as it turned out, the extension of the franchise in Great Britain went hand in hand with gradual changes in the social structure, which would probably have justified it in his eyes. The fact that, two centuries later, his country has Queen, Lords and Commons, as well as universal suffrage, is an indication of the value placed on continuity and evolutionary change by its people. However, one must not ignore the impact of one important historical event in turning Britain away from the path of radicalism. That event was the French Revolution, which, far more than the American Revolution, illustrated the grave dangers inherent in a doctrinaire approach to popular sovereignty. The Reign of Terror and the disillusioning developments that followed it not only vindicated Tucker in some of his less popular views but also acted as an object lesson which may have helped save his countrymen from a similar ordeal – a much more important outcome for Tucker.

Notes

NB: Place of publication London, unless otherwise stated; BL = British Library.

CHAPTER 1

1. Gloucester Public Library, Tucker Letters, Tucker to Adams, 6 June 1779.
2. Scottish Record Office, Kames Collection, Tucker to Kames, 15 Feb 1764.
3. Walter Ernest Clark, *Josiah Tucker, Economist* (New York, 1903) p. 23.
4. A copy of the parish register can be found at the library of the Society of Genealogists in London.
5. Public Records Office, Treasury Board Papers, LXXVIII, 34. An alternative reading for the wording in the parish register would be that Tucker's father was a salt officer at Nevern, but there is no evidence that salt tax was ever collected there.
6. Francis Green and Catherine Octavia Higgon, 'The Tuckers of Sealyham', *West Wales Historical Records*, VIII (Carmarthen, 1919–20).
7. T. Y. Lewis, 'Nevern', *Transactions of the Cardiganshire Antiquarian Society*, VII (Aberystwyth, 1930) 28.
8. Letter from the Vicar of Nevern to the author.
9. Mary Curtis, *The Antiquities of Laugharne and Pendine, Carmarthenshire, South Wales* (1871).
10. Josiah Tucker, *Instructions for Travellers* (1757) p. 39.
11. D. J. Davies, *The Economic History of South Wales prior to 1880* (Cardiff, 1933) p. 90.
12. Edward Hughes, *Studies in Administration and Finance 1558–1825 with Special Reference to the History of Salt Taxation in England* (Manchester, 1934), contains a detailed history of the salt tax.
13. Ibid., pp. 199–200.
14. See John Humphrey Davies, 'Cardiganshire Freeholders in 1760', *West Wales Historical Records*, III (Carmarthen, 1912–13) 73–116. The other records are located in the National Library of Wales, Aberystwyth.
15. Daniel Defoe, *A Tour through England and Wales*, ed. G. D. H. Cole (1928) vol. II, p. 59. This is the Everyman edition of part of *Tour Thro' the Whole Island of Great Britain* (1724).
16. D. J. Davies, *Economic History of South Wales*, p. 132.
17. Dr Richard Pococke, *The Travels Through England of Dr. Richard Pococke in 1750, 1751 and Later Years*, ed. J. J. Cartwright (1888–9) vol. II, p. 181.
18. *Biograph Mirror*, 1789, pp. 47–8.
19. Nicholas-Carlisle, *A Concise Description of the Endowed Grammar Schools in England and Wales* (1818) vol. II, p. 935.

274   Dean Tucker and Eighteenth-Century Thought

20. Letter from Headmaster of Ruthin School to the author, quoting a report in his possession.
21. Carlisle, *Concise Description of the Endowed Grammar Schools*, vol. II, p. 937.
22. *Public Characters of 1798–99*, 4th edn (1803) pp. 162–3.
23. Ralph Bigland, *The Original History of the City of Gloucester* (1819) p. 108.
24. Charles Edward Mallet, *A History of the University of Oxford* (1927) vol. III, p. 133.
25. [Nicholas Amhurst], *Terrae-filius or the Secret History of the University of Oxford in Several Essays* (1726) pp. 51–2.
26. Quoted in A. D. Godley, *Oxford in the Eighteenth Century* (1908).
27. Mallet, *History of the University of Oxford*, vol. III, p. 2.
28. Godley, *Oxford in the Eighteenth Century*, p. 17.
29. Ibid., p. 19.
30. Quoted ibid., p. 46.
31. Amhurst, *Terrae-filius*, p. 187.
32. Godley, *Oxford in the Eighteenth Century*, p. 15.
33. Ibid., p. 252.
34. BL Add. MSS. 4319, Tucker to Birch, 20 July 1757.
35. Rev. Luke Tyerman, *The Life and Times of the Rev. John Wesley, M.A.*, 2nd edn (1871–2) vol. I, pp. 85–6.
36. Godley, *Oxford in the Eighteenth Century*, pp. 189–90.
37. Ibid., p. 196.
38. Ibid., p. 35.
39. Rev. Norman Sykes, *Church and State in England in the XVIIIth Century* (Cambridge, 1934) p. 78.
40. C. D. Broad, *Five Types of Ethical Theory* (1930) pp. 6–7.

CHAPTER 2

1. Daniel Defoe, *A Tour through England and Wales*, ed. G. D. H. Cole (1928) vol. II, p. 36.
2. W. E. Minchinton, 'Bristol – Metropolis of the West in the Eighteenth Century', *Transactions of the Royal Historical Society*, 5th ser., IV (1954) 71.
3. For this section I have relied on the previously quoted monograph by W. E. Minchinton and his Introduction to *The Trade of Bristol in the Eighteenth Century*, ed. W. E. Minchinton, Bristol Record Society Publication XX (Bristol, 1957), as well as Bryan Little, *The City and County of Bristol* (1954).
4. Richard Pares, *A West India Fortune* (1950) p. 212.
5. See, for example, *Cui Bono* (Gloucester, 1781) letters III and V. (For full title of this work, see Ch. 9, n. 13.)
6. See Bristol Public Library, B13794, Richard Woodward to Tucker, 13 July 1753; and BL Add. MSS. 11275, fo. 138, Tucker to Rev. C. N. Forster, 19 May 1755.
7. Charles J. Abbey, *The English Church and its Bishops 1700–1800* (London, 1887) vol. I, pp. 301–2.
8. *Gentleman's Magazine*, IX (1739) 238. A copy of the broadsheet itself may be found among Archbishop Secker's papers at Lambeth Palace.
9. Ibid., pp. 239–42.

Notes

10. Ibid., pp. 242–3.
11. Ibid., p. 294.
12. Ibid., p. 292.
13. Ibid., pp. 294–7.
14. *The Life of Mr. Geo. Whitefield by an impartial Hand* (1739) pp. 57–8.
15. Luke Tyerman, *The Life and Times of the Rev. John Wesley, M.A.*, 2nd edn (1871–2) vol. I, p. 244.
16. John Wesley, *Journal* (Epworth, 1926) vol. II, p. 341, 4 Apr 1740.
17. H. B. Workman, *Methodism* (Cambridge, 1912) pp. 109–10.
18. Henry Bett, *The Spirit of Methodism* (1937) p. 130.
19. Rupert Davies, *Methodism* (Harmondsworth, 1963) p. 11.
20. Abbey, *The English Church*, vol. I, p. 290.
21. Josiah Tucker, *A Brief History of the Principles of Methodism* (Oxford, 1742). The quotes are from the Preface.
22. James Boswell, *Life of Johnson* (1906) vol. I, p. 390.
23. Tucker, *Brief History*, pp. 7–11.
24. Ibid., pp. 12–13, 21.
25. Ibid., pp. 36–7.
26. Ibid., p. 37, quoting from the Preface to vol. II of Wesley's *Hymns* (1739) pp. 6–7.
27. Ibid., pp. 38–9.
28. Ibid., p. 32.
29. Ibid., pp. 45–6, 51.
30. John Wesley, *The Principles of a Methodist, Occasioned by a Late Pamphlet, Entitled, A Brief History of the Principles of Methodism*, 2nd edn (Bristol, 1746) p. 3.
31. Bernard Semmel, *The Methodist Revolution* (New York, 1973) pp. 54, 64, 78, 85.
32. Wesley, *Principles*, pp. 20, 22.
33. John Wesley, *Works* (1872) vol. VIII, pp. 284–5.

CHAPTER 3

1. Josiah Tucker, *A Series of Answers to Certain Popular Objections* (Gloucester, 1776), p. 94n.
2. Josiah Tucker, *Reflections on the Expediency of a Law for the Naturalization of Foreign Protestants*, pt II (1752) Appendix, p. 55.
3. Ibid., pp. 65–6.
4. G. Munro Smith MD, *A History of the Bristol Royal Infirmary* (Bristol and London, 1917) p. 23.
5. Josiah Tucker, *Hospitals and Infirmaries, Considered as Schools of Christian Education for the Adult Poor and as Means Conducive towards a National Reformation of the Common People* (Bristol, 1746) pp. 8–10.
6. Ibid., p. 30.
7. Smith, *History of the Bristol Royal Infirmary*, p. 26.
8. Ibid., pp. 34 and 31.
9. Tucker, *Hospitals and Infirmaries*, pp. 11–13.
10. Ibid., p. 11.
11. Josiah Tucker, *Two Dissertations on Certain Passages of Holy Scripture ... Wherein the Cavils and Objections of the Late Mr. Chubb ... are Particularly Considered and Refuted* (1749) p. 4.

12. Josiah Tucker, *An Impartial Inquiry into the Benefits and Damage Arising to the Nation from the Present Very Great Use of Low Priced Spiritous Liquors* . . . (1751) Advertisement.
13. Ibid., p. 28.
14. Josiah Tucker, *An Earnest and Affectionate Address to the Common People of England Concerning Their Usual Recreations on Shrove Tuesday* (n.d.) pp. 3–4. This pamphlet is advertised in Tucker's *Reflections on the Expediency of Opening the Trade to Turkey* (1753).
15. Josiah Tucker, *The Important Question Concerning Invasions, a Sea-War, Raising the Militia, and Paying Subsidies for Foreign Troops; Fairly and Impartially Stated on Both Sides, and Humbly Referred to the Judgment of the Public: Being a New Edition of the Papers First Published in the Evening Advertiser* (1755) p. 8.
16. Ibid., pp. 39, 41.
17. Ibid., p. 62.

CHAPTER 4

1. Josiah Tucker, *A Brief Essay on the Advantages and Disadvantages which Respectively Attend France and Great Britain with Regard to Trade* . . . (*Essay on Trade*), 3rd edn, corrected with additions (1753) pp. i–ii.
2. Bruno Suviranta, *The Theory of the Balance of Trade in England. A Study in Mercantilism* (Helsingfors, 1923) p. 25.
3. Tucker, *Essay on Trade*, p. iv.
4. Ibid., pp. iv–vii.
5. Joseph Schumpeter, in his *Economic Doctrine and Method* (1954) p. 29, says, 'Tucker produced more solid results [than Hume]; in his work the subject matter of economics began as it were to settle down.'
6. See John Ramsay McCulloch, *The Literature of Political Economy* (1845) for assessments of Tucker's writings on this basis.
7. The bicentenary of the publication of *The Wealth of Nations* in 1976 has added to the substantial literature on Adam Smith. Donald Winch, *Adam Smith's Politics* (Cambridge, 1978), contains a useful bibliography. Some disagreement has arisen as to Smith's real stance. For the purposes of this work I have adopted the traditional view that, despite the exceptions and reservations to be found in his writings, he believed that national wealth would be maximised by a policy of minimal intervention by the state.
8. Tucker, *Essay on Trade*, p. viii.
9. Adam Smith, *An Inquiry into the Nature and Causes of the Wealth of Nations*, with an Introduction by Edwin Cannan (New York, 1937) p. 248.
10. *A Catalogue of the Library of Adam Smith*, ed. James Bonar (1894) p. 115. It was the Glasgow edition of 1756.
11. See Philip Arnold Gibbon, *Ideas of Political Representation in Parliament 1651–1832* (Oxford, 1914).
12. For example in Edgar S. Furniss, *The Position of the Laborer in a System of Nationalism* (Boston, Mass., and New York, 1920) p. 132.
13. Smith, *Wealth of Nations*, p. 81.
14. Adam Smith, *Lectures on Justice, Police, Revenue and Arms*, with an Introduction and notes by Edwin Cannan (1896) p. 157.

15. Smith, *Wealth of Nations*, p. 89.
16. Ibid., p. 897.

CHAPTER 5

1. See John Latimer, *The Annals of Bristol in the Eighteenth Century* (Bristol, 1893) p. 290; and *Gentleman's Magazine*, XXI (1751) 186.
2. Josiah Tucker, *Reflections on the Expediency of a Law for the Naturalization of Foreign Protestants in Two Parts. Part I Containing Historical Remarks on the Disposition and Behaviour of the Natives of this Island, in Regard to Foreigners; Occasioned by the Rejection of the Late Naturalization Bill* (1751) pp. iii–iv.
3. Ibid., p. v.
4. Quoted ibid., p. 44.
5. Josiah Tucker, *Reflections on the Expediency of a Law for the Naturalization of Foreign Protestants in Two Parts. Part II Containing Important Queries . . .* (1752) p. xv.
6. Adam Smith, *An Inquiry into the Nature and Causes of the Wealth of Nations*, ed. Edwin Cannan (New York, 1937), p. 436.
7. The entire correspondence is to be found in Historical MSS. Commission, *Eleventh Annual Report* (1887), Appendix IV, pp. 371–9, 382. The pamphlet is sometimes mistakenly attributed to the author's son, as by Jacob Viner in his Introduction to Rae's biography of Adam Smith.
8. Thomas W. Perry, *Public Opinion Propaganda, and Politics in Eighteenth Century England. A Study of the Jew Bill of 1753* (Cambridge, Mass., 1962).
9. Josiah Tucker, *A Letter to a Friend Concerning Naturalization . . .* (1753) pp. 2–4.
10. Perry, *Public Opinion*, p. 21.
11. Josiah Tucker, *A Second Letter to a Friend Concerning Naturalization* (1753) p. 4.
12. BL Add. MS. 35398, fo. 168, Yorke to Birch, 4 Oct 1753.
13. Josiah Tucker, *An Humble Address and Earnest Appeal . . .* (Gloucester, 1775) p. 16n. (For the full title of this work, see Ch. 9, n. 6.)
14. Josiah Tucker, *Reflections on the Expediency of Opening the Trade to Turkey*, 2nd edn (1755) pp. 4–6.
15. Alfred C. Ward, *A History of the Levant Company* (Oxford, 1935) accepts Tucker's criticisms as legitimate.
16. Perry, *Public Opinion*, pp. 40–1.

CHAPTER 6

1. Historical MSS. Commission, *Eleventh Annual Report* (1887), Appendix, pt IV, Tucker to Lord Townshend, 5 Apr 1752.
2. Josiah Tucker, *Four Tracts together with Two Sermons on Political and Commercial Subjects* (Gloucester, 1774) pp. ix–xi.
3. Scottish Records Office, Kames Collection, Tucker to Kames, 18 Oct 1761.
4. Ibid., Tucker to Kames, 16 Feb 1764.
5. Josiah Tucker, *The Elements of Commerce and Theory of Taxes* (privately printed, 1755) p. 1. Since copies of this work are extremely hard to find, the page numbers of the following quotations in the text will refer to the reprint in

Josiah Tucker, A Selection from his Economic and Political Writings, ed. Robert Livingston Schuyler (New York, 1931).
6. Adam Smith, *An Inquiry into the Nature and Causes of the Wealth of Nations*, ed. Edwin Cannan (New York, 1937) p. 14.
7. Ibid., p. 423.
8. Josiah Tucker, *Instructions for Travellers* (privately printed, 1757) p. 1.
9. Bristol Public Library, B13794, Richard Woodward to Tucker, 13 July 1753. In this letter he describes the expansion of the city of Liverpool.
10. R. J. White, *The Age of George III* (1968) p. 169.
11. Josiah Tucker, *The Case of Going to War for the Sake of Procuring, Enlarging, or Securing of Trade, Considered in a New Light* (1763), being a fragment of a greater work.
12. Jeremy Bentham, *Works*, ed. John Bowring (Edinburgh, 1843) vol. II, p. 546.
13. Josiah Tucker, *Four Tracts on Political and Commercial Subjects*, 3rd edn (Gloucester, 1776) p. vii.
14. *The Letters of David Hume*, ed. J. Y. T. Greig (Oxford, 1932) vol. I, pp. 270–1.
15. Scottish Record Office, Kames Collection, Tucker to Kames, 6 July 1758.
16. Bernard Semmel, 'The Hume–Tucker Debate and Pitt's Trade Proposals', *Economic Journal*, Dec 1965. There is another discussion of the exchange in J. M. Low, 'An Eighteenth Century Controversy in the Theory of Economic Progress', *Manchester School of Economic and Social Studies*, II, no. 3 (Sep 1952).
17. BL Add. MSS. 4319, Tucker to Birch, 19 May 1760.
18. W. E. Clark, *Josiah Tucker, Economist* (New York, 1903) p. 67.

CHAPTER 7

1. T. H. B. Oldfield, *The Representative History of Great Britain and Ireland* (1816) vol. IV, p. 416.
2. Peter Thomas Underdown, 'The Parliamentary History of the City of Bristol, 1750–1790' (unpublished MA dissertation, University of Bristol, 1948) pp. 8–9. I have relied on this thorough study for local background material.
3. *Dictionary of National Biography*, vol. II, p. 530, for Birch, and vol. VII, p. 459, for Forster.
4. BL Add. MSS. 4319.
5. Ibid., Tucker to Birch, 30 Mar 1754.
6. Ibid., Tucker to Birch, 2 Apr 1754.
7. BL Add. MSS. 32735, fos 48–9.
8. BL Add. MSS. 32995, fos 97, 102, 113.
9. See Claud Nugent, *Memoir of Robert, Earl Nugent* (1898).
10. Sir Lewis Namier, *England in the Age of the American Revolution* (1930) p. 383.
11. Sir Lewis Namier and John Brooke, *The History of Parliament, The House of Commons, 1754–1790* (1964) vol. III, p. 220.
12. Josiah Tucker, *A Review of Lord Clare's Conduct as Representative of Bristol* (Gloucester, 1776).
13. BL Add. MSS. 4319, 21 Mar 1754.
14. Ibid., Tucker to Birch, 30 Mar 1754.
15. Some of these are found with Tucker's letters in BL Add MSS. 4319.

16. Ibid., fo. 247.
17. For Philipps, see W. R. Williams, *The Parliamentary History of the Principality of Wales* (Brecknock, 1895) p. 157.
18. David Nicholas, 'The Welsh Jacobites', *Transactions of the Honourable Society of Cymmrodorion*, (1949), pp. 467–74.
19. See William Llewellin, 'David Morgan, the Welsh Jacobite', *Cambrian Journal* (Tenby) 1861, pp. 297–333.
20. BL Add. MSS. 4319, Tucker to Birch, 23 Mar 1754.
21. Ibid., Tucker to Birch, 13 Apr 1754. The cutting is from the *Bristol Weekly Intelligencer*, 13 Apr 1754.
22. Ibid., Tucker to Birch, 29 Apr 1754.
23. BL Add. MSS. 32,736, Nugent to Newcastle, 1 Aug 1754.
24. BL Add. MSS. 11,275, Tucker to Forster, 27 Aug 1754.
25. Ibid., Tucker to Forster, 6 Dec 1755.
26. Ibid., Tucker to Forster, 31 Dec 1755.
27. Ibid., Tucker to Forster, 24 Jan 1756.
28. Ibid., Tucker to Forster, 25 Feb 1756.
29. Ibid., Tucker to Forster, 27 Feb 1756, enclosure.
30. BL Add. MSS. 35,692, Tucker to Hardwicke, 13 Mar 1756.
31. BL Add. MSS. 11,275, Tucker to Forster, 25 Feb 1756.
32. Ibid., Tucker to Forster, 27 Feb 1756.
33. Ibid., Tucker to Forster, 3 Mar 1756.
34. Ibid., Tucker to Forster, 7 Mar 1756.
35. Ibid., Tucker to Forster, 17 Mar 1756.
36. BL Add. MSS. 35,692, Tucker to Hardwicke, 13 Mar 1756.
37. Oldfield, *Representative History*, vol. IV, p. 416.
38. Sir Lewis Namier, *The Structure of Politics at the Accession of George III*, 2nd edn (1957) p. x.
39. Josiah Tucker, *A Review of Lord Clares Conduct*, p. 6.
40. BL Add. MSS. 32,866, Newcastle to Nugent, 31 July 1756.
41. BL Add. MSS. 4319, Tucker to Birch, 23 Aug 1756.
42. BL Add. MSS. 32,867, Nugent to Newcastle, 3 Sep 1756.
43. BL Add. MSS. 32,868, Nugent to Newcastle, 4 Mar 1758.
44. BL Add. MSS. 4319, Tucker to Birch, 22 July 1758.
45. BL Add. MSS. 35,692, Tucker to Hardwicke, 6 Dec 1760.
46. Selwyn to Lord Holland, 19 Mar 1761; Earl of Ilchester, *Letters to Henry Fox, Lord Holland* (1915), p. 145, as quoted in Namier, *The Structure of Politics*, p. 78.

CHAPTER 8

1. Alfred Gregory, *Robert Raikes Journalist and Philosopher* (1877) p. 62.
2. Josiah Harris, *Robert Raikes, the Man and His Works* (Bristol and London, 1899) p. 58.
3. Ibid.
4. Gregory, *Raikes*, p. 81.
5. Harris, *Raikes*, p. 189.
6. Tucker's reply is given in *European Magazine*, July–Dec 1799, p. 378, and

Gentleman's Magazine, LXXXVI (1799) 1003. Warburton's comment first appeared in Rt. Rev. Thomas Newton, Works (1782) vol. I, p. 60.
7. Letters from a Late Eminent Prelate, ed. Richard Hurd, 2nd edn (1809) Warburton to Hurd, 11 Nov 1769.
8. Scottish Record Office, Kames Collection, Tucker to Kames, 11 Feb 1758.
9. Ibid., Tucker to Kames, n.d.
10. [Josiah Tucker], *The Manifold Causes of the Increase of the Poor Distinctly Set Forth; Together with a Set of Proposals for Removing and Preventing Some of the Principal Evils, and for Lessening Others* (n.d.) p. iv. The Advertisement is signed 'Josiah Tucker' and dated 26 May 1760, at Gloucester.
11. Ibid., p. 5.
12. Sidney and Beatrice Webb, *English Poor Law History, Part I: The Old Poor Law* (1963) p. 267.
13. Scottish Record Office, Kames Collection, Tucker to Kames, 26 Dec 1763.
14. Ibid., Tucker to Kames, 15 Feb 1764.
15. Royal Society of Edinburgh, Hume MSS., Tucker to Hume, VII, letter 79, 27 July 1765.
16. *The Letters of David Hume*, ed. J. Y. T. Greig (Oxford, 1932) vol. II, p. 180, Hume to Turgot, 16 June 1768.
17. Ibid., p. 182n., Tucker to Hume, 25 June 1768.
18. Ibid., p. 183, Hume to Turgot, 8 July 1768.
19. Ibid., p. 203n., referring to a letter from Morellet to Hume of 16 May 1769.
20. *Mémoires de l'Abbé Morellet* (Paris, 1821) vol. I, p. 205.
21. W. Walker Stephens, *The Life and Writings of Turgot*, reprint of 1895 edn (New York, 1971) pp. 291–2, Turgot to Tucker, 12 Sep 1770.
22. Josiah Tucker, *A Sermon Preached in the Parish-Church of Christchurch, London, on Wednesday, May the 7th, 1766* ... (1766).
23. Josiah Tucker, *Six Sermons on Important Subjects* (Bristol, 1772).
24. Josiah Tucker, *An Apology for the Present Church of England, as by Law Established Occasioned by a Petition Said to be Preparing by Certain Clergymen, and Others to be Laid before Parliament, for Abolishing Subscription, in a Letter to One of the Petitioners* (Gloucester, 1772) p. 11.
25. Andrew Kippis DD, *A Vindication of the Protestant Dissenting Ministers, with Regard to Their Late Application to Parliament*, 2nd edn (1773) p. 13.
26. Josiah Tucker, *Letters to the Rev. Dr. Kippis Occasioned by His Treatise Entitled A Vindication* ... (Gloucester, 1773) p. 5.
27. Josiah Tucker, *Religious Intolerance No Part of the General Plan either of the Mosaic or Christian Dispensation Proved by Scriptural Inferences and Deductions after a Method Entirely New* (1774).
28. Josiah Tucker, *A Brief and Dispassionate View of the Difficulties Attending the Trinitarian Arian and Socinian Systems: Occasioned by the Fierce Controversies Now on Foot in Divers Parts of the Kingdom Respecting Those Subjects: And Designed to Assist Candid, Humble, and Modest Inquirers in Their Searches after Gospel Truths* (Gloucester, 1774) p. 6.
29. Josiah Tucker, *Seventeen Sermons on Some of the Most Important Points on Natural and Revealed Religion, Respecting the Happiness Both of the Present and of a Future Life* (1776) pp. 137–9.

Notes

CHAPTER 9

1. Josiah Tucker, *A Letter from a Merchant in London to His Nephew in North America* (1766) p. 5.
2. Josiah Tucker, *Four Tracts and Two Sermons on Political and Commercial Subjects* (Gloucester, 1774) p. xii.
3. Josiah Tucker, *The Respective Pleas and Arguments of the Mother Country and the Colonies Distinctly Set Forth* (1775).
4. Edmund Burke, *Speeches and Letters on America Affairs* (London and New York, 1908) p. 44.
5. Josiah Tucker, *A Letter to Edmund Burke, Esq*. . . . (Gloucester and London, 1775) p. 56.
6. Josiah Tucker, *An Humble Address and Earnest Appeal to Those Respectable Personages in Great Britain and Ireland, who, by Their Great and Permanent Interest in Landed Property, Their Liberal Education, Elevated Rank, and Enlarged Views, are the Ablest to Judge, and the Fittest to Decide, Whether a Connection with, or Separation from the Continental Colonies of America, be Most for the National Advantage and the Lasting Benefit of These Kingdoms*, 3rd edn (1776). The 1st edn appeared in 1775.
7. Burke, *Speeches*, pp. 79–80.
8. Josiah Tucker, *A Series of Answers to Certain Popular Objections against Separating from the Rebellious Colonies and Discarding Them Entirely; being the Concluding Tract of the Dean of Gloucester, on the Subject of America Affairs* (Gloucester and London, 1776).
9. Gloucester Public Library, Tucker Letters, Tucker to Adams, 26 Oct 1777.
10. Ibid., Tucker to Adams, 18 Dec 1777.
11. Josiah Tucker, *Dean Tucker's Reflections on the Terrors of Invasion, Republished by a Friend to His Country* (1806).
12. Gloucester Public Library, Tucker Letters, Tucker to Adams, 22 Sep 1779.
13. Josiah Tucker, *Cui Bono? or, an Inquiry, What Benefit Can Arise either to the English or the Americans, the French, Spaniards, or Dutch, from the Greatest Victories, or Successes in the Present War, Being a Series of Letters, Addressed to Monsieur Necker, Late Controller General of the Finances of France* (Gloucester, 1781) p. 5.

CHAPTER 10

1. John Wesley, *Works* (1872) vol. xii, p. 315, letter 296 to Christopher Hopper, 26 Dec 1775.
2. Samuel Johnson, *Political Tracts* (1776) pp. 256–7.
3. William Roberts, *Memoirs of the Life and Correspondence of Mrs. Hannah More*, 2nd edn (1834) vol. i, p. 70.
4. Ibid., p. 71n.
5. Ibid., p. 58.
6. Ibid., p. 58n.
*7. Ibid., pp. 115–16.
8. Josiah Tucker, *A Treatise Concerning Civil Government* (1781) p. 367.
9. William Molyneux, *The Case of Ireland's Being Bound by Acts of Parliament in England Stated* (1698) pp. 169–70.

10. J. W. Gough, *The Social Contract*, 2nd edn. (Oxford, 1957) p. 135n.
11. John Cartwright, *The Legislative Right of the Commonalty Vindicated or, Take Your Choice!*, 2nd edn (1777) p. 46.
12. John Cartwright, *The People's Barrier against Undue Influence and Corruption* ... (1780) p. 27.
13. *The Letters of David Hume*, ed. J. Y. T. Greig, 2 vols (Oxford, 1932) vol. I, p. 48, Hume to Hutcheson, Jan 1743.
14. Roberts, *Memoirs of Mrs More*, vol. I, p. 210.
15. Joseph Towers, *A Vindication of the Political Doctrine of Mr. Locke* ... (1781).
16. Jonathan Boucher, *A View of the Causes and Consequences of the American Revolution* (1797) p. 531n.

CHAPTER 11

1. Gloucester Public Library, Tucker Letters, Tucker to Adams, 23 Feb 1780.
2. Ibid., Tucker to Adams, 4 Apr 1780.
3. William Roberts, *Memoirs of the Life and Correspondence of Mrs. Hannah More*, vol. I, p. 194, Tucker to Mrs More, 3 Feb 1781.
4. Ibid., p. 219.
5. Found with Tucker letters in the Gloucester Public Library.
6. Roberts, *Memoirs of Mrs More*, vol. I, p. 196, Tucker to Mrs More, 3 Feb 1781.
7. *Satirical Poems by William Mason with Notes by Horace Walpole*, ed. Paget Toynbee (Oxford, 1926) p. 32.
8. Horace Walpole, *Letters*, vol. XXVIII, p. 233, Walpole to Mason, 27 Nov 1775.
9. Ibid., vol. XXIX, p. 125, Walpole to Mrs More, 30 Mar 1781.
10. Toynbee, *Satirical Poems by William Mason*, pp. 107, 109.
11. Walpole, *Letters*, vol. XXIX, pp. 131–2, Mason to Walpole, 21 Apr 1781.
12. Ibid., p. 134, Walpole to Mason, 25 Apr 1781.
13. Soame Jenyns, *Works* (Dublin, 1790) vol. I, p. 170.
14. Ibid., vol. II, p. 185.
15. 'Malcolm M'Greggor' (William Mason), *The Dean and the Squire, A Political Ecologue* (1782) p. iii.
16. Josiah Tucker, *Four Letters on Important National Subjects, Addressed to the Right Honourable The Earl of Shelburne, His Majesty's First Lord Commissioner of the Treasury* (1783, misdated 1773) pp. 2–3. Tucker's critic was Samuel Eskwich, who wrote an answer to his *Humble Address and Earnest Appeal*.
17. Public Records Office, SP 37/6/79/2, Tucker to Shelburne, 11 Jan 1767.
18. Josiah Tucker, *Reflections on the Present Low Price of Coarse Wools, Its Immediate Causes, and Its Probable Consequences* (1782) p. 9.
19. John Ramsay McCulloch, *The Literature of Political Economy* (1845) p. 239.
20. Josiah Tucker, *Reflections on the Present Matters in Dispute between Great Britain and Ireland; and on the Means of Converting these Articles into Marked Benefits to Both Kingdoms* (1785) p. 14.
21. Thomas Clarkson, *The History of the Rise, Progress, and Accomplishment of the Abolition of the Mason Stone-Trade* (1808) pp. 304, 368.
22. Anon., *Arguments for and against an Union between Great Britain and Ireland Considered; to Which is Prefixed a Proposal on the Same Subject, by Josiah Tucker, D.D., Dean of Gloucester* (1798).

Notes 283

23. The Rev. Dr. Clarke, *Union or Separation Written Some Years Since by the Reverend Dr. Tucker, Dean of Gloucester* . . . (1799). Another edition was published the same year in Dublin.
24. *Gentleman's Magazine* new ser. XIV (1840), correspondence of Mrs Jones, Tucker to Mrs Jones, 12 Jan 1783.
25. BL Add. MSS. 5419, Tucker to William Seward, 29 Oct 1790.
26. *Gentleman's Magazine*, LXIII (1793) 1063.
27. *The Parliamentary History of England* (1817) vol. XXX, pp. 330, 333.
28. William Seward, *Anecdotes of Distinguished Persons Chiefly of the Present and Two Preceding Centuries*, 4th edn (1798) vol. I, p. iv.
29. Jacob Viner, *The Long View and the Short* (Glencoe, Ill. 1958) p. 407. The review originally appeared in *Journal of Political Economy*, XL (1932). The volume reviewed was *Josiah Tucker, a Selection from his Economic and Political Writings*, ed. Robert Livingston Schuyler (New York, 1931).
30. Ibid., p. 406.
31. James Bonar, *The Tables Turned* (1931) p. 38.
32. Walter Earnest Clark, *Josiah Tucker Economist. A Study in the History of Economics* (New York, 1903) p. 5. (Repr. by AMS Press, New York, 1968.)
33. Ibid., pp. 225–6.
34. Henry Higgs, *The Physiocrats* (1897) p. 31n. Clark mistakenly refers to Quesnay's other article 'Fermiers'.
35. Viner, *The Long View and the Short*, p. 407.
36. Charles W. Cole, 'The Heavy Hand of Hegel,' in *Nationalism and Internationalism*, ed. Edwin Mead Earle (New York, 1930) p. 75.
37. Viner, *The Long View and the Short*, p. 244. On the next page he even goes so far as to say that Smith 'had not succeeded in completely freeing himself from mercantilistic delusions'.
38. *Precursors of Adam Smith*, ed. Ronald L. Meek (1973) pp. 176–7.
39. Bernard Semmel, *The Rise of Free Trade Imperialism* (Cambridge, 1970).
40. Bernard Semmel, 'The Hume–Tucker Debate and Pitt's Trade Proposals', *Economic Journal*, Dec 1965, p. 759.
41. Ibid., p. 768.
42. Ibid., p. 770.
43. Semmel, *Rise of Free Trade Imperialism*, pp. 228–9.
44. Karl Marx, *Capital*, Foreign Language Publishing House edn (Moscow, 1959) vol. I p. 760.
45. Ibid., p. 760n.
46. D. W. Brogan, *The Price of Revolution* (1951) p. 3.
47. Ibid., p. 4.
48. T. B. Macaulay, *Essays*, ed. F. C. Montague (1903) vol. I, p. 531.
49. For a brief account of this incident, see S. E. Morrison and H. S. Commager, *The Growth of the American Republic* (New York, 1955) vol. I, pp. 274–6.

Index

Adams, Samuel, 185, 204, 269
Adams, Dr William, 206, 240–1
Alien duty, 81–3
Allen, Ralph, 164–5
American Revolution, 19, 168, 182, 239, 242, 257, 265, 267–8, 270
Amhurst, Nicholas, 6–7, 9
Amusements, 45–6, 54, 116–17, 163–4
d'Angeul, Plumart, 52, 78, 107, 260
Artificial wants, 25, 91

Beckford, Richard, 136, 145–6, 148–9
Bentham, Jeremy, 126, 218, 267
Berkeley, George, 7, 13, 123
Birch, Thomas, 84, 132, 134–7, 140, 145, 158–9
Birmingham, 17, 56, 100, 109
Blackstone, William, 8, 218
Bonar, James, 258–9
Boston Tea Party, 185, 269
Boucher, Jonathon, 239
Bounties, 99, 190
Bristol, 16–21, 33, 56, 60, 133–40, 142–6, 148–9, 151, 155–6, 159, 166–7, 206, 255
Broad, C. D., 13
Brogan, D. W., 265
Burke, Edmund, 175, 177, 194–200, 216, 219, 241, 264–7
Butler, Joseph, 13–16, 21, 31, 106, 135, 211

Calvinism, 31–3
Canada, 104, 125, 187, 191, 208, 213
Cantillon, Richard, 103
Carolina, Fundamental Constitution for the Government of, 250
Carte, Thomas, 41

Cartwright, Major John, 237
Cassandra, 168, 212
Child, Sir Josiah, 76, 107
Child labour, 111, 163
Chubb, Thomas, 41–3
Church of England, 10–13, 22, 29–30, 73, 108, 175–7
City of London, 83, 87, 133, 146
Clark, W. E., 132, 258–60
Clarkson, Thomas, 255
Class struggle, 113
Cloth, 85–6, 112, 114, 253
Congress, 185, 190, 193, 227
Crow, Mrs, 241–2
Cyclical philosophy of history, 131

Declaratory Act (1766), 194, 227
Defoe, Daniel, 4, 17
De Witt, John, 103
Division of labour, 91, 129
Divorce, 95

East India Company, 103, 143, 254
Elizabeth I, 72, 104
English, character of, 117–19
Erasmus, Desiderius, 178–9

Factory system, 112, 114
Feathers Tavern Petition, 175
Filmer, Sir Robert, 225, 227, 251
Forster, Nathaniel, 134–6, 147–52, 154
Franklin, Benjamin, 172, 201–2, 204, 210
Freedom, of a corporation, 71–2, 81, 133
French Revolution, 19, 245, 256–7, 264–5, 220

Garrick, David, 215–16
Gibbon, Edward, 6–7, 31, 139
Gin-drinking, 76
Glorious Revolution, 43–4, 83, 225
Gloucester, 159–60, 162–6, 169, 255
Goldsmith, Oliver, 139, 258
Gough, J. W., 231–2
Grenville, George, 8, 182, 202

Hancock, John, 204
Hardwicke, Philip Yorke, 1st Earl of, 80, 84, 135, 142–3, 149, 154, 160
Henderson, John, 241–2
Higgs, Henry, 260
Hobbes, Thomas, 15, 232, 250
Hooker, 237
Hudson's Bay Company, 61–3, 104, 143
Hume, David, 103, 126, 128, 131–2, 164, 166, 170–2, 218, 263, 267
Hutcheson, Francis, 218, 238

Immigration, 55–6
Industrial Revolution, 110, 163, 253
Infant industry, 99, 115
Infirmary, Bristol Royal, 39–40
Interest rate, 120, 130
Ireland, 56, 60–1, 68, 131–2, 205, 250, 255

Jacobites, 7–8, 37, 41, 43, 142, 197–8, 206, 219, 227
Jenyns, Soame, 243–4
Jewish Naturalisation Act (1753) (Jew Bill), 80, 85, 95
Jews, 43, 70, 79–80, 83–4, 95, 143
Johnson, Samuel, 8, 31, 135, 214–15, 241–3, 258

Kames, Henry Home, Lord, 89, 131, 166, 169, 209
Keynes, J. M., 261
Kippis, Andrew, 177–8

Laissez-faire, 49–50, 69, 100, 115, 260–1

Landowners, 51, 96, 99, 115, 196, 198
Laugharne, Carmarthenshire, 1, 2
Law, William, 28, 31, 35
Liverpool, 17–18, 20
Locke, John, 192, 217–28, 231–2, 235, 237–9, 242–3, 249–53
London, 17, 22, 137, 147–9
Loughborough, Alexander Wedderburn, 1st Baron, 258
Lovell, Christopher, 41
Loyalists, American, 205, 212–13, 239, 267

Macaulay, Mrs Catherine, 216
Macaulay, Thomas B., 267
Machinery, labour-saving, 109–11, 163
Manchester, 17, 123
Mandeville, Bernard, 15–16, 67
Marriage, 93–6, 101, 109
Marriage Act, 143–4
Marx, Karl, 114, 264
Mason, William, 242–5
Meek, Ronald L., 262
Mercantilism, 49–50
Methodism, 8, 22–36, 175
Minchinton, W. E., 17
Molyneux, William, 218–19, 224, 226
Money, 102–3, 105, 126, 129
Monopoly, 20, 61–3, 66, 72, 82, 92, 100, 104–5, 130, 254
Montesquieu, 103, 107, 111
Moravian Brethren, 22, 30, 32, 34
More, Hannah, 215–16, 238, 240–1
Morgan, David, 142–3
Myrdal, Gunnar, 264

Namier, Sir Lewis, 139, 155, 160
Naturalisation, 70, 72, 81, 95
Necker, Jacques, 208–10
Newcastle, Thomas Pelham-Holles, 1st Duke of, 138–9, 146–8, 157–9
Norwich, 17, 123
Nugent, Robert (later Lord Clare and Earl Nugent), 70, 79, 136–40, 143–50, 154, 157, 159

Oldfield, T. E. B., 133, 155

Paine, Thomas, 204
Pelham, Henry, 44, 70, 80, 86, 139
Perry, Thomas W., 80, 82, 86
Petty, Sir William, 76
Philipps, Sir John, 140, 142–4, 146
Physiocrats, 49, 78, 172, 258, 260
Pitt, William, the Elder, 1st Earl of Chatham, 8, 124, 165
Pitt, William, the Younger, 245, 263
Pococke, Richard, 4
Poor, 40–1, 46, 53–4, 57–9
Pope, Alexander, 139, 164
Population, 56, 59, 76, 93
Price, Richard, 206, 212, 218–9, 222, 226–7, 239
Priestley, Joseph, 192, 207, 218–22, 225

Quesnay, Pierre, 98, 260

Raikes, Robert, 164, 255
Reynolds, Joshua, 215–16, 258
Richmond, Charles Lennox, 3rd Duke of, 208, 248
Rousseau, Jean-Jacques, 218, 220, 222, 251, 266
Ruthin School, 5

St John's College, Oxford, 5, 7
St Mawes, Cornwall, 138–9
Schuyler, R. C., 258, 262
Scotland, 56, 68, 127–31, 143, 249
Sea Sergeants, Ancient and Honourable Society of, 141–3
Self-love, 91–3
Seligman, Edwin, R.A., 259
Selwyn, George, 160–1
Semmel, Bernard, 34, 132, 262–3
Seven Years' War, 47, 204
Seward, William, 255, 257–8
Shaftesbury, Anthony Ashley Cooper, 1st Earl of, 53
Shaftesbury, Anthony Ashley Cooper, 3rd Earl of, 217
Shays, Daniel, 269
Shelburne, William Petty, 2nd Earl of (later 1st Marquis of Lansdowne), 197, 219, 245–8, 250, 252, 256, 263
Slavery, 20, 112, 254–5
Smith, Adam, 15, 49–52, 57, 60–1, 65–7, 76–7, 91–2, 94, 96, 101, 110–11, 113, 126, 163, 166, 172, 185, 256–7, 258–60, 262–3
Smith, Jarrit, 151–4, 156–7
Smuggling, 52, 61, 184, 194, 199
Social mobility, 119–20
Society of Merchant Adventurers, 134
Spencer, John, 151–4, 156–7
Stephen, Leslie, 29, 36
Stamp Act, 182–3, 185–7, 189, 192, 194, 201–2
Steadfast Society, 134, 136, 152
Stuart, Prince Charles, the Young Pretender, 8, 37–8, 142
Swift, Jonathan, 13, 53

Taxes, 54, 59–60, 66–7, 94, 116, 182–3, 218, 224
Thirty-nine Articles, 175–8
Tilsley, John, 163
Towers, Joseph, 240, 249
Townshend, Charles, 3rd Viscount, 79, 88
Townshend, Charles, 79, 185
Tucker, Josiah
  Life
    ancestry and birth, 1–2
    education, 5–9
    Curate of St Stephens, 17
    Rector of All Saints, 21
    marriage to Elizabeth Woodward, 21
    first appearance in print, 23
    Bristol elections, 133–55
    Dean of Gloucester, 159
    and Bishop Warburton, 165
    and Lord Kames, 166–70
    and Hume, 170–2
    and Turgot, 172
    and Burke, 194–5, 216
    and Hannah More, 215
    marriage to Mrs Crow, 240

Tucker, Josiah – *Cont.*
and Lord Shelburne, 245–6
gives up St Stephens, 256
death, 257
Writings
An Apology for the Present Church of England as by Law Established (1772), 175–9
A Brief Essay on the Advantages and Disadvantages which Respectively Attend France and Great Britain with Regard to Trade (1749), 48, 70, 78–9, 106–7, 166, 254, 260
A Brief and Dispassionate View of the Difficulties Attending the Trinitarian, Arian, and Socinian Systems (1774), 180 – 1
A Brief History of the Principles of Methodism (1742), 31–4
A Calm Address to All Parties in Religion, Concerning Disaffection to the Present Government (1745), 37–9
The Case of Going to War for the Sake of Procuring, Enlarging, or Securing of Trade, Considered in a New Light (1763), 121, 186
'Charity School Sermon' (1776), 173–4
Cui Bono? (1781), 208, 256
An Earnest and Affectionate Address to the Common People of England Concerning Their Usual Recreations on Shrove Tuesday (1753), 45–6
The Elements of Commerce and Theory of Taxes (1755), 48, 79, 88–9, 121
Four Letters on Important National Subjects, Addressed to the Right Honourable the Earl of Shelburne (1783), 245, 254
Four Tracts together with Two Sermons (1774), 88, 121, 126, 181–2, 186, 190, 201, 259, 262
'The Great Question Resolved, Whether a Rich Country Can Stand a Competitor with a Poor Country, etc.' (1774), 126–32.
Hospitals and Infirmaries, Considered as Schools of Christian Education etc. (1746), 39–41
An Humble Address and Earnest Appeal, etc. (1775), 196, 244
An Impartial Inquiry into the Benefits and Damage Arising to the Nation from the Present Very Great Use of Low-Priced Spirituous Liquors (1751), 44–5
The Important Question Concerning Invasions (1755), 46–7
Instructions for Travellers (1757), 3, 14, 48, 105, 165
A Letter from a Merchant in London to His Nephew in North America, Relative to the Present Posture of Affairs in the Colonies (1766), 182, 186
A Letter to Edmund Burke (1775), 194, 196, 206, 217
Letter to a Friend Concerning Naturalisation (1753), 80–3
Letters to the Rev. Dr. Kippis (1773), 177–9
The Manifold Causes of the Increase of the Poor (1760), 168–9
Reflections on the Expediency of a Law for the Naturalisation of Foreign Protestants, Part I (1751), Part II (1752), 70–9
Reflections on the Expediency of Opening the Trade to Turkey (1753), 85–6
Reflections on the Present Low Price of Coarse Wools (1782), 253
Reflections on the Present Matters in Dispute between Great Britain and Ireland (1785), 254
Reflections on the Terrors of Invasion (1779), 207
Religious Intolerance No Part of the General Plan either of the Mosaic or Christian Dispensation, etc. (1774), 181
The Respective Pleas and Arguments of

Index

the Mother Country and the Colonies Distinctly Set Forth (1775), 190
A Review of Lord Vis. Clare's Conduct as Representative of Bristol (1775), 140
Second Letter to a Friend Concerning Naturalisation (1753), 80, 83–4
A Series of Answers to Certain Popular Objections against Separating from the Rebellious Colonies etc. (1776), 201–2, 206, 217
Seventeen Sermons (1776), 39, 181
Six Sermons on Important Subjects (1772), 39, 174–5
Treatise Concerning Civil Government (1781), 44, 217, 221, 227, 239, 243, 245, 249, 252
'The True Interest of Great Britain Set Forth in Regard to the Colonies' (1774), 186
Two Dissertations on Certain Passages of Holy Scripture etc. (1749), 41–4
Turgot, Anne-Robert-Jacques, 78, 126, 171–2, 208, 211–12
Turkey Company (Levant Co.), 61–2, 84–6, 104
Turkey trade, 82, 143, 145

Underdown, P. E., 134
Unemployment, 74–5
Union Club, 134, 136, 150

Viner, Jacob, 258, 260–1
Voting qualifications, 53, 58, 93, 221, 235–6

Wales, 1–5, 56, 142, 170
Walpole, Horace, 242–3, 245
Walpole, Robert, 124
War, 97, 130, 166–8, 236
Warburton, William, 108, 158, 164–5
Washington, George, 233, 269
Wesley, John, 8, 11, 22, 28–36, 156, 164, 214
Whisky Rebellion, 269
Whitefield, George, 8, 22–8, 31–4
White, R. J., 121
Women, 66, 94, 96, 108, 221, 237, 249
Whig interpretation of history, 267
Woodward, Elizabeth, 21
Woodward, Richard, 21, 106

York, Philip, 84, 135
Young, Arthur, 121

Zinzendorf, Count von, 22, 33

GPSR Compliance
The European Union's (EU) General Product Safety Regulation (GPSR) is a set of rules that requires consumer products to be safe and our obligations to ensure this.

If you have any concerns about our products, you can contact us on

ProductSafety@springernature.com

In case Publisher is established outside the EU, the EU authorized representative is:

Springer Nature Customer Service Center GmbH
Europaplatz 3
69115 Heidelberg, Germany

www.ingramcontent.com/pod-product-compliance
Lightning Source LLC
Chambersburg PA
CBHW031519100426

42873CB00013B/129